THEORY OF REGULAR ECONOMIES

Series on Mathematical Economics and Game Theory

Series Editor: Tatsuro Ichiishi *(The Ohio State University)*

Published

Vol. 1:   Theory of Regular Economies
by Ryo Nagata

Vol. 2:   Theory of Conjectural Variations
by C. Figuières, A. Jean-Marie, N. Quérou & M. Tidball

Series on Mathematical Economics and Game Theory

Vol. 1

THEORY OF REGULAR ECONOMIES

Ryo Nagata

Waseda University, Japan

World Scientific

NEW JERSEY · LONDON · SINGAPORE · BEIJING · SHANGHAI · HONG KONG · TAIPEI · CHENNAI

Published by

World Scientific Publishing Co. Pte. Ltd.

5 Toh Tuck Link, Singapore 596224

USA office: Suite 202, 1060 Main Street, River Edge, NJ 07661

UK office: 57 Shelton Street, Covent Garden, London WC2H 9HE

British Library Cataloguing-in-Publication Data
A catalogue record for this book is available from the British Library.

SURI KEIZAIGAKU NO SHINTENKAI by Ryo Nagata
Copyright © 2001. All rights reserved.
Original Japanese edition published by Waseda University Press.
This US edition is published by arrangement with Waseda University Press, Tokyo, Japan
through Tuttle-Mori Agency, Inc., Tokyo, Japan.

ISBN 981-238-849-4

Printed in Singapore by World Scientific Printers (S) Pte Ltd

Preface

This is the English revised edition of my Japanese monograph, *A Frontier of Mathematical Economics: the Theory of Regular Economies*, Waseda University Press, Tokyo, 2001. As recommended by Professor Tatsuro Ichiishi, the editor of the series *Mathematical Economics and Game Theory*, I thoroughly rewrote the original book. Revised portions are too numerous to mention individually, and some new chapters (i.e. Introduction, chapters 6 and 12) have been supplemented. I believe that the book has improved much through the revision process.

The aim of the present book is to provide a systematic treatment of the theory of regular economies, one of the most advanced topics in modern general equilibrium theory, emphasizing the basic idea, tools and important applications. The theory itself is relatively new but is getting more and more important not only in general equilibrium theory but also in many other areas as well.

Hence, the subject of the book is very significant but highly mathematical, implying that readers are required to understand quite a volume of mathematics before proceeding to the economical analysis. Furthermore, most of the mathematics required here are not familiar to many students specializing in economics. Thus, quite a few similar works give a separate exposition on the necessary mathematics as a whole, see e.g. Mas-Colell (1985), Villanacci et al. (2002). Although this way of presenting analyses may be efficient, it is true that many readers will be burdened with a large quantity of mathematics and may be reluctant to read the entire work.

In order for the reader to save much effort on the mathematics and to shortly understand how successfully the mathematics is used for the economical problem, I decided to gradually introduce the mathematics in this book. Specifically, at the beginning of each chapter I put the minimum requisite mathematics for the economical analysis of the chapter; thus, most chapters consist of two divisions: Mathematical Preliminaries and Economical Analysis. In such a formation of the book, I particularly took notice of two points: (1) providing the mathematics step by step from the fundamental level to the advanced level as the chapters proceed, and (2) arranging the economical issues relevant to the mathematics provided in such a way that the economical arguments are kept consistent throughout each chapter. I believe this approach was successful.

I hope this book will prove useful both as a graduate text on one advanced topic of general equilibrium theory and as an introduction, for economists and academics interested in the application of mathematics to economics, to current research in a frontier area of general equilibrium theory. The mathematical prerequisite for this book is simply a solid foundation in basic analysis, linear algebra and elementary topology.

Now, acknowledgments would be in order to certain people. I want to express my special thanks to Professor Tatsuro Ichiishi who provided the opportunity to create the English version of my original book. Without his offer, the present edition would not have been realized. I am greatly indebted to Doctor Tatsuji Owase, from whom I learned how to do research in economic theory. Even after his retirement, he has always been generous in providing advice and encouragement to my research. I would like to address my thanks to many people who read my original edition and provided helpful comments, in particular an anonymous referee who recommended my book for the English edition. In manipulating T_EX and, particularly, constructing figures in the text, I received assistance from Research-assistant Hisatoshi Tanaka to whom I am deeply grateful. In addition, I wish to thank one of my graduate students, Yoshimoto Honda, who helped me with some figures. Finally, I must tender my sincere gratitude to Professor Timothy Seul who read all my manuscripts and gave me a large number of valuable advice concerning English expression. If the present book proves more or less readable, it is certainly owing to his patient cooperation. Needless to say, any remaining errors and inaccuracies are my own.

Ryo Nagata

Contents

Introduction

Let's think of terms containing 'economy' prefixed with some adjectives: a capitalistic economy, a socialistic economy, a barter economy, a monetary economy, a closed economy, an open economy, European economy, Asian economy, etc. In most cases, the meanings of those terms are easily understandable through the accompanying adjective. In other words, these adjectives appropriately inform us of what aspects of an economy matter.

Now how about a regular economy? What does the adjective 'regular' mean? Following the analogy of the terms mentioned above, it may be expected to convey a regularity in some economic sense. However this is not the case with this term. We shall give an exposition on how this term differs from others.

First of all, it should be noted that this term is not concerned with a general economy but with an economy theoretically translated. In economics, it is the convention to view an economy as follows:

The observed state of an economy can be viewed as an equilibrium resulting from the interaction of a large number of agents with partially conflicting interests (Debreu (1974)).

Thus, only an equilibrium state of an economy matters for regular economies.

If a regular economy is concerned with an equilibrium state of an economy, then the adjective 'regular' is intuitively expected to imply some economic regularity of an equilibrium such as Pareto efficiency. But this intuition is wrong, which is the second point. Indeed, the adjective stems from mathematics and does not have anything to do with economic characters. Specifically, the origin of the word is a regular value (or a regular point) which is concerned with some property of a differentiable map.

Thus, the term regular economies is solely used in a theoretical and mathematical context, which makes the word less popular than others even though it has already gained a firm footing in the field of mathematical economics (see Nicola (2000)). Accordingly, the term is conceptually abstract and rigorous. We shall give the strict definition of regular economies in subsequent chapters while here we are going to briefly explain how the notion is brought about.

Recall the basic view of an economy alluded to above. That is to say, the observed state of an economy is theoretically seen as an equilibrium, which should be in turn dependent upon some fundamentals underlying the economy. After all, an equilibrium state, no matter what it may be, is not realized until the components constructing an economy itself are given. Thus, it is legitimate to first draw a clear distinction between the state of an economy and the framework of an economy, then considering the relation between them. It goes without saying that different frameworks yield different states (i.e. equilibria), which naturally leads to a mapping between frameworks and states. In light of the mapping, it is possible to distinguish a certain normality and abnormity among the frameworks. The normal property itself is characterized by a regular value of the map. Accordingly, if an economy is formed by the framework of such a normality, then it is called a regular economy.

Now that we have roughly grasped the meaning of "regular" in regular economies, we should proceed to inquire what is the use of regular economies. In particular, it is interesting to see what kind of benefit the concept of regular economies provides in terms of economics. We shall discuss this issue in what follows.

In order to understand the economic significance of regular economies, it is advisable to consider in what context they initially appeared in the economic literature. The term of regular economies was first used by Debreu (1970) in his investigation of the uniqueness problem of general competitive equilibrium. The general competitive equilibrium is the key concept of the abstract model of the economic reality, corresponding to *the observed state of an economy*. The existence of such an equilibrium has been rigorously proved in the most fundamental model, called the Arrow-Debreu model, albeit with some assumptions. In order for the economic view stated in the previous section to make sense, the existence of such an equilibrium is certainly indispensable while the uniqueness of the equilibrium is also desirable. However, it has been well known that the uniqueness of the equilibrium is theoretically obtained only under the very restrictive assumptions, which implies that presuming the uniqueness of the equilibrium in a general economy is illegitimate. Then we are naturally led to this question: what about the number of equilibria in an economy on the basis of the similar assumptions of those assuring the existence of the equilibrium?

On this issue, Debreu showed that not all, but almost all, economies have *locally unique* equilibria, which means that in a neighborhood of an equilibrium there exists no other equilibrium. The course of his reasoning is as follows. First specify numerical parameters that describe the framework of an economy, then consider the admissible set of those parameters that is called the space of economies. Accordingly, a point of the space corresponds to a specific economy, thus each point of the space is itself called an economy. Secondly, devise a map that associates an economy with the set of its equilibria. A regular value induced by the map specifies an economy, which has locally unique and in fact a finite number of equilibria. In the process an economy corresponding to a regular value is called a regular economy. The important thing about regular economies is that, through Sard's theorem, almost all economies in the space of economies are regular. This fact assures the generality of regular economies, which enables us to say that contrary to the uniqueness of the equilibrium, the local uniqueness of equilibria is the general phenomenon. Debreu also showed that locally each equilibrium is smoothly dependent on the parameters specifying an economy, which implies that in general a drastic change in an equilibrium is not induced by a small perturbation of an economy.

It follows from Debreu's argument that the economic significance of regular economies is twofold, one in an individual sense and the other in an aggregate sense. More specifically, (1) each regular economy shows a specific structure of the equilibrium set and (2) the whole of regular economies occupies a specific position in all economies (i.e. the space of economies). In particular, the latter is quite a new view in economics though it is intrinsically equivalent to a mathematical concept, genericity. It is, however, worth noting that these two phases are closely related in the analysis. Undoubtedly this approach has opened up a new way in the economical analysis. Moreover,

Since the publication of Debreu's seminal paper, genericity analysis has dominated the equilibrium analysis literature (Zhou (1997a)).

Then, we shall briefly see how this original idea has been thereafter developed and applied.

First we should note that the theory of regular economies begins with specifying the economic parameters. Thus it is possible in the theory to consider various kinds of economies according to the parameters we choose. Not only the standard Walrasian economy but also a non-Walrasian economy is conceivable. Indeed, Laroque and Polemarchakis (1978) and Wiesmeth (1979) have investigated the structure of the non-Walrasian equilibrium set by means of the approach of regular economies. On the other hand, within the standard Walrasian economy, a variety of models can be treated. As is well known, it is conventional in the research of the Walrasian economy to separate a pure exchange economy and a production economy for analytical convenience. In the former case, what can be regarded as specifying parameters are, above all, initial endowments, utility functions and/or individual excess demand functions among consumers. In fact, Debreu's model is only based on initial endowments whereas Delbaen (1970), Dierker and Dierker (1972), etc., have chosen individual excess demand functions as well as initial endowments for the parameters. Furthermore, Smale (1974a) has harked back to utility functions, which are surely more primitive parameters. In the case of a production economy, parameters specifying production must be added. Production functions are typical parameters on which Fuchs (1974) has built a model and analysed the structure of the equilibrium set in terms of regular economies, while Smale (1974c) has chosen a parametrized production possibility set to develop a similar argument. Moreover, production technology itself can be freely specified in the theory. Mas-Colell (1975, 1977b) and Kehoe (1980, 1982, 1983) have picked up the linear production technology, using an activity vector as a parameter of production. All the arguments provided so far are based on a finite model; that is, the number of agents and goods are all finite. On the other hand, the theory can accept an atomless economy consisting of infinite agents (Hildenbrand (1974), Dierker (1975)).

Not only the orthodox Walrasian economy but also an anomalous Walrasian economy can be acceptable in the theory. In this regard, the incomplete market model should be referred to. This is the model that represents a certain imperfection of markets. Specifically, incomplete markets indicate that *asset* markets are incomplete, which means that the number of asset markets is insufficient when compared to conceivable states in the future. It has been known that the approach of regular economies is particularly effective for the analysis of the incomplete market model. In fact, it may be safely said that the theory of GEI (general equilibrium with incomplete asset markets), which has been established as an important field, is intrinsically based upon the theory of regular economies (for the GEI model, see Geanakoplos (1990), Magill and Shafer (1991), Magill and Quinzii (1996) and Villanacci et al. (2002)). We shall discuss the GEI model with a special emphasis on the application of regular economies (see chapters 11, 12).

Next, we should refer to the considerable aspects of the equilibrium set corresponding to various frameworks of economies provided above. As we have mentioned, Debreu investigated local uniqueness or finiteness of the equilibrium set as well as the smooth independence of each equilibrium on underlying parameters. We do not, however, have to confine ourselves to those aspects. The mathematical structure of the theory of regular economies allows us to consider a wider range of properties with regard to the equilibrium set. First of all we can examine the most fundamental problem about the equilibrium; that is, the existence of an equilibium for which the theory of regular economies provides a distinctive approach (Dierker (1972)) on which we shall argue in the text (see chapter 4). In this connection, it is worth noting that the investigation of the existence of an equilibium from the viewpoint of regular economies is of great use especially for the GEI model, which is one of the reasons why the theory of GEI depends on the theory of regular economies. Secondly, another important problem about the equilibrium, that is, the stability of an equilibrium, is also the subject of the theory of regular economies. In fact, a very unique approach to this issue has been developed from the viewpoint of regular economies and some suggestive consequences have been deduced (Dierker (1972), Varian (1975)) on which we shall discuss in the text (see chapter 5). The third property to be considered is, of course, the efficiency of an equilibium. However, as is well known, an equilibrium allocation in a standard Walrasian model is substantially equivalent to an efficient allocation. Thus, even with the theory of regular economies, we would have few comments on this issue as far as a standard Walrasian model is concerned. Consequently, the efficiency of an equilibrium only matters when we consider an anomalous Walrasian economy. In fact, an equilibrium allocation in the GEI model has been shown not necessarily to be efficient (Hart (1975)). Hence, in the text we shall investigate the efficiency problem of an equilibrium in the GEI model from the viewpoint of regular economies. Finally, as a special issue, the convergence of a competitive equilibrium to the core has been dealt with in terms of regular economies (Debreu (1975), Grodal (1975)). So far we have argued the benefit of the theory with a special emphasis on the construction of the theory itself. It is, however, worth noting the pregnancy of mathematical tools adopted in the theory. Mathematically, the theory of regular economies is mainly dependent on concepts and tools of differential topology. They had not been used in the economic literature before the theory of regular economies appeared. The theory then clearly showed how useful these new mathematical appliances are for the economic analysis. For instance, the existence of an equilibrium, the finiteness of equilibria and the local uniqueness of equilibria alluded to above are all derived entirely by means of new mathematical methods. In addition, what is more important, these new methods are suitable not only for the theory of regular economies but also for other fields. To mention a few, one of the methods provided in the theory of regular economies has been used to show the uniqueness of the Cournot-Nash equilibrium in an oligopoly market (Kolstad and Mathiesen (1987), Vives (1999)), the transfer problem of international economics has been investigated through the method of regular economies (Balasko (1978b)) and the existence of a voting-equilibrium has been argued through the method of regular economies (Schofield (1984)).

Now some comments on the organization of the book would be in order. This book is divided into three parts. The first part, consisting of five chapters, presents the fundamentals of the theory of regular economies. Throughout Part 1, we only deal with a pure exchange economy and presume that the specifying framework of an economy only consists of the initial endowments among agents in order to make matters simple. First, Debreu's original model is introduced in chapter 1 as the motivation, where the basic idea of the theory should be suggested. Then, the core notion of the theory is summarized in terms of genericity in chapter 2, where the basic method of the theory should be revealed. In chapter 3 the elaborated formalization of regular economies is presented, which has evolved from Debreu's model. Since the formalization has a broad applicability, it is now approved as the standard formula of regular economies. On the basis of this formalization, the rest of Part 1 develops some distinctive consequences the theory provides. An exposition is given in chapter 4 on the special method to show the existence of an equilibrium in regular economies, which is based on a specialized mathematical concept, i.e. the homotopy invariance of the modulo 2 degree. In chapter 5, some suggestive outcomes concerning the stability of equilibria in regular economies are derived through the application of a profound mathematical claim, i.e. the Poincaré-Hopf theorem.

Part 2 introduces utility functions of the agents as another specifying parameter of an economy while we still remain in a pure exchange economy model. The utility function causes a special difficulty for the theory that is immune to the initial endowments; that is, we have to be concerned with a functional space. Thus, chapter 6 is devoted to the study of the structure of the space of utility functions. We introduce the Whitney topology to the space and describe some properties concerning the topology. In order to consider genericity with a functional space, another mathematical notion called transversality is required. Therefore, chapter 7 provides some basic properties concerning transversality in connection with regular economies. Then, in chapter 8 we describe two central transversality theorems for the genericity analysis and thereafter apply them to the regular economies with utility functions as well as initial endowments as parameters of an economy. Chapter 9 deals with the existence and the finiteness of equilibria in such regular economies, where the modulo 2 intersection number is successfully employed as the transversality version of the modulo 2 degree mentioned above.

One may safely say that Part 1 and Part 2 present the basis of the theory. In contrast, Part 3 is concerned with the development and the application of the theory. Chapter 10 contains one of the important expansions of the basic model, that is, the introduction of production. Actually, there are some ways to introduce production into regular economies. We particularly pay attention to the way initiated by Mas-Colell (1975, 1977b) and Kehoe (1980, 1982, 1983) in which the production technology is expressed as the configuration of linear activities. We choose their argument not only because constant returns to scale is important in a practical sense, but also because their method is uniquely computational, providing a new scope for regular economies. The rest of Part 3 is devoted to the GEI theory that is one of the outstanding applications of regular economies. In contrast to the complete market model, the incomplete market model has been known to show various structural imperfections. Hart pointed out quite some time ago (1974) that the GEI model does not necessarily possess an equilibrium, which is a serious problem for the theory. This difficulty was not overcome until the method of regular economies was adopted. In chapter 11, we show how successfully the method of regular economies works to get rid of this difficulty. Then, chapter 12 deals with another difficulty of the GEI model, that is, the inefficiency of equilibria. Unfortunately, one can not escape from this crisis even with the method of regular economies. Instead, through the method, one can determine with mathematical accuracy how common inefficiency is among the equilibria of the GEI model.

Part 1

Foundations of Regular Economies

Chapter 1

What Is a Regular Economy?

In this chapter we show how a concept of regular economies is generated. The concept of regular economies is very different from other economical concepts in that it does not assume any particular economical character. Indeed, the term "regular" stems from some mathematical concept, i.e. a regular value, and does not imply any a priori regularity in an economical sense. In a sense the theory of regular economies is rather a particular way of analysis for economics than the economic theory itself. Thus, from the nature of the matter, we need some mathematical knowledge before proceeding toward an understanding of the concept of regular economies. We first present mathematical equipment and then explain how the concept evolves.

1.1   Mathematical Preliminaries

1.1.1   *Manifolds and Tangent Spaces*

Let $\boldsymbol{R}$ denote the real numbers and $\boldsymbol{R}^n$ denote n-dimensional Euclidean space with a standard Euclidean topology. In the following we consider $\boldsymbol{R}^n$ to be an ambient space. Roughly speaking, if a subset M of $\boldsymbol{R}^n$ has locally the same structure as $\boldsymbol{R}^m$ where $m \leq n$, then M is called an m-dimensional manifold. To be precise,

Definition 1.1 $M \subseteq \boldsymbol{R}^n$ is a m-dimensional manifold if each point x of M has a neighborhood $W \cap M$ that is diffeomorphic to an open subset U of $\boldsymbol{R}^m$. Note that W is itself an open subset in $\boldsymbol{R}^n$. $n - m$ is called the codimension of M in $\boldsymbol{R}^n$.

3

In general, X of $\boldsymbol{R}^n$ is diffeomorphic to Y of $\boldsymbol{R}^n$ if there exists a smooth map called a diffeomorphism $f : X \to Y$ such that f carries X homeomorphically onto Y and that both f and f^{-1} are smooth where a smooth map is the map that has continuous partial derivatives of all orders. A smooth map is also called the map of class C^∞.

In the above definition, a diffeomorphism $\phi : U \to W \cap M$ is called a parametrization of the neighborhood $W \cap M$ and the inverse diffeomorphism ϕ^{-1} is called a coordinate system on $W \cap M$. Each component function of ϕ^{-1} is called a coordinate function.

Intuitively, a manifold in $\boldsymbol{R}^n$ is the subset with following properties. That is , it has the same structure everywhere and has no boundary as well as no ragged part. As an example, consider the circle

$$S^1 = \{(x, y) \in \boldsymbol{R}^2 \mid x^2 + y^2 = 1\}$$

which is the very manifold. Indeed, for any point (x, y) in the upper semicircle, take the upper semicircle itself as its neighborhood.

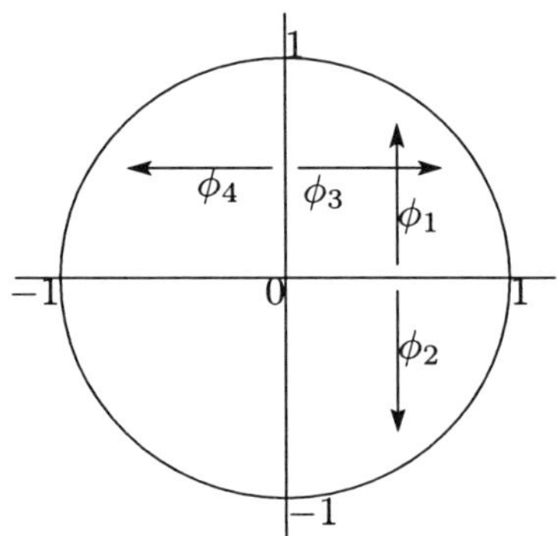

Fig. 1.1

Then the map ϕ_1 from the open interval $(-1, +1)$ onto the upper semicircle defined by

$$\phi_1(x) = (x, \sqrt{1 - x^2})$$

constitutes a parametrization of the neighborhood (see the above figure). In fact, its inverse $\phi_1^{-1} : (x, y) \to x$ is certainly smooth. For any point of the lower semicircle a parametrization ϕ_2 is similarly defined from the open interval $(-1, +1)$ onto the lower semicircle as follows:

$$\phi_2(x) = (x, -\sqrt{1 - x^2}).$$

To cover the two axis points $(1, 0)$ and $(-1, 0)$, we can take

$$\phi_3(y) = (\sqrt{1 - y^2}, y),$$
$$\phi_4(y) = (-\sqrt{1 - y^2}, y)$$

respectively mapping the open interval $(-1, +1)$ onto the right and left semicircle. Thus, the circle is a one-dimensional manifold.

Some important manifolds are as follows.

Example 1.1   An open subset in $\boldsymbol{R}^n$ is itself an n-dimensional manifold in $\boldsymbol{R}^n$.

Example 1.2   0-dimensional manifold: This is a discrete set by the definition.

Example 1.3   submanifold: Let A be a subset of a manifold M in $\boldsymbol{R}^n$. If A is itself a manifold in $\boldsymbol{R}^n$, A is called a submanifold of M. It is known that if A is a submanifold of M, then for any point $x \in A \subset M$ there exists an open subset W in $\boldsymbol{R}^n$ and a coordinate system $\varphi : W \cap M \to \boldsymbol{R}^m, \varphi(x') = (\varphi_1(x'), \ldots, \varphi_m(x'))$ such that the restriction of φ on $W \cap A$ carries any x' to $(\varphi_1(x'), \ldots, \varphi_h(x'), 0, \ldots, 0)$ where h $(\leq m)$ is the dimension of A.

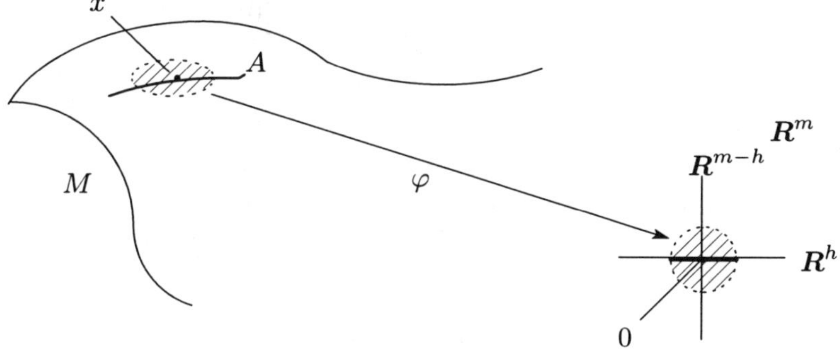

Fig. 1.2

Accordingly, the composite of the projection $\Pi : \boldsymbol{R}^m \to \boldsymbol{R}^h$ and the above restriction constitutes a coordinate system on $W \cap A$ (see Fig. 1.2). One calls $m - h$ the codimension of A in M.

Example 1.4 product manifold: Let M and K be manifolds respectively in $\boldsymbol{R}^n$ and $\boldsymbol{R}^l$. We suppose $dimM = m$ and $dimK = k$. For any point (x, y) of $M \times K$, we can find an open set $W \subset \boldsymbol{R}^m$ and a parameterization $\phi : W \to M$ around x whereas similarly there is an open set $U \subset \boldsymbol{R}^k$ and a parameterization $\psi : U \to K$ around y. Pick the map $\phi \times \psi : W \times U \to M \times K$ defined by

$$\phi \times \psi(w, u) = (\phi(w), \psi(u)),$$

then obviously $W \times U$ is an open set in $\boldsymbol{R}^m \times \boldsymbol{R}^k = \boldsymbol{R}^{m+k}$ and $\phi \times \psi$ is a parametrization around (x, y). It follows that $M \times K$ is a manifold with $m + k$ dimension, which is called a product manifold.

Now we turn to the tangent space of a manifold which plays a crucial role in the analytical argument. Intuitively speaking, the tangent space of a manifold is the closest flat approximation to the manifold at each point. The flat approximation is virtually identified with a linear space, i.e. $\boldsymbol{R}^m$. Since analytical operations are easily defined on $\boldsymbol{R}^m$, we can develop the differential analysis regarding maps defined on a manifold by means of the tangent space.

In order to define the tangent space of a m-dimensional manifold M, we need the derivative of a parametrization. For any point x of M, we can take a parametrization $\phi : U \to V$ such that $\phi^{-1}(x) = 0$ where $V = W \cap M$. Then we consider the map $d\phi_0 : \boldsymbol{R}^m \to \boldsymbol{R}^n$ defined by

$$d\phi_0(h) = \lim_{t \to 0} \frac{\phi(th) - \phi(0)}{t}$$
$$= \lim_{t \to 0} \frac{\phi(th) - x}{t}$$

which is well defined because ϕ is a diffeomorphism between U and V. This map is called the derivative of ϕ at 0. $d\phi_0$ is the best linear approximation to ϕ at 0. The reason is as follows. Consider Taylor's series about 0 generated by $\phi : U \to V$

$$\phi(h) = \phi(0) + J\phi(0) \cdot h + R(h)$$
$$= x + J\phi(0) \cdot h + R(h)$$

where $J\phi(0)$ is the Jacobian matrix of ϕ at 0 and $R(h)$ is the remainder. This formula tells us that ϕ can be approximated by a linear function near 0. From the above equation, we obtain

$$\phi(th) - x = tJ\phi(0) \cdot h + R(th).$$

Thus,

$$\lim_{t \to 0} \frac{\phi(th) - x}{t} = J\phi(0) \cdot h + \lim_{t \to 0} \frac{R(th)}{t}$$
$$= J\phi(0) \cdot h.$$

It follows that the derivative $d\phi_0$ is nothing but a linear transformation whose matrix-representation is $J\phi(0)$. Note that $J\phi(0)$ is of rank m because of the property of ϕ. By the derivative $d\phi_0$, the tangent space of M is defined as follows.

Definition 1.2 The tangent space of a m-dimensional manifold M at x is the image of the derivative $d\phi_0$. The tangent space, which we denote $T_x M$, is itself a vector subspace of $\mathbf{R}^n$ whose dimension is m. An element of $T_x M$ is called a tangent vector to M at x.

Thus, $T_x M$ is considered to be the m-dimensional hyperplane in $\mathbf{R}^n$ through the origin that is parallel to the hyperplane which best approximates M near x (see Fig. 1.3).

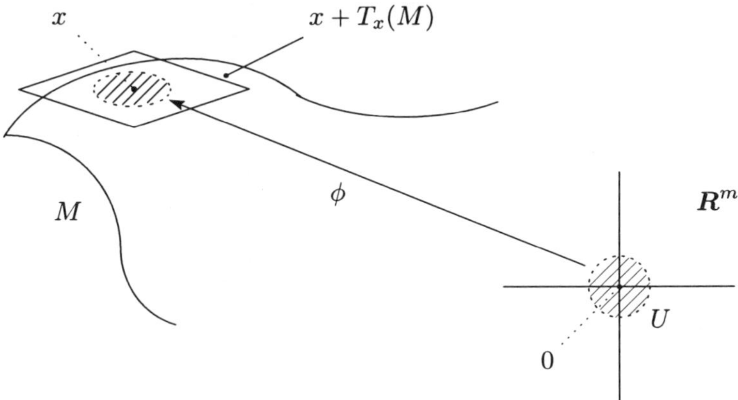

Fig. 1.3

As a concrete example, consider the tangent space of the circle S^1 mentioned above. We pick up a particular point $\bar{x} = (0, 1)$ on S^1 and describe $T_{\bar{x}} S^1$ explicitly. To this end , take a parametrization $\phi^1(x) = (x, \sqrt{1 - x^2})$ and compute $d\phi_0^1 : \mathbf{R} \to \mathbf{R}^2$. Note that $\phi^1(0) = \bar{x}$. Since $d\phi_0^1 = J\phi^1(0)$, we obtain that $d\phi_0^1 = (1, 0)^t$ where a superscript t designates the transpose. Thus, the desired tangent space $d\phi_0^1(\mathbf{R})$ is the set $\{(r, 0) \in \mathbf{R}^2 | r \in \mathbf{R}\}$

which is the horizontal axis X in $\boldsymbol{R}^2$. $\bar{x} + X$ is indeed the hyperplane which is tangent to S^1 at $\bar{x}$ (see Fig. 1.4).

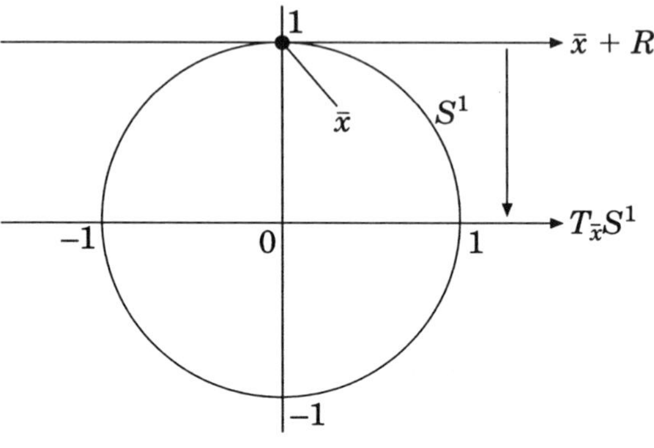

Fig. 1.4

Since the tangent space of a submanifold is of particular importance, we refer to it as a special example of the tangent space.

Example 1.5 the tangent space of a submanifold: Let A be a h-dimensional submanifold of a m-dimensional manifold M ($h \leq m$). The

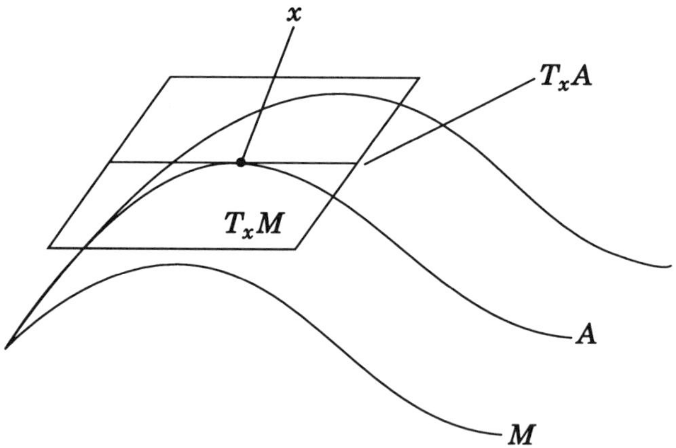

Fig. 1.5

tangent space of A at x, i.e. T_xA is the h-dimensional vector subspace of T_xM (see Fig. 1.5).

This property is easily obtained by the relation of the coordinate systems between A and M (see example 1.3).

1.1.2 *Differentiable Maps and Their Derivatives*

We now consider a map between manifolds. A differentiability of such a map is naturally defined by means of a parametrization of each manifold.

Definition 1.3 Let $M \subset \boldsymbol{R}^n$, $K \subset \boldsymbol{R}^l$ be two manifolds. Suppose that $dim M = m$ and $dim K = k$. A map $f : M \to K$ is differentiable at $x \in M$ if for a parametrization $\phi : U \to M$ about x and a parametrization $\psi : V \to K$ about $f(x)$, the composite $\psi^{-1} \circ f \circ \phi : U \to V$ is differentiable at $\phi^{-1}(x)$, where $U \subset \boldsymbol{R}^m$, $V \subset \boldsymbol{R}^k$ and U is small enough.

If $f : M \to K$ is differentiable at every point of M, f is simply called differentiable on M. In addition, if $\psi^{-1} \circ f \circ \phi$ is smooth, that is, infinitely continuously differentiable at $\phi^{-1}(x)$, f is called smooth at x. In this monograph, for convenience of explanation, we shall be mostly concerned with smooth maps .

For a smooth map, we can deduce by analogy, with the derivative of a parametrization, a linear map called the derivative at each point which is a linear approximation of the map around the point.

Definition 1.4 Let f be a smooth map between a m-dimensional manifold $M(\subset \boldsymbol{R}^n)$ and a k-dimensional manifold $K(\subset \boldsymbol{R}^l)$. The derivative of f at x, which we denote df_x, is a linear map from $T_x M$ to $T_{f(x)} K$ defined by

$$df_x = d\psi_0 \circ dg_0 \circ (d\phi_0)^{-1}$$

where ϕ, ψ are parametrizations about x and $f(x)$ respectively and $g = \psi^{-1} \circ f \circ \phi$ whereas $\phi(0) = x$, $\psi(0) = f(x)$.

Note in the above definition that $d\phi_0 : \boldsymbol{R}^m \to T_x M$ is a linear isomorphism so that $(d\phi_0)^{-1}$ makes sense. The property of the derivative df_x as a linear map depends on the derivative $dg_0 : \boldsymbol{R}^m \to \boldsymbol{R}^k$, more specifically, the Jacobian matrix of g at 0 since $d\phi_0$ and $d\psi_0$ are both linear isomorphisms.

Some of important derivatives are as follows.

Example 1.6 The derivative of the identity map: The identity map (denoted by I) from M to M has the identity map as its derivative at each point. That is, $dI_x = I : T_x M \to T_x M$ for any $x \in M$.

Example 1.7   The derivative of the inclusion map: The inclusion map (denoted by i) from a submanifold A of M to M has the inclusion map as its derivative at each point. That is, $di_x = i : T_x A \to T_x M$ for any $x \in A$.

Example 1.8   The derivative of a constant map: The derivative of a constant map $f : M \to K$ defined by $f(x) = \bar{y}$ for any $x \in M$ is also a constant map $df_x : T_x M \to T_{\bar{y}} K$ in which $df_x(v) = 0$ for any $v \in T_x M$ and any $x \in M$ since the singleton $\{\bar{y}\} \in K$ is considered to be a 0-dimensional submanifold in K.

Example 1.9   The derivative of a linear map: The derivative of a linear map $L : \boldsymbol{R}^n \to \boldsymbol{R}^l$ at $x \in \boldsymbol{R}^n$ is L itself.

Example 1.10   Chain rule: Let f be a smooth map from a manifold M to a manifold K and g be another differentiable map from a manifold K to a manifold P. Then the derivative of the composite $g \circ f$ at any point $x \in M$ is as follows.

$$d(g \circ f)_x = dg_{f(x)} \circ df_x.$$

In other words, the derivative of the composite is equal to the composite of the derivatives.

1.1.3   *Regular Values*

Let M and K be two manifolds. If $dim M \geq dim K$, we have a very important concept about a smooth map $f : M \to K$.

Definition 1.5   Let f be a smooth map from M to K. f is called a submersion at $x \in M$ if its derivative $df_x : T_x M \to T_{f(x)} K$ is surjective. If f is a submersion at $x \in M$, x is called a regular point of f. A point in M that is not a regular point of f is called a critical point of f. If every point in M is a regular point of f, f is simply called a submersion on M.

It is obvious from the definition that a regular point makes sense only if $dim M \geq dim K$. Note that x is a regular point of f if and only if the derivative of f at x, i.e. df_x, has the maximal rank. A regular value is deduced by a regular point.

Definition 1.6   For a smooth map $f : M \to K$, a point $y \in K$ is a regular value of f if every point in $f^{-1}(y)$ is a regular point of f. A point in K that is not a regular value of f is called a critical value of f.

Note that if $f^{-1}(y) = \emptyset$, then y is logically a regular value of f since the premise of the assertion is not valid. Some authors call a critical point (value) a singular point (value). Regarding a regular value, we can derive some very deep and interesting propositions on which the theory of regular economies is intrinsically based. Before proceeding to that argument, we are now in a position to give the definition of a regular economy.

1.2 Economical Analysis

The most abstract and fundamental question behind the theory of regular economies is this. What kind of properties can we observe in almost all conceivable economies? In terms of the theory of regular economies, economies and properties in question are specified in such a way that an economy should be formally described by a general competitive equilibrium model and properties should be concerned with the structure of the equilibrium set associated with each economy. Thus the question investigated in the theory should be as follows. What kind of structure does the set of equilibria have in almost all general equilibrium models? A "regular" economy is a key concept to cope with this problem.

Our goal in this section is to show how a "regular" economy is generated in the simplified framework.

1.2.1 *Basic Model*

Before reaching our goal, there are some prerequirements to meet. One of them is specification of an economy. As is mentioned above, an economy should be described by a general competitive equilibrium model. In this regard, we adopt the simplest economic model, that is, a pure exchange model where there is no production. Needless to say, the theory is applicable to the economy with production and, indeed, we deal with that case in Chapter 10.

The economy consists of I consumers ($i = 1, \ldots, I$) and L consumption goods($l = 1, \ldots, L$). A consumer is permitted to buy and sell any consumption good with a given price within its budget. Since we consider the pure exchange economy, a consumer's budget is solely made of its initial endowment of each good. That is to say, i-th consumer's income just amounts to $\boldsymbol{p} \cdot \boldsymbol{\omega}^i$ where $\boldsymbol{p}$ designates a given price vector $(p_1, \ldots, p_L)$ and $\boldsymbol{\omega}^i$ its initial endowment vector $(\omega_1^i, \ldots, \omega_L^i)$ which is also given to the consumer

$(i = 1, \ldots, I)$. Let w^i denote $\boldsymbol{p} \cdot \boldsymbol{\omega}^i$. We assume that the trade behavior of consumer i is characterized by its demand function $f^i : \boldsymbol{R}^L \times \boldsymbol{R} \to \boldsymbol{R}^L$ which carries $(\boldsymbol{p}, w^i)$ to its quantity demanded for each good $(i = 1, \ldots, I)$. Since the demand function is a vector-valued function, it will be written in component form as $f^i(\boldsymbol{p}, w^i) = (f_1^i(\boldsymbol{p}, w^i), \ldots, f_L^i(\boldsymbol{p}, w^i))$. Note that if $f_l^i(\boldsymbol{p}, w^i) - \omega_l^i > (<)0$, consumer i demands (supplies) the quantity of the difference for good l. So $f^i(\boldsymbol{p}, w^i) - \boldsymbol{\omega}^i$ is called the net demand function of consumer i and the value of each element of the net demand function is called the net quantity demanded for the corresponding good by i $(i = 1, \ldots, I)$. In general, the quantity demanded for good l by i is denoted by x_l^i and the vector composed of the quantity demanded for all goods is designated by $\boldsymbol{x}^i$, i.e. $\boldsymbol{x}^i = (x_1^i, \ldots, x_L^i)$, $i = 1, \ldots, I$.

We make the following assumptions with regard to the ingredients of the model.

Assumption 1.1   Every price is strictly positive. That is, $\boldsymbol{p} \in \boldsymbol{R}_{++}^L$.

Assumption 1.2   The initial endowment for each good of every consumer is strictly positive. That is, $\boldsymbol{\omega}^i \in \boldsymbol{R}_{++}^L$, $i = 1, \ldots, I$.

Assumption 1.3 $f^i : \boldsymbol{R}_{++}^L \times (0, +\infty) \to \boldsymbol{R}_+^L$ $(i = 1, \ldots, I)$ satisfies

(1) $f^i \in C^\infty(\boldsymbol{R}_{++}^L \times (0, +\infty), \boldsymbol{R}_+^L)$,

(2) f^i is homogeneous of degree 0 with respect to $\boldsymbol{p}$ and w^i, since $w^i = \boldsymbol{p} \cdot \boldsymbol{\omega}^i$, f^i turns out to be homogeneous of degree 0 with respect to $\boldsymbol{p}$,

(3) for any $\boldsymbol{p}$ and w^i, we have $\boldsymbol{p} \cdot f^i(\boldsymbol{p}, w^i) = w^i$.

Assumption 1.3 (2) enables us to normalize a price vector, confining it in a strictly positive $(L - 1)$-dimensional simplex $S_{++}^{L-1} = \{\boldsymbol{p} \in \boldsymbol{R}_{++}^L \mid \sum_{l=1} p_l = 1\}$. This normalization economically implies that we can only deal with relative prices.

A pure exchange model is the simplest model of a competitive economy because a perfectly competitive market opens for every good though no product is involved in a market. Therefore, every agent, i.e. consumer, is supposed to behave as a price taker. A price for each good itself is determined by an auctioneer who adjusts the market condition through a tâtonnement process. As a result, we reach the specific situation where the aggregate demand is equal to the aggregate supply in every market, which is called an equilibrium. The fundamental idea of economics is that "the observed state of an economy can be viewed as an equilibrium" (Debreu

(1974)). Thus, we need to describe an equilibrium condition as the last ingredient to form our basic model.

Definition 1.7   A general equilibrium (or simply equilibrium) state is the situation where the aggregate demand is equal to the aggregate supply in every market, that is,

$$\sum_{i=1} f^i(\boldsymbol{p}, w^i) = \sum_{i=1} \boldsymbol{\omega}^i.$$

A price vector that gives rise to an equilibrium state is called a system of equilibrium prices or an equilibrium price vector.

Needless to say, the equilibrium condition can also be written as

$$\sum_{i=1} f^i(\boldsymbol{p}, \boldsymbol{p} \cdot \boldsymbol{\omega}^i) = \sum_{i=1} \boldsymbol{\omega}^i.$$

1.2.2   *The Space of Economies*

Since, as we stated before, the subject of the theory of regular economies is to investigate a property in 'almost all' economies, the theory should be developed on the basis of the whole set of "economies". The set of economies is only conceivable in an analytical sense if an economy can be represented by some analytical characteristics. In general the analytical characteristics contributing a framework for modelling an economy are called economy parameters. Consider such parameters regarding our model, i.e, a general competitive equilibrium model mentioned above. As such we can mention the initial endowment and the demand function of each consumer as well as the numbers of consumers and goods. In this monograph we neglect the birth and the death of consumers and goods so that we are left with choices of the initial endowment and the demand function of each consumer. In Part 1 we only consider the former as the economy parameter specifying an economy, which implies that the demand functions of all consumers are given. In other words, it is an allocation of consumers' initial endowment vectors $(\boldsymbol{\omega}^1, \ldots, \boldsymbol{\omega}^I)$ that specifies a pure exchange economy. Thus, we are able to identify an economy with an allocation of consumers' initial endowment vectors. Let ω denote $(\boldsymbol{\omega}^1, \ldots, \boldsymbol{\omega}^I)$ in the following.

Definition 1.8   The whole set of conceivable allocations of consumers' initial endowment vectors is called the space of economies denoted by $\mathcal{E}$. That is, $\mathcal{E} = (\boldsymbol{R}^L_{++})^I = \boldsymbol{R}^{LI}_{++}$.

An economy parameter $\omega \in \mathcal{E}$ is often simply called an economy. However, note that the space of economies is not a priori fixed but dependent on what kind of parameters we choose. Indeed, in Part 2 we will try to extend the space of economies given in the above definition.

Given an $\omega \in \mathcal{E}$, a pure exchange economy is specified. Then, what are we supposed to do next? As provided above, an equilibrium has been seen as an abstraction from a state of our real economy, so that it is no wonder that most theoretical issues have taken place with regard to the properties of an equilibrium. This is also the case in the theory of regular economies. We are especially concerned with the structure of equilibria as a set. Is the set of equilibria empty or not? Is the set of equilibria a singleton, finite or a continuum? If it is a continuum, does it have a definite dimension or not? Indeed, historically the theory of regular economies originated from an issue of uniqueness of an equilibrium (see Debreu (1970)).

The remarkable feature of the theory of regular economies consists in investigating those issues always in connection with the underlying economy. Specifically, we associate an economy ω with its set of equilibria which we denote $W(\omega)$. So it remains for us to determine the characteristics that represent an equilibrium. Though in the literature a couple $((\boldsymbol{x}^i)_i, p)$ which yields an equilibrium state is very often used as such a characteristic, we only adopt a system of equilibrium prices to describe an equilibrium state. So $W(\omega)$ should be interpreted as a set of systems of equilibrium prices for an economy ω.

1.2.3 *Regular Economies*

Now we are in a position to answer the question " What is a regular economy?" The term regular stems from a regular value. In a word, a regular economy is an economy as a regular value. Therefore, it formally follows from the definition of a regular value that a regular economy requires some smooth map from one manifold to the space of economies as another manifold. The point is how we should construct the smooth map as well as the domain manifold. In view of our issue alluded to above, we are required to construct it in such a way that the set of equiribria is associated with the underlying economy.

There are several ways to accomplish this among which we adopt for a while (chapters 1 and 2) the one developed by Debreu who initiated the theory of regular economies (see Debreu (1970)). This way is rather artificial but good enough to illuminate how to define regular economies.

The story begins with the following map $F : S_{++}^{L-1} \times (0, +\infty) \times \boldsymbol{R}_{++}^{L(I-1)} \to \boldsymbol{R}^{LI}$ defined by

$$F(\boldsymbol{p}, w^1, \boldsymbol{\omega}^2, \ldots, \boldsymbol{\omega}^I) = (f^1(\boldsymbol{p}, w^1) + \sum_{i=2} f^i(\boldsymbol{p}, \boldsymbol{p} \cdot \boldsymbol{\omega}^i) - \sum_{i=2} \boldsymbol{\omega}^i, \boldsymbol{\omega}^2, \ldots, \boldsymbol{\omega}^I).$$

This is a smooth map between two manifolds (note that $S_{++}^{L-1} \times (0, +\infty) \times \boldsymbol{R}_{++}^{L(I-1)}$ is a product manifold). Note that the range manifold includes the space of economies. A relation between an economy and its equilibrium set is deduced by the map through the following proposition.

Proposition 1.1   *For any economy $\omega \in \mathcal{E}$, a price vector $\boldsymbol{p}$ is a system of equilibrium prices if and only if*

$$F(\boldsymbol{p}, w^1, \boldsymbol{\omega}^2, \ldots, \boldsymbol{\omega}^I) = (\boldsymbol{\omega}^1, \ldots, \boldsymbol{\omega}^I).$$

Proof. $\leftarrow$: If

$$F(\boldsymbol{p}, w^1, \boldsymbol{\omega}^2, \ldots, \boldsymbol{\omega}^I) = (\boldsymbol{\omega}^1, \ldots, \boldsymbol{\omega}^I),$$

we have

$$f^1(\boldsymbol{p}, w^1) + \sum_{i=2} f^i(\boldsymbol{p}, \boldsymbol{p} \cdot \boldsymbol{\omega}^i) - \sum_{i=2} \boldsymbol{\omega}^i = \boldsymbol{\omega}^1.$$

Multiplying through by $\boldsymbol{p}$, then we have $w^1 = \boldsymbol{p} \cdot \boldsymbol{\omega}^1$ since $\boldsymbol{p} \cdot f^i(\boldsymbol{p}, \boldsymbol{p} \cdot \boldsymbol{\omega}^i) = \boldsymbol{p} \cdot \boldsymbol{\omega}^i$, $i = 2, \ldots, I$, and $\boldsymbol{p} \cdot f^1(\boldsymbol{p}, w^1) = w^1$ by definition. Thus the above equation implies

$$\sum_{i=1} f^i(\boldsymbol{p}, \boldsymbol{p} \cdot \boldsymbol{\omega}^i) = \sum_{i=1} \boldsymbol{\omega}^i$$

which is nothing but an equilibrium condition.

   $\to$: If a price vector $\boldsymbol{p}$ is a system of equilibrium prices for ω, we have

$$f^1(\boldsymbol{p}, \boldsymbol{p} \cdot \boldsymbol{\omega}^1) + \sum_{i=2} f^i(\boldsymbol{p}, \boldsymbol{p} \cdot \boldsymbol{\omega}^i) - \sum_{i=2} \boldsymbol{\omega}^i = \boldsymbol{\omega}^1$$

which is equivalent to that

$$F(\boldsymbol{p}, w^1, \boldsymbol{\omega}^2, \ldots, \boldsymbol{\omega}^I) = (\boldsymbol{\omega}^1, \ldots, \boldsymbol{\omega}^I)$$

and

$$f^1(\boldsymbol{p}, w^1) = f^1(\boldsymbol{p}, \boldsymbol{p} \cdot \boldsymbol{\omega}^1).$$

Among the above two equations, the former implies the latter because we have shown that if the former holds, $w^1 = \boldsymbol{p} \cdot \boldsymbol{\omega}^1$. $\qquad\square$

Consider the inverse image $F^{-1}(\omega)$ for any economy $\omega \in \mathcal{E}$. If two elements $(\boldsymbol{p}, w^1, \boldsymbol{\omega}^2, \ldots, \boldsymbol{\omega}^I)$, $(\boldsymbol{p}', w^{1\prime}, \boldsymbol{\omega}^{2\prime}, \ldots, \boldsymbol{\omega}^{I\prime})$ in $F^{-1}(\omega)$ are distinct, then $\boldsymbol{p} \neq \boldsymbol{p}'$ because otherwise $w^1 = \boldsymbol{p} \cdot \boldsymbol{\omega}^1 = \boldsymbol{p}' \cdot \boldsymbol{\omega}^1 = w^{1\prime}$, which is a contradiction. Thus, the foregoing proposition assures that for any $\omega \in \mathcal{E}$, $W(\omega)$ (the set of systems of equilibrium prices for ω) is equipotent to $F^{-1}(\omega)$, which we denote $W(\omega) \sim F^{-1}(\omega)$, where "Set A is equipotent to set B" means that there exists a bijection between A and B. Since $F^{-1}(\omega)$ can be regarded as a relative topological space in $S_{++}^{L-1} \times (0, +\infty) \times \boldsymbol{R}_{++}^{L(I-1)}$ which is endowed with the standard Euclidean topology, we obtain the induced topology in $W(\omega)$ through the bijection:$F^{-1}(\omega) \to W(\omega)$. Note that with respect to those topologies, $F^{-1}(\omega)$ and $W(\omega)$ are homeomorphic, which we denote $F^{-1}(\omega) \simeq W(\omega)$. It follows from the fact that $F^{-1}(\omega) \simeq W(\omega)$ that we are allowed to investigate $F^{-1}(\omega)$ in place of $W(\omega)$ so far as the topological structure is concerned. In other words, by virtue of the foregoing map F, we can replace the relation of ω and $W(\omega)$ by the one of ω and $F^{-1}(\omega)$.

Finally we can give the definition of a regular economy.

Definition 1.9   An economy $\omega \in \mathcal{E}$ is a regular economy if ω is a regular value of F. If ω is a critical value of F, then it is called a critical economy.

We see from the above definition that a "regular" economy is wholly dependent on a mathematical concept "regular value". Then, why is a regular value our particular concern in the context of our economical analysis? What's more, does a regular value ever exist in the space of economies $\mathcal{E}$? (Note that $\mathcal{E}$ is only a subset of the range of F.) It turns out in the next chapter that mathematical properties concerning regular values give the answers to those questions that involve remarkably significant economical interpretations. More specifically, only if an economy $\omega \in \mathcal{E}$ is a regular economy, $W(\omega)$ has a particular structure. Moreover, only regular economies occupy a particularly significant position in the space of economies.

Chapter 2

Regular Economies and Genericity

A specific structure of the equilibrium set of a regular economy and a specific position that regular economies occupy in the space of economies are related by a mathematical concept called "genericity" which is the keyword of the theory of regular economies. In this chapter, first we give a precise exposition of genericity in terms of the regular values of a smooth map. Then, on the basis of the genericity we show many significant aspects regular economies assume in the space of economies.

2.1 Mathematical Preliminaries

2.1.1 *Preimage Theorem*

Regular values have some remarkable properties. Our interest here in this subsection is, among others, in the property concerning the preimage of a regular value. First of all, we need the following lemma.

Lemma 2.1 *Let f be a smooth map from a m-dimensional manifold M to a k-dimensional manifold K $(m \geq k)$. Suppose that $\bar{x} \in M$ is a regular point of f, and $\bar{y} = f(\bar{x})$. Then there exist parametrizations around $\bar{x}$ and $\bar{y}$ such that $\psi^{-1} \circ f \circ \phi(x_1, \ldots, x_m) = (x_1, \ldots, x_k)$ where $\phi(0) = \bar{x}$ and $\psi(0) = \bar{y}$.*

This lemma is known as the Local Submersion Theorem (for the proof, see Guillemin and Pollack (1974) p. 20). If we identify any point in a manifold with its values of coordinate functions, then the above lemma asserts that around a regular point f is locally equivalent to the canonical submersion where the canonical submersion is the standard projection of $\boldsymbol{R}^m$ onto $\boldsymbol{R}^k$ in which $(x_1, \ldots, x_m) \mapsto (x_1, \ldots, x_k)$.

17

We are led to the following theorem called the Preimage Theorem by this lemma.

Theorem 2.1 *Let f be a smooth map from a m-dimensional manifold M to a k-dimensional manifold $K(m \geq k)$. Suppose that $y \in K$ is a regular value of f. Then the preimage $f^{-1}(y)$ is a submanifold of M with $dim f^{-1}(y) = dim M - dim K$ (i.e. $m - k$).*

Proof.   Since any point $\bar{x} \in f^{-1}(y)$ is a regular point of f, we obtain by the foregoing lemma that around $\bar{x}$ and y

$$f(x_1, \ldots, x_m) = (x_1, \ldots, x_k)$$

where we identify any point in the neighborhoods of $\bar{x}$ and y with its values of the corresponding coordinate functions. Thus around $f^{-1}(y) \cap V$, $f^{-1}(y)$ is composed of the points with the coordinates $(0, \ldots, 0, x_{k+1}, \ldots, x_m)$ since we can assume that y corresponds to $(0, \ldots, 0)$. Alternatively put, for the neighborhood of $\bar{x}$ (denoted by V) any point of $f^{-1}(y) \cap V$ always has a particular coordinate form $(0, \ldots, 0, x_{k+1}, \ldots, x_m)$ so that only coordinate functions corresponding to $(x_{k+1}, \ldots, x_m)$ form a coordinate system on $f^{-1}(y) \cap V$. Since a point $\bar{x} \in f^{-1}(y)$ is arbitrary, the theorem follows. $\square$

Corollary 2.1   *Let f, M and K be the same as the ones in the previous theorem. Suppose that $y \in K$ is a regular value of f. Then at any point $x \in f^{-1}(y)$, $df_x^{-1}(0)$ is equal to $T_x(f^{-1}(y))$ where $df_x : T_x M \to T_y K$ is the derivative of f at x.*

Proof.   Since f is a constant map on $f^{-1}(y)$, at any point $x \in f^{-1}(y)$ df_x carries any point(tangent vector) of $T_x(f^{-1}(y))$ to 0. On the other hand, $df_x : T_x M \to T_y K$ is surjective for x is a regular point of f. Thus the dimension of the kernel $df_x^{-1}(0)$ is equal to $dim M - dim K$ $(= m - k)$ which is, by the above theorem, nothing but the dimension of $f^{-1}(y)$. $\square$

It follows from the above corollary that df_x is linear isomorphic on the complementary subspace of $T_x(f^{-1}(y))$ in $T_x M$.

We are especially concerned with the case in which $dim M = dim K$. The following proposition is immediately obtained.

Proposition 2.1   *If $dim M = dim K$, for any regular value $y \in K$ of $f : M \to K$, $f^{-1}(y)$ constitutes a discrete set.*

Proof.   By theorem 2.1 $dim f^{-1}(y) = 0$, so that it forms a discrete set (see example 1.2). $\square$

It is possible for us to obtain a strengthened result through the following lemma.

Lemma 2.2 *A compact discrete set in $\boldsymbol{R}^n$ is a finite set.*

Proof. Let X be a compact discrete set in $\boldsymbol{R}^n$. Suppose that X is an infinite set. Since X is discrete, there exists a relatively open neighborhood around each point x of X that includes no point of X but x. Thus those open neighborhoods corresponding to each point form an open covering of X. It is, however, obvious that any finite family of sets from the covering can not cover X, which contradicts the compactness of X. $\qquad\square$

Proposition 2.2 *If $dimM = dimK$ and M is compact, then for any regular value $y \in K$ of $f : M \to K$, $f^{-1}(y)$ is a finite set.*

Proof. Since f is continuous, $f^{-1}(y)$ is closed in M (note that a singleton $\{y\}$ is a closed set in K). Thus $f^{-1}(y)$ is compact so that by the above lemma it is a finite set. $\qquad\square$

What if M is not compact? Then the properness of a smooth map f leads to the same consequence.

Definition 2.1 A smooth map $f : M \to K$ is proper if for any compact set C in K, $f^{-1}(C)$ is compact in M.

Proposition 2.3 *If $dimM = dimK$ and a smooth map $f : M \to K$ is proper, then for any regular value $y \in K$ of f, $f^{-1}(y)$ is a finite set.*

Proof. Since f is proper, $f^{-1}(y)$ is compact, for a regular value y is compact in K as a singleton set. $\qquad\square$

2.1.2 *Lebesgue Measure Zero*

Our next concern is about a position that regular values themselves occupy in the range of a smooth map. Before proceeding to the topic, we need to refer to Lebesgue measure zero which is a measure of the "smallness" of a set in the ambient space.

Definition 2.2 A subset A in $\boldsymbol{R}^n$ has Lebesgue measure zero if for any given ϵ, it is possible to cover A by a sequence of cubes in $\boldsymbol{R}^n$ having total n-dimensional volume less than ϵ.

Lebesgue measure zero is often simply called measure zero.

Example 2.1   A single point in $\boldsymbol{R}$. A line in $\boldsymbol{R}^2$. A plane in $\boldsymbol{R}^3$. A hyperplane in $\boldsymbol{R}^n$. A k-dimensional affine space in $\boldsymbol{R}^n$ ($k < n$). They all have Lebesgue measure zero.

The concept of Lebesgue measure zero can be easily extended to sets in manifolds.

Definition 2.3   A subset C in a m-dimensional manifold M has Lebesgue measure zero in M if for a parametrization $\phi : U \to V$ around any point of C, $\phi^{-1}(C \cap V)$ has Lebesgue measure zero in $\boldsymbol{R}^m$.

Example 2.2   A submanifold K in M has Lebesgue measure zero in M if $dim K < dim M$. In particular, a curve in $\boldsymbol{R}^2$, a surface in $\boldsymbol{R}^3$, and a hypersurface in $\boldsymbol{R}^n$ all have Lebesgue measure zero.

Intuitively, a set of Lebesgue measure zero seems very "thin" in the ambient space. Indeed, the complement of any Lebesgue measure zero set is "fat" in the following sense.

Proposition 2.4   *The complement of a set of Lebesgue measure zero in $\boldsymbol{R}^n$ is dense in $\boldsymbol{R}^n$.*

Proof.   Let A be a set of Lebesgue measure zero and B be the complement of A in $\boldsymbol{R}^n$. Suppose that there exists a point $x \in \boldsymbol{R}^n$ and its neighborhood N_x such that $N_x \cap B = \emptyset$. Then obviously $N_x \subseteq A$. Since N_x contains an open ball around x in $\boldsymbol{R}^n$, A includes an open set in $\boldsymbol{R}^n$, which contradicts that A has Lebesgue measure zero. Thus at any point in $\boldsymbol{R}^n$, any neighborhood of the point intersects B. $\square$

Considering definition 2.3, we may say that if a subset C in an m-dimensional manifold M has Lebesgue measure zero in M, then the complement of C in M is dense in M.

It is, however, noteworthy that Lebesgue measure zero is compatible with density. We would be able to understand why it goes on with the following proposition concerning Lebesgue measure zero.

Proposition 2.5   *The union of a countable family of sets of Lebesgue measure zero has Lebesgue measure zero.*

Proof.   Let $A_1, A_2, \ldots$ be a sequence of sets of Lebesgue measure zero. For any given ϵ (> 0), let $\{Q_i^n\}_{i=1}^{\infty}$ be a sequence of cubes covering A_n with total volume less than $\epsilon/2^n$, ($n = 1, 2, \ldots$). Then obviously $\bigcup_{n=1}^{\infty} A_n \subseteq \bigcup_{n=1}^{\infty} \bigcup_{i=1}^{\infty} Q_i^n$ and the latter set has a total volume less than $\sum_{n=1}^{\infty} \epsilon/2^n = \epsilon$. $\square$

It follows from this proposition that in particular the whole set of rational numbers has Lebesgue measure zero in $\boldsymbol{R}$. However, as is well known, the set itself is dense in $\boldsymbol{R}$! Thus the intuitive way of saying that a set of Lebesgue measure zero is "thin" and a dense set is "fat" is very misleading.

To strengthen Lebesgue measure zero another concept of closedness is often taken into account. Indeed, if a set of Lebesgue measure zero is closed, then it becomes nowhere dense, so that it is a meager set (for a meager set, see Dugundji (1989), Chap. XI, § 10). Moreover, a closed subset of Lebesgue measure zero is incompatible with density because a closed dense set is the ambient space itself. Consequently, the precise image of the "thinness" of a set should be based not only on Lebesgue measure zero but also on closedness. In this connection, the complement of a closed subset of Lebesgue measure zero is dense *and* open, which should be considered to be a precise index of the "fatness" of a set.

2.1.3 *Sard's Theorem*

We now turn to another remarkable property concerning regular values, which is related to the position they occupy in the range. The key to the whole story is the following theorem that is well known as Sard's theorem.

Theorem 2.2 *Let f be a smooth map from $\boldsymbol{R}^m$ to $\boldsymbol{R}^k (m \geq k)$. Then the set of critical values of f has Lebesgue measure zero in $\boldsymbol{R}^k$. Thus the set of regular values of f is dense in $\boldsymbol{R}^k$.*

For the proof of the theorem, see Milnor (1969), § 3.
The manifold version of the above theorem is straightforward.

Theorem 2.3 *Let f be a smooth map from an m-dimensional manifold M to an k-dimensional manifold K $(m \geq k)$. Then the set of critical values of f has Lebesgue measure zero in K. Thus the set of regular values of f is dense in K.*

Now we consider the requirements for the set of critical values of f to be closed so as to attain the real fat set of regular values. To this end, we first notice how the set of critical *points* behaves.

Proposition 2.6 *The set of critical points of a smooth map $f : M \to K$ $(dim M \geq dim K)$ is closed in M .*

Proof. We will demonstrate the proposition by showing that the complement of the set of critical points of a smooth map f in M, which is nothing but the set of regular points of f, is open in M. Let R be the set of regular points of f. Fix a point $\bar{x}$ of R, then there exist parametrizations around $\bar{x}$ and $\bar{y} = f(\bar{x})$ such that the map $\tilde{f} = \psi^{-1} \circ f \circ \phi : U \to V$ is a submersion at 0 where $\phi(0) = \bar{x}$ and $\psi(0) = \bar{y}$. Thus the matrix representation of the derivative $d\tilde{f}_0$, which we denote $\tilde{F}_0$, has full rank. Since at any point $x \in U$ sufficiently close to 0 each element of the matrix representation of the derivative $d\tilde{f}_x$, which we denote $\tilde{F}_x$, is close enough to the corresponding element of $\tilde{F}_0$, $\tilde{F}_x$ also has full rank, so that $\tilde{f}$ is a submersion at x. This implies that any point of a neighborhood of $\bar{x}$ is a regular point. Since $\bar{x}$ was arbitrarily chosen from R, our claim follows. $\qquad\square$

It follows from the above proposition that if $f : M \to K$ is a closed map, then the set of critical values of f has a closed property as well as Lebesgue measure zero where a closed map is defined as follows.

Definition 2.4   A map $f : X \to Y$ is called closed if the image of each closed set in X is closed in Y.

Note that the above definition is written in a general form where X and Y are topological spaces.

Interestingly enough, a closed map is closely related to a previously mentioned proper map.

Proposition 2.7   *Let X and Y be both locally compact Hausdorff spaces. Then a continuous map $f : X \to Y$ is proper if and only if f is a closed map and $f^{-1}(y)$ is compact for any $y \in Y$.*

For the proof of the proposition, see Bourbaki (1965), Chap. 1, § 10.

Since finite dimensional manifolds are locally compact Hausdorff spaces, we have

Proposition 2.8   *If a smooth map f from a m-dimensional manifold M to a k-dimensional manifold K ($m \geq k$) is proper, then the set of regular values of f is open and dense in K.*

Proof.   If f is proper, the set of critical values of f is closed and has Lebesgue measure zero. Thus the the set of regular values of f, which is the complement of the set of critical values of f in K, is open and dense in K. $\qquad\square$

2.1.4 *Genericity*

According to the mathematical convention concerning properties associated with points, if some property is invalid only on the set of Lebesgue measure zero, then the property is said to be valid at almost all points or almost everywhere. Genericity is the generalization of this notion.

Suppose that the totality of admissible environments under consideration is described by some parameters. Roughly speaking, a generic property is such a property that holds in a very large set of parameters. For the formal definition of genericity, we presume that the parameter space is endowed with a certain topology.

Definition 2.5 Let X be the parameter space with some topology. If the set $\{x \in X \,|\, x \; satisfies \; property \; P\}$ is dense in X, then P is a generic property with respect to X.

In particular, if X is a finite dimensional manifold, a property that fails to hold in a set of Lebesgue measure zero is properly generic. Accordingly, in view of the arguments of foregoing subsections, regular values could have something to do with genericity. Indeed, if we consider a k-dimensional manifold K to be a parameter space, then for any given smooth map $f : M \to K$ a property common to all regular values of f is a generic property with respect to K. Consequently, given a smooth map $f : M \to K$ $(dim M \geq dim K)$, the property that the preimage by f constitutes a $(m-k)$-dimensional submanifold in M is generic with respect to K. This observation plays a very important role in the following economical analysis.

In the literature, the term "genericity" is often confined to the case in which the parameter space is a functional space $C^{\infty}(M, K)$, i.e. the set of all smooth maps from M to K. We will deal with such a case in Part 2 where we will consider each agent's preference to be one of the parameters that describe the economy.

2.2 Economical Analysis

2.2.1 *Regular Economies and Genericity*

First, recall how a regular economy is specified. An economy $\omega \in \mathcal{E}$ is a regular economy if ω is a regular value of the following map $F : S_{++}^{L-1} \times$

$$(0, +\infty) \times \boldsymbol{R}_{++}^{L(I-1)} \to \boldsymbol{R}^{LI}.$$

$$F(\boldsymbol{p}, w^1, \boldsymbol{\omega}^2, \ldots, \boldsymbol{\omega}^I) = \left(f^1(\boldsymbol{p}, w^1) + \sum_{i=2} f^i(\boldsymbol{p}, \boldsymbol{p} \cdot \boldsymbol{\omega}^i) - \sum_{i=2} \boldsymbol{\omega}^i, \boldsymbol{\omega}^2, \ldots, \boldsymbol{\omega}^I \right).$$

For $\omega, \mathcal{E}, , f, w$ and $\boldsymbol{p}$, see Chap. 1, § 2. Thus, through Sard's Theorem we immediately obtain

Theorem 2.4　*The set of regular economies is dense in $\mathcal{E}$ (the space of economies).*

Proof.　Since $S_{++}^{L-1} \times (0, +\infty) \times \boldsymbol{R}_{++}^{L(I-1)}$ and $\boldsymbol{R}^{LI}$ are obviously finite dimensional manifolds and F is smooth, the set of regular values of F, which we denote R, is dense in $\boldsymbol{R}^{LI}$. On the other hand, $\mathcal{E}$ is nothing but $\boldsymbol{R}_{++}^{LI}$, which is open in $\boldsymbol{R}^{LI}$. Thus $R \cap E$ is dense in $\mathcal{E}$. $\qquad\square$

Needless to say, the set of critical economies forms a set of Lebesgue measure zero.

Thus, a property common to every regular economy is generic with respect to $\mathcal{E}$. Alternatively put, a property that holds in regular economies can be observed in almost all economies. The basic idea of the theory of regular economies consists in investigating a generic property with respect to economies through regular economies. In this connection, we should keep it in mind that a 'property' is exclusively concerned with the structure of the equilibrium set. In the following we will show some properties as such.

2.2.2　*Local Uniqueness of Equilibria as a Generic Property*

What is a conceivable generic property concerning regular economies? In this connection, recall the suggestion stated in 2.1.4. That is, given a smooth F, then the property that the preimage by F constitutes a definite dimensional submanifold is generic with respect to $\mathcal{E}$. This observation leads to the following claim.

Theorem 2.5　*For any regular economy $\omega \in E$, the set of equilibrium price vectors $W(\omega)$ is a discrete set. In other words, the local uniqueness of equilibria is generic with respect to economies.*

Proof.　The dimension of the domain of $F(S_{++}^{L-1} \times (0, +\infty) \times \boldsymbol{R}_{++}^{L(I-1)})$ is LI which is equal to the dimension of $\boldsymbol{R}^{LI}$. It follows from the Preimage Theorem that the preimage of any regular value by F constitutes a submanifold with dimension 0. Thus $F^{-1}(\omega)$ is discrete for any regular economy ω. However, for any economy ω, $F^{-1}(\omega) \simeq W(\omega)$, so that for any regular economy ω, $W(\omega)$ also turns out to be discrete. $\quad\square$

Note that on the contrary, the uniqueness of equilibrium requires very severe assumptions on the demand functions(to be precise, the aggregate excess demand function) such as the gross substitutability or the weak axiom of social revealed preference, etc (See Mas-Colell, Whinston and Green (1995), 17. F).

2.2.3 *Finiteness of Equilibria as a Generic Property*

We could strengthen the result obtained in the previous subsection with a modest assumption on the demand function.

Theorem 2.6 asserts that the set of regular economies forms a dense set in $\mathcal{E}$ and the set of equilibrium price vectors of every regular economy is a discrete set. However, as we suggested before (see propositions 2.3 and 2.8), if the map F is proper, we will have a strengthened and preferable result; that is to say, not only the set of regular economies is open and dense in $\mathcal{E}$ but also the set of equilibrium price vectors of every regular economy is finite. It is, however, easily seen that F is itself not proper since the range manifold of F is $\boldsymbol{R}^{LI}$. Thus, we consider a constrained properness regarding F by restricting conceivable compact sets not in $\boldsymbol{R}^{LI}$ but in $\boldsymbol{R}^{LI}_{++}$ which is nothing but the space of economies $\mathcal{E}$ to be considered. Specifically, we check if $F^{-1}(C)$ is compact in $S^{L-1}_{++} \times (0, +\infty) \times \boldsymbol{R}^{L(I-1)}_{++}$ for any compact set C in $\boldsymbol{R}^{LI}_{++}$ where $S^{L-1}_{++} \times (0, +\infty) \times \boldsymbol{R}^{L(I-1)}_{++}$ and $\boldsymbol{R}^{LI}_{++}$ are both considered to be relative topological spaces. Then we see that some condition is needed on the map f^1 of F to assure the constrained properness for F. Indeed, if $f^1(\boldsymbol{p}, w^1)$ has a bounded value for some $\boldsymbol{p} \in S^{L-1}_{++}$ and infinity of w^1, then the preimage of some bounded point in $\boldsymbol{R}^{L(I-1)}_{++}$ by F may be unbounded in the domain, which obviously leads to the invalidity of the constrained properness for F. So we consider the following assumption for f^1.

Assumption 2.1 If a sequence $(\boldsymbol{p}^q, w^{1q})$ in $S^{L-1}_{++} \times (0, +\infty)$ converges to a point $(\boldsymbol{p}^0, w^{10})$ in $(S^{L-1}_+ \setminus S^{L-1}_{++}) \times (0, +\infty)$, then

$$\lim_{q \to +\infty} \|f^1(\boldsymbol{p}^q, w^{1q})\| = +\infty$$

where $\| \cdot \|$ designates the Euclidean norm.

In view of the desirability of the goods, this assumption does not seem so restrictive.

This assumption enables us to obtain the constrained properness for F.

Lemma 2.3   *Under assumption 2.1, the preimage of any compact set in $\mathcal{E}$ by F is compact in $S_{++}^{L-1} \times (0, +\infty) \times \boldsymbol{R}_{++}^{L(I-1)}$.*

Proof.   Let K be an arbitrary compact set in $\mathcal{E}$. To demonstrate that $F^{-1}(K)$ is compact in $S_{++}^{L-1} \times (0, +\infty) \times \boldsymbol{R}_{++}^{L(I-1)}$, it suffices to show that any sequence in $F^{-1}(K)$ has a subsequence which converges to a point in $S_{++}^{L-1} \times (0, +\infty) \times \boldsymbol{R}_{++}^{L(I-1)}$. Pick any sequence $(\boldsymbol{p}^q, w^{1q}, \boldsymbol{\omega}^{2q}, \ldots, \boldsymbol{\omega}^{Iq})_q$ from $F^{-1}(K)$. It is easily seen from the construction of F that the sequence contains a convergent subsequence in $S_+^{L-1} \times (0, +\infty) \times \boldsymbol{R}_{++}^{L(I-1)}$. Let $(\boldsymbol{p}^0, w^{10}, \boldsymbol{\omega}^{20}, \ldots, \boldsymbol{\omega}^{I0})$ be the limit point of the subsequence. It is sufficient to show that $\boldsymbol{p}^0 \in S_{++}^{L-1}$ and $0 < w^{10} < +\infty$. Noting that $\boldsymbol{p}^0(f^1(\boldsymbol{p}^0, w^{10}) + \sum_{i=2} f^i(\boldsymbol{p}^0, \boldsymbol{p}^0 \cdot \boldsymbol{\omega}^{i0}) - \sum_{i=2} \boldsymbol{\omega}^{i0}) = w^{10}$, we obtain the boundedness of w^{10} since $\boldsymbol{p}^0 \in S_+^{L-1}$ while the continuity of F assures the boundedness of $f^1(\boldsymbol{p}^0, w^{10}) + \sum_{i=2} f^i(\boldsymbol{p}^0, \boldsymbol{p}^0 \cdot \boldsymbol{\omega}^{i0}) - \sum_{i=2} \boldsymbol{\omega}^{i0}$. Consequently it remains to be shown that $\boldsymbol{p}^0 \in S_{++}^{L-1}$. Suppose that $\boldsymbol{p}^0 \in S_+^{L-1} \setminus S_{++}^{L-1}$. Then, by Assumption 2.1 $\|f^1(\boldsymbol{p}^0, w^{10})\| = +\infty$, which implies that the sequence $(f^1(\boldsymbol{p}^q, w^{1q}) + \sum_{i=2} f^i(\boldsymbol{p}^q, \boldsymbol{p}^q \cdot \boldsymbol{\omega}^{iq}) - \sum_{i=2} \boldsymbol{\omega}^{iq})_q$ is unbounded. However, $F(\boldsymbol{p}^q, w^{1q}, \boldsymbol{\omega}^{2q}, \ldots, \boldsymbol{\omega}^{Iq}) = (f^1(\boldsymbol{p}^q, w^{1q}) + \sum_{i=2} f^i(\boldsymbol{p}^q, \boldsymbol{p}^q \cdot \boldsymbol{\omega}^{iq}) - \sum_{i=2} \boldsymbol{\omega}^{iq}, \boldsymbol{\omega}^{2q}, \ldots, \boldsymbol{\omega}^{Iq}) \in K$, which is a contradiction because K is compact. Thus, we have that $\boldsymbol{p}^0 \in S_{++}^{L-1}$. $\square$

For simplicity, let U be the domain of F (i.e. $S_{++}^{L-1} \times (0, +\infty) \times \boldsymbol{R}_{++}^{L(I-1)}$) and V be the preimage of $\mathcal{E}$ by F (i.e. $F^{-1}(\mathcal{E})$).

Lemma 2.4   *Under assumption 2.1, for any closed set C in U the complement of $F(C \cap V)$ in $\mathcal{E}$ is open in $\mathcal{E}$.*

Proof.   By the foregoing lemma, a restriction of F on V (denoted by $F|_V$) is proper, thus a closed map. Since $C \cap V$ is obviously closed in V, $F(C \cap V) = F|_V(C \cap V)$ is closed in $\mathcal{E}$. Thus, its complement in $\mathcal{E}$ is open in $\mathcal{E}$. $\square$

We are now ready to present a desirable result concerning regular economies.

Theorem 2.6   *Under assumption 2.1, the set of regular economies is open and dense in $\mathcal{E}$ and the set of equilibrium price vectors for every regular economy is finite. Thus, under the assumption, the finiteness of equilibria is generic with respect to $\mathcal{E}$.*

Proof. Through proposition 2.6 the set of critical points of F is closed in U. Thus, under the assumption, the set of regular economies is open in $\mathcal{E}$ by lemma 2.4. On the other hand, any regular economy ω can be considered to be compact in $\mathcal{E}$ as a singleton set, so that by lemma 2.3 $F^{-1}(\omega)$ is compact in U. Since $F^{-1}(\omega)$ is known to be a discrete set, it turns out to be finite (see lemma 2.1). Thus the set of equilibrium price vectors $W(\omega)$ is also finite since $F^{-1}(\omega) \simeq W(\omega)$. $\qquad\square$

Thus it turns out that assumption 2.1 is very crucial in obtaining the desirable result. The assumption, however, may seem specific in the sense that consumer 1 is privileged there. It actually is much more general than it appears, for in the assumption consumer 1 is only a representative of consumers who possess the property provided there. The point of the assumption is that there exists at least one consumer who has the property in question. Consumer 1 is just a naming of such a consumer in the assumption.

Chapter 3

Formalization of Regular Economies

In view of the introductory arguments in the previous chapters, we may summarize the analytical skeleton of the theory of regular economies as follows. That is, for the space of economies or a bigger space including the space of economies (say K), there exists a set represented by a manifold (say M) and a smooth map (say f) from $M \to K$ such that a regular economy is defined by a regular value of f and the structure of the equilibrium set of each regular economy is analytically characterized by f, M and K. Thus it may be safely said that the theory of regular economies itself is composed of an appropriate triple (M, f, K). It follows that how well the theory works is especially dependent on how we prescribe f and M. So far we have considered F as f and $S_{++}^{L-1} \times (0, +\infty) \times \boldsymbol{R}_{++}^{L(I-1)}$ as M. However, F is too artificial though very skillfully constructed. In this chapter we present a more general formalization of regular economies which has been developed through the works of Dierker (1974), Smale (1974a), Balasko (1975a), Debreu (1976) and so on. Then we show how well the altered formalization functions by investigating the continuity of an equilibrium with respect to economies as well as local uniqueness and finiteness of equilibria. We finally give a very useful characterization of regular economies on the basis of the general formalization.

3.1 Mathematical Preliminaries

First note that the mathematical concepts explained below in 3.1.1 and 3.1.2 are not substantially utilized in the economical analysis of this chapter although they are crucially applied later (see chapter 11). Rather, those concepts, somehow, serve as a technical precept or a reference criterion to obtain a general formalization of regular economies.

29

3.1.1   *Fibre Bundles*

Recall the product manifold which consists of two manifolds, M and K (see example 1.3). We consider the projection π_1 of $M \times K$ on M defined by $\pi_1(x, y) = x$ for any $(x, y) \in M \times K$. Then, obviously π_1 is a submersion and $\pi_1^{-1}(x)$ is diffeomorphic to $x \times K$ for any $x \in M$. We have the same situation for the other projection $\pi_2 : M \times K \to K$. Generalization of this construction leads us to the notion of a fibre bundle.

Definition 3.1   If there exists a smooth surjective map π from a $m + k$-dimensional manifold P to a m-dimensional manifold M and a k-dimensional manifold K which satisfy the following condition, then a triple (P, π, M) is called a fibre bundle with fibre K. The condition is this; for any $x \in M$ there exists an open neighborhood U of x in M such that we have a diffeomorphism $\sigma : \pi^{-1}(U) \to U \times K$ which fulfills that $\pi_1 \circ \sigma = \pi$ where π_1 is the projection of $U \times K$ on U. P is called the total space, M is called the base space and the differentiable map π is called the projection of the bundle.

    Thus, we may say that the total space is built up by assembling the family of submanifolds $\pi^{-1}(x)(= \{y \in P | x = \pi(y)\})$ over M since π is a submersion. Intuitively, P can be seen as a bundle of fibres which grow one at a point of M.

Example 3.1   A triple $(M \times K, \pi_1, M)$ mentioned in the beginning is the simplest fibre bundle, which is sometimes called the product bundle over M with fibre K. For its structure, see the figure below.

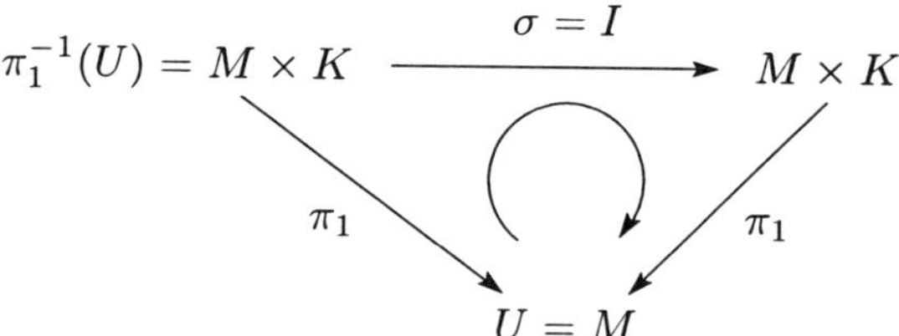

Fig. 3.1

3.1.2 *Vector Bundles*

A fibre bundle with a vector space as a fibre is especially called a vector bundle which has a wide applicability. It is formally defined as follows.

Definition 3.2 A (k-dimensional) vector bundle is a triple (P, π, M) where $\pi : P \to M$ is a smooth surjective map, every $\pi^{-1}(x)$ has the structure of a k-dimensional vector space such that every point of M has a neighborhood U in M for which there exists a homeomorphism

$$f : \pi^{-1}(U) \to U \times \mathbf{R}^k$$

such that for every $x \in U$

$$f|_{\pi^{-1}(x)} : \pi^{-1}(x) \to x \times \mathbf{R}^k$$

is a linear isomorphism.

Example 3.2 Let M be a m-dimensional manifold. Consider the disjoint union of tangent spaces at every point of M, that is, $\bigcup_{x \in M} T_x M$ which we denote TM. If we consider a map $\pi : TM \to M$ which associates $v \in T_x M$ with x, then we have a vector bundle (TM, π, M) called the tangent bundle.

We will come back to the tangent bundle later in chapter 11 where this bundle will play a crucial role.

3.1.3 *Family of Maps*

Here we introduce a useful concept, 'family of maps', which we shall use for characterizing regular economies in a specific way.

In addition to the two manifolds M, K, we consider the third manifold P. An element of P plays a part of a parameter which specifies a smooth map from M to K. Suppose that $F_p : M \to K$ is a collection of smooth maps, parametrized by $p \in P$. Then, the collection can be expressed by the map $F : P \times M \to K$ defined by $F(p, x) = F_p(x)$. Roughly speaking, a family of maps is a map which generates a collection of maps, just like the above F. To be precise,

Definition 3.3 Let M, K and P be manifolds. Then, a smooth map $F : P \times M \to K$ is called a smooth family of maps.

It is common practice to write $F(p, x) = F_p(x)$. We shall declare a very important lemma concerning a smooth family of maps.

Lemma 3.1   *Let $F : P \times M \to K$ be a smooth family of maps. If a point $y \in K$ is a regular value of F, then the set*

$$\{p \in P \mid y \text{ is a regular value of } F_p : M \to K\}$$

is equal to the set

$$\{p \in P \mid p \text{ is a regular value of } \pi|_{F^{-1}(y)}\}$$

where $\pi|_{F^{-1}(y)}$ is a restriction of the projection $\pi : P \times M \to P$ to $F^{-1}(y)$.

Proof.   Let P_1 be the set

$$\{p \in P \mid y \text{ is a regular value of } F_p : M \to K\}$$

and P_2 be the set

$$\{p \in P \mid p \text{ is a regular value of } \pi|_{F^{-1}(y)}\}.$$

First note that $dF_{(p,x)}(T_{(p,x)}(P \times M)) = dF_{(p,x)}(T_{(p,x)}(P \times x)) + dF_{(p,x)}(T_{(p,x)}(p \times M))$.

By assumption, y is a regular value of F, so that for any $(p, x) \in F^{-1}(y)$ we have

$$dF_{(p,x)}(T_{(p,x)}(P \times x)) + dF_{(p,x)}(T_{(p,x)}(p \times M)) = T_y K \qquad (3.1)$$
$$dF_{(p,x)}(T_{(p,x)}(F^{-1}(y))) = 0 \qquad (3.2)$$

(for the latter equation see corollary 2.1).

Suppose that $p \in P_1$. Then, for any $x \in F_p^{-1}(y)$ we have

$$dF_{p,x}(T_x M) = T_y K.$$

In addition, for that (p, x) it obviously holds that

$$dF_{p,x}(T_x M) = dF_{(p,x)}(T_{(p,x)}(p \times M).$$

Thus, by (3.1), we have

$$dF_{(p,x)}(T_{(p,x)}(P \times x)) \subset dF_{(p,x)}(T_{(p,x)}(p \times M)).$$

This results in the following (note (3.2)).

$$T_{(p,x)}(P \times x) \subset T_{(p,x)}(p \times M) + T_{(p,x)}(F^{-1}(y)) \qquad (3.3)$$

Now consider the derivative $d\pi_{(p,x)} : T_{(p,x)}(P \times M) \to T_p P$ of the projection $\pi : P \times M \to P$ at any $(p, x) \in P \times M$. Obviously we have $d\pi_{(p,x)}(a, b) = a$ for any $(a, b) \in T_{(p,x)}(P \times M) = T_{(p,x)}(P \times x) \times T_{(p,x)}(p \times M)$. Hence,

$$d\pi_{(p,x)}(T_{(p,x)}(p \times M) + T_{(p,x)}(F^{-1}(y))) = d\pi_{(p,x)}(T_{(p,x)}(F^{-1}(y)))$$

and

$$d\pi_{(p,x)}(T_{(p,x)}(P \times x)) = T_p P.$$

Here we recall (3.3). By applying $d\pi_{(p,x)}$ to both sides, we have

$$T_p P \subset d\pi_{(p,x)}(T_{(p,x)}(p \times M)) + T_{(p,x)}(F^{-1}(y))) = d\pi_{(p,x)}(T_{(p,x)}(F^{-1}(y)))$$

which implies that at a pair of any x and the relevant p which are included in $F^{-1}(y)$, the derivative of the restriction $\pi|_{F^{-1}(y)}$ is surjective; that is, p is a regular value of $\pi|_{F^{-1}(y)}$. Thus, we have $p \in P_2$. It is easily seen that the above argument is invertible, so that the proof is completed. $\qquad\square$

Recalling Sard's theorem, this lemma asserts that if a point of a range is a regular value of a smooth family of maps, then the point is also a regular value of almost all component maps constructing the family.

This lemma is important not only because it gives rise to a useful characterization of regular economies, but also because it provides a cornerstone to construct transversality theorems that will play a major role in Part 2.

3.2 Economical Analysis

3.2.1 Equilibrium Manifold and Regular Economies

For the convenience of exposition, we adopt the same framework as the first chapter. That is, we consider a pure exchange economy where L goods and I consumers exist. Each consumer i is characterized by its initial endowment vector ω^i in $\boldsymbol{R}^L_{++}$ and its demand function f^i defined on $\boldsymbol{R}^L_{++} \times (0, +\infty)$. Consumers' demand functions are given which satisfy the assumption 1.3. Thus, the data which specifies an economy is only the allocation of initial endowments among I consumers, which we denote $\omega \ (= (\omega^1, \ldots, \omega^I))$. ω is simply called an 'economy' and the conceivable set of ω, $\boldsymbol{R}^{LI}_{++}$, is called the space of economies which is denoted by $\mathcal{E}$ for simplicity. Every price is assumed to be strictly positive. It is easily seen that each consumer's demand function is homogeneous of degree 0 with respect to p, so that we can normalize a price vector to obtain S_{++}^{L-1} (the strictly positive $L - 1$-dimensoinal simplex in $\boldsymbol{R}^L$) as the conceivable set of price vectors.

Now then, we consider the aggregate excess demand function $G : \mathcal{E} \times S_{++}^{L-1} \to \boldsymbol{R}^L$ defined as follows.

$$G(\omega, \boldsymbol{p}) = \sum_{i=1}^{I} f^i(\boldsymbol{p}, \boldsymbol{p} \cdot \boldsymbol{\omega}^i) - \sum_{i=1}^{I} \boldsymbol{\omega}^i.$$

Needless to say, an equilibrium state is the situation in which $G(\omega, \boldsymbol{p}) = 0$. Note that G is a vector valued function. Let $G_1, \ldots, G_L$ be the component functions of G. The following proposition concerning an equilibrium state is straightforward.

Proposition 3.1 $G(\omega, \boldsymbol{p}) = 0$ *if and only if* $\tilde{G}(\omega, \boldsymbol{p}) = 0$ *where* $\tilde{G} = (G_1, \ldots, G_{L-1}) : \mathcal{E} \times S_{++}^{L-1} \to \boldsymbol{R}^{L-1}$.

Proof.   Through the assumption 1.3 regarding a demand function, we have so called Walras' law; that is, $\boldsymbol{p} \cdot G(\omega, \boldsymbol{p}) = 0$ for any $\boldsymbol{p} \in S_{++}^{L-1}$, which directly leads to the claim. $\square$

In this chapter, as in the previous chapters, we consider an equilibrium state to be represented by the equilibrium price vector alone.

Now let's turn to our main topic, i.e. a general formalization of regular economies. We are considering the relation between an economy and its equilibrium in the space of economies. Thus we have only two relevant sets, $\mathcal{E}$ and S_{++}^{L-1}. Therefore, let a simple product bundle $(\mathcal{E} \times S_{++}^{L-1}, \pi, \mathcal{E})$ over $\mathcal{E}$ with fibre S_{++}^{L-1} be our launching site. We consider how to restrict $\pi^{-1}(\omega)$ $(= (\omega, S_{++}^{L-1}))$ to $(\omega,$ *equilibria of* $\omega)$. To this end, first note that the map $\tilde{G}$ introduced above allows us to have the set of a pair of an economy and its equilibrium, that is, the set $\{(\omega, \boldsymbol{p}) \in \mathcal{E} \times S_{++}^{L-1}| \ \tilde{G}(\omega, \boldsymbol{p}) = 0\}$, which we call the equilibrium set and denote M. M has a remarkable property.

Proposition 3.2   *The equilibrium set M forms an LI-dimensional submanifold in* $\mathcal{E} \times S_{++}^{L-1}$.

Proof.   It is easily seen that in the matrix representation of the derivative $d\tilde{G}_{(\omega, \boldsymbol{p})}$ of $\tilde{G}$ at any $(\omega, \boldsymbol{p}) \in \mathcal{E} \times S_{++}^{L-1}$, the first $(L - 1) \times L$ submatrix is written as follows.

$$
\begin{pmatrix}
p_1\frac{\partial f_1^1}{\partial w^1} - 1 & p_2\frac{\partial f_1^1}{\partial w^1} & \cdots & p_{L-1}\frac{\partial f_1^1}{\partial w^1} & p_L\frac{\partial f_1^1}{\partial w^1} \\
p_1\frac{\partial f_2^1}{\partial w^1} & p_2\frac{\partial f_2^1}{\partial w^1} - 1 & \cdots & p_{L-1}\frac{\partial f_2^1}{\partial w^1} & p_L\frac{\partial f_2^1}{\partial w^1} \\
\vdots & \vdots & \vdots & \vdots & \vdots \\
p_1\frac{\partial f_{L-1}^1}{\partial w^1} & p_2\frac{\partial f_{L-1}^1}{\partial w^1} & \cdots p_{L-1}\frac{\partial f_{L-1}^1}{\partial w^1} - 1 & p_L\frac{\partial f_{L-1}^1}{\partial w^1}
\end{pmatrix}
$$

where w^1 denotes the income of consumer 1 and f_k^1 denotes the demand function for the k-th good of consumer 1 ($k = 1, \ldots, L - 1$). This matrix operates on the subspace $\boldsymbol{R}^L$ in the tangent space $\boldsymbol{R}^{LI} \times \boldsymbol{R}^{L-1}$ at $(\omega, \boldsymbol{p})$.

Since this matrix has obviously full rank and $(\omega, \boldsymbol{p})$ is arbitrary, $\tilde{G}$ is a submersion on $\mathcal{E} \times S_{++}^{L-1}$. Hence, every point of $\boldsymbol{R}^{L-1}$ is a regular value of $\tilde{G}$ and so is $0 \in \boldsymbol{R}^{L-1}$. Through the Preimage Theorem, $\tilde{G}^{-1}(0) \ (= M)$ constitutes a submanifold in $\mathcal{E} \times S_{++}^{L-1}$ the dimension of which is $LI + L - 1 - (L - 1) = LI$. $\qquad\square$

This leads to the following definition.

Definition 3.4 The equilibrium manifold is the equilibrium set with a manifold structure.

For simplicity, we use the same term M to denote the equilibrium manifold in the remainder of this chapter.

Thus, if we restrict the projection π of the simple product bundle $(\mathcal{E} \times S_{++}^{L-1}, \pi, \mathcal{E})$ on $M \ (\subset \mathcal{E} \times S_{++}^{L-1})$, then the set $\{(\omega, \ equilibria \ of \ \omega)\}$ for any $\omega \in \mathcal{E}$ is represented by the preimage of the restriction $\pi|_M^{-1}(\omega)$.

This observation leads us to the following formalization of regular economies.

Definition 3.5 An economy $\omega \in \mathcal{E}$ is called a regular economy if it is a regular value of the restriction of the projection π in the product bundle $(\mathcal{E} \times S_{++}^{L-1}, \pi, \mathcal{E})$ on the equilibrium manifold M. An economy which is not a regular economy is called a critical economy.

In Fig. 3.2 in the next page, we have shown what is going on in the formalization. Since at a regular economy the projection of the tangent space of M at every point of $\pi|_M^{-1}(\omega)$ must form $\boldsymbol{R}^{LI}$ itself, it is easily seen in the diagram that all but ω_1, ω_2 and ω_3 are regular economies in the horizontal axis.

The above formalization is general in that its background is a simple product bundle made out of all the relevant sets which is always readily defined in various frameworks of economies. In addition, this formalization

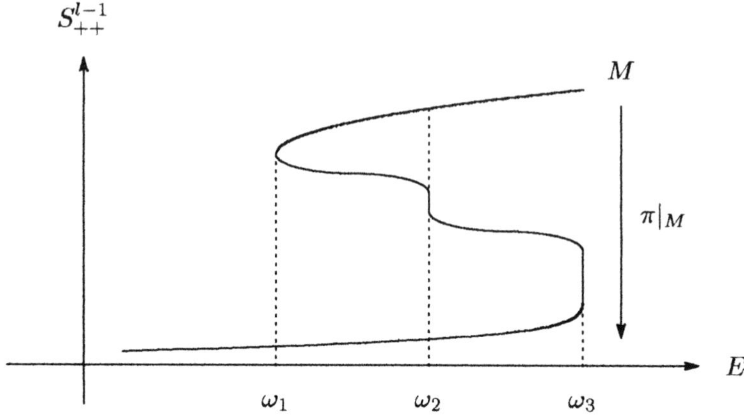

Fig. 3.2

has its own benefit for analysis in the sense that $\pi|_M^{-1}(\omega)$ is just equal to $(\omega, W(\omega))$ while according to the previous definition (definition 1.9), we have only that $W(\omega) \simeq F^{-1}(\omega)$.

3.2.2 *Local Uniqueness and Finiteness of Equilibria in the General Formalization*

We can easily demonstrate that the propositions concerning regular economies stated in chapter 2 also hold for the regular economies in the general formalization, i.e. definition 3.5.

Theorem 3.1 *The set of regular economies is dense in $\mathcal{E}$ and the set of equilibrium price vectors for every regular economy is a discrete set. Thus, local uniqueness of equilibria is generic with respect to economies.*

Proof. Since the restriction $\pi|_M$ of π to M is obviously smooth, the set of critical values of $\pi|_M$ has Lebesgue measure 0, so that the set of regular values of $\pi|_M$ is dense. On the other hand, by proposition 3.2 the dimension of M is equal to the one of $\mathcal{E}$, thus the preimage $\pi|_M^{-1}(\omega)$ for a regular economy ω is a discrete set according to the Preimage Theorem. As mentioned above, $\pi|_M^{-1}(\omega) = (\omega, W(\omega))$, which leads to the claim. $\square$

We need a similar assumption to assumption 2.1 in order to obtain a strengthened and preferable consequence regarding regular economies. As suggested at the end of chapter 2, although consumer 1 is privileged in the assumption, actually we do not need to treat him so specially. Here, we are allowed to represent explicitly the anonymity in the assumption.

Assumption 3.1 If a sequence $(\boldsymbol{p}^q, w^{1q})$ in $S_{++}^{L-1} \times (0, +\infty)$ converges to a point $(\boldsymbol{p}^0, w^{10})$ in $(S_{+}^{L-1} \setminus S_{++}^{L-1}) \times (0, +\infty)$, then for at least one consumer i its demand function $f^i(\boldsymbol{p}, w^i)$ has the following property.

$$\lim_{q \to +\infty} \|f^i(\boldsymbol{p}^q, w^{iq})\| = +\infty$$

where $\| \cdot \|$ designates the Euclidean norm.

Then we have a desired consequence for regular economies.

Theorem 3.2 *Under assumption 3.1, the set of regular economies is open and dense in $\mathcal{E}$ and the set of equilibrium price vectors for every regular economy is finite. Thus, under the assumption, the finiteness of equilibria is generic with respect to $\mathcal{E}$.*

Proof. It suffices to show that $\pi|_M$ is proper. Let K be an arbitrary compact set in $\mathcal{E}$. Our goal is to show that $\pi|_M^{-1}(K)$ is compact in M. To this end, pick any sequence $(\omega^q, \boldsymbol{p}^q)_q$ out of $\pi|_M^{-1}(K)$. Then $(\omega^q, \boldsymbol{p}^q)_q$ is bounded since for any q, $\pi|_M(\omega^q, \boldsymbol{p}^q) = \omega^q$, which is in a compact set K whereas S_{++}^{L-1} containing $\boldsymbol{p}^q$ is obviously bounded. Thus the sequence has a convergent subsequence. Let $(\omega^0, \boldsymbol{p}^0)$ be the limit point of the subsequence. First we show that $\omega^0 \in \mathcal{E}$ and $\boldsymbol{p}^0 \in S_{++}^{L-1}$. The former condition is trivial since for any q, ω^q is contained in K which is a compact subset of $\mathcal{E}$. To show the latter condition, suppose that $\boldsymbol{p}^0$ is not an element of S_{++}^{L-1}, which implies that $\boldsymbol{p}^0 \in (S_{+}^{L-1} \setminus S_{++}^{L-1})$. Then, by assumption 3.1 we have that $\tilde{G}(\omega^0, \boldsymbol{p}^0) \neq 0$. Thus, for a point $(\omega^q, \boldsymbol{p}^q)$ close enough to $(\omega^0, \boldsymbol{p}^0)$, we also have $\tilde{G}(\omega^q, \boldsymbol{p}^q) \neq 0$ because of the continuity of $\tilde{G}$. But this implies that $(\omega^q, \boldsymbol{p}^q) \notin M$, which is a contradiction. Now that $\omega^0 \in \mathcal{E}$ and $\boldsymbol{p}^0 \in S_{++}^{L-1}$, $\tilde{G}(\omega^0, \boldsymbol{p}^0) = 0$ because of the continuity of $\tilde{G}$, which implies that $(\omega^0, \boldsymbol{p}^0) \in M$. Since $\omega^0 \in K$ and $(\omega^0, \boldsymbol{p}^0) \in M$, we obtain that $(\omega^0, \boldsymbol{p}^0) \in \pi|_M^{-1}(K)$, which implies that $\pi|_M^{-1}(K)$ is compact. $\qquad\square$

3.2.3 *Dependence of Equilibria on Regular Economies in the General Formalization*

Here, we consider an interesting question "How do equilibria correspond to regular economies?" More specifically, we are trying to see how equilibria react to the change of regular economies where the term 'change' should be interpreted as a quantitative shift of initial endowments among the consumers because we have defined an economy as an allocation of initial endowment vectors among them.

Since we have considered the equilibria of an economy ω ($\in \mathcal{E}$) to be the set of its equilibrium price vectors $W(\omega)$, the above issue leads us to the investigation into the mathematical property of a correspondence which associates ω with $W(\omega)$. This correspondence is called the Walras correspondence. It is very hard to see the global structure of the Walras correspondence itself (see Balasko (1975a)). However, if we confine ourselves to regular economies and take assumption 3.1 into account, then we are able to establish a specific local behavior of the correspondence.

Theorem 3.3 *Under assumption 3.1, for any regular economy there exists a neighborhood of it in $\mathcal{E}$ such that all the economies in the neighborhood have the same number of equilibria.*

Proof. Let ω be an arbitrary regular economy. Since $\pi|_M^{-1}(\omega)$ is a finite set by theorem 3.2, let $(\omega, \boldsymbol{p}^q)_{q=1,\ldots,k}$ represent the set $\pi|_M^{-1}(\omega)$. Needless to say, $\boldsymbol{p}^1, \ldots, \boldsymbol{p}^k$ are all equilibrium price vectors for ω. Since each $(\omega, \boldsymbol{p}^q)$ is a regular point of $\pi|_M$ and $dim M = dim \mathcal{E}$, by the inverse function theorem there exists a neighborhood U_q of it in $\mathcal{E}$ such that $\pi|_M$ is a diffeomorphism on U_q (for the inverse function theorem, see for example Rudin (1976), theorem 9.24). We may assume that all $U_q's$ are disjoint with each other, for the set $(\omega, \boldsymbol{p}^q)_{q=1,\ldots,k}$ is discrete. Let V_q be the image $\pi|_M(U_q)$ for $q = 1, \ldots, k$. Since $\pi|_M$ is bijective on each U_q, $\pi|_M$ is an open map as well as a closed map on U_q, so that both U_q and V_q are open ($q = 1, \ldots, k$). Now we consider the following set V in $\mathcal{E}$.

$$V = \bigcap_{q=1} V_q - \pi|_M(M - \bigcup_{q=1} U_q).$$

Since the set $M - \bigcup_{q=1} U_q$ is closed in M, under assumption 3.1 the image $\pi|_M(M - \bigcup_{q=1} U_q)$ is closed. Thus V is a open set obviously including ω. It follows from the construction of V that for any economy ω' in V, $\pi|_M^{-1}(\omega')$ consists of k points, which implies that every economy in V has the same number of the equilibrium price vectors. $\square$

Incidentally, under assumption 3.1 the set of regular economies is open; thus in the theorem we may presume that all the economies (with the same number of equilibria) in the neighborhood are regular economies.

According to the above theorem, for any regular economy there exists a neighborhood in which all the economies has the same number of the equilibrium price vectors. So, let the number of equilibria be k and $(\boldsymbol{p}^q(\omega))_{q=1}^k$ represent the equilibrium price vectors corresponding to an economy in the neighborhood. Then the proof of the above theorem leads to the precise way of dependence of equilibria on regular economies as well.

Theorem 3.4 *Each $\boldsymbol{p}^q(\omega)$ turns out to be a smooth map on the relevant neighborhood $(q = 1, \ldots, k)$.*

Proof. For any given regular economy ω, let V be its neighborhood derived in the proof of theorem 3.3. Obviously V is diffeomorphic to an appropriate neighborhood U_q' of $(\omega, \boldsymbol{p}^q)$ through $\pi|_M$, $q = 1, \ldots, k$. Thus, $\pi|_M^{-1}$ defined on V brings about k's diffeomorphisms:$V \to U_q'$, $q = 1, \ldots, k$. Then the composite of the projection $\pi_p : E \times S_{++}^{L-1} \to S_{++}^{L-1}$ and each of the diffeomorphisms leads to the desired map $\boldsymbol{p}^q(\cdot)$, $q = 1, \ldots, k$. $\square$

Thus, if we admit assumption 3.1, a slight change of regular economies in terms of the initial endowments only causes a very small alteration of each equilibrium price. Moreover, the alteration of equilibrium prices takes place smoothly in response to the change of an economy.

3.2.4 *Specific Characterization of Regular Economies in the General Formalization*

The formalization of regular economies stated in 3.2.1 permits a specific characterization of regular economies that is useful for further analysis.

Recall the truncated aggregate excess demand function $\tilde{G} = (G_1, \ldots, G_{L-1}) : \mathcal{E} \times S_{++}^{L-1} \to \boldsymbol{R}^{L-1}$. In the construction of the function, if we consider $\mathcal{E}$ of the domain to be a parameter space, then $\tilde{G}$ can be seen as a smooth family of maps. Furthermore, it is worth noting that $\tilde{G}$ has 0 as a regular value (see the proof of proposition 3.2). Thus, by applying lemma 3.1, we immediately have the following proposition.

Proposition 3.3 *An economy $\omega \in \mathcal{E}$ is a regular economy if and only if 0 is a regular value for the map $\tilde{G}_\omega$ where $\tilde{G}_\omega$ denotes the map $\tilde{G}(\omega, \cdot) : S_{++}^{L-1} \to \boldsymbol{R}^{L-1}$.*

Proof. Since 0 is a regular value of $\tilde{G}$, the set

$$\{\omega \in \mathcal{E} \mid 0 \ is \ a \ regular \ value \ of \ \tilde{G}_\omega : S_{++}^{L-1} \to \boldsymbol{R}^{L-1}\}$$

is equal to the set

$$\{\omega \in \mathcal{E} \mid \omega \ is \ a \ regular \ value \ of \ \pi|_{\tilde{G}^{-1}(0)}\}$$

where $\pi|_{\tilde{G}^{-1}(0)}$ is a restriction of the projection $\pi : \mathcal{E} \times S_{++}^{L-1} \to \mathcal{E}$ to $\tilde{G}^{-1}(0)$ (see lemma 3.1). The latter set

$$\{\omega \in \mathcal{E}|\ \omega \ \text{is a regular value of}\ \pi|_{\tilde{G}^{-1}(0)}\}$$

is nothing but the set of regular economies in the general formalization, so that the claim is immediate. $\qquad\qquad\square$

This characterization of regular economies is convenient in a twofold sense. That is, first we can use a definite map $\tilde{G}_\omega$ to see if an economy ω is a regular one or not. Secondly, for any regular economy ω, $\tilde{G}_\omega^{-1}(0)$ represents the set of equilibrium price vectors for the economy.

Chapter 4

The Number of Equilibria in Regular Economies

The purpose of this chapter is to discuss the number of equilibria in regular economies. We have seen that the set of equilibria for a regular economy is a discrete set. We have also shown that the set turns out to be finite if we admit an assumption regarding the demand function (assumption 3.1). Thus, investigating the number of equilibria under the assumption proves to be an interesting undertaking. People may think that before proceeding to the issue, it remains to be seen if an equilibrium exists at all for regular economies. Although it is true that the arguments of previous chapters do not assure the existence of equilibria, it is interesting to note that the establishment of the number of equilibria necessarily implies the existence of equilibria for a regular economy.

In the first section, we give a full exposition of a specific mathematical tool called the modulo 2 degree of a smooth map. This is just what enables us to reconcile the existence with the number of equilibria. Then, in the economical analysis, we first address the general existence problem of an equilibrium for all the economies (including regular economies) satisfying assumption 3.1. After that, we turn to the main issue of the number of equilibria for regular economies.

4.1 Mathematical Preliminaries

4.1.1 *Modulo 2 Degree*

The concept of the modulo 2 degree of a smooth map is concerned with the number of elements in the preimage of a regular value of the map. Thus the concept makes sense only if the preimage always forms a finite set for a regular value. Therefore we presume for the sake of the concept that (1) the

41

domain manifold M is compact, (2) the range manifold K is connected and (3) $dim M = dim K$. Indeed, in this setting, any smooth map $f : M \to K$ has a finite preimage of a regular value (see proposition 2.1).

Roughly speaking, the modulo 2 degree of a smooth map determines whether the number of elements in the finite preimage of a regular value is even or odd. For the precise definition, we need a preliminary notion called the modulo 2 residue class.

Definition 4.1 The modulo 2 residue class of a finite set A is the set of integers k that makes $k - \sharp A$ multiples of 2 where $\sharp A$ designates the number of elements in A. The modulo 2 residue class of a finite set A is denoted by $\sharp A \ mod \ 2$.

It is easily seen that the modulo 2 residue class is either all the even numbers or all the odd numbers. Thus, if $\sharp A \ mod \ 2$ consists of all the even numbers, then we abbreviate it to $\sharp A \ mod \ 2 = 0$ while if it consists of all the odd numbers, we abbreviate it to $\sharp A \ mod \ 2 = 1$. Incidentally, if two finite sets A, B have the same modulo 2 residue class, then we express that $\sharp A = \sharp B \ (mod \ 2)$. Then we have the definition of the modulo 2 degree of a smooth map.

Definition 4.2 Let M, K be two manifolds fulfilling the three conditions mentioned above. The modulo 2 degree of a smooth map $f : M \to K$ is the modulo 2 residue class of the preimage $f^{-1}(y)$ of a regular value y, which we denote $deg_2 f$.

It is worth noting our usage of the term $deg_2 f$. If for two distinct regular values y, y', $\sharp f^{-1}(y) \ mod \ 2 \neq \sharp f^{-1}(y') \ mod \ 2$, then we are not allowed to write it in such a way. In order for the notation to be consistent, it must be guaranteed that the modulo 2 residue class of the preimage is common to all regular values. In the following, we will show that it actually holds.

Before proceeding to the proof, however, we need to provide some mathematical concepts and tools that are not only useful for the proof itself but also indispensable for the economical analysis in this chapter.

4.1.2 *Manifolds with Boundary*

Here we enlarge the class of manifolds. So far a manifold has been considered to be the set without boundary. In fact, if a m-dimensional manifold $M \ (\subset \boldsymbol{R}^n)$ has the boundary, any neighborhood of a boundary point can not be diffeomorphic to any open set in $\boldsymbol{R}^m$. However, what if we think of a closed half-space in $\boldsymbol{R}^m$ instead of $\boldsymbol{R}^m$ itself when defining m-dimensional manifolds? The definition of a closed half-space in $\boldsymbol{R}^m$ is as follows.

Definition 4.3   A closed half-space in $\boldsymbol{R}^m$ is the set $\boldsymbol{H}^m$ defined by

$$\boldsymbol{H}^m = \{(x_1, \ldots, x_m) \in \boldsymbol{R}^m \mid x_m \geq 0\}.$$

The boundary of $\boldsymbol{H}^m$ is, of course, the set $\{(x_1, \ldots, x_m) \in \boldsymbol{R}^m | x_m = 0\}$, which we denote $\partial \boldsymbol{H}^m$. $\partial \boldsymbol{H}^m$ is nothing but a hyperplane or a $(m-1)$-dimensional affine space in $\boldsymbol{R}^m$. Note in addition that $\partial \boldsymbol{H}^m$ itself is a $(m-1)$-dimensional manifold in $\boldsymbol{R}^m$.

By means of $\boldsymbol{H}^m$, we are allowed to extend the notion of manifolds as follows.

Definition 4.4   A subset M in $\boldsymbol{R}^n$ is a m-dimensional manifold with boundary if every point x in M has a neighborhood V $(= W \cap M,\ W$ is an open set in $\boldsymbol{R}^n)$ that is diffeomorphic to an open set U in $\boldsymbol{H}^m$ where U is written as $Y \cap \boldsymbol{H}^m$ for some open set Y in $\boldsymbol{R}^m$. As before, the diffeomorphism from U to V is called a parameterization of V and its inverse is called a coordinate system on V. The boundary of M, denoted ∂M, consists of those points that belong to the image of $\partial \boldsymbol{H}^m$ under some parameterization.

Note in the definition that a parameterization has a smooth extension from U' to $\boldsymbol{R}^n$ where U' is an open set in $\boldsymbol{R}^m$ that includes U so that the parameterization is smooth on the boundary of $\boldsymbol{H}^m$.

The complement of ∂M in M is called the interior of M, denoted $Int(M)$. Since $Int(M)$ could be M, or equivalently, ∂M could be empty, manifolds as defined earlier also qualify as manifolds with boundary, thus the above definition really means the extension of the notion of manifolds.

We give some examples of manifolds with boundary.

Example 4.1   A closed interval [a, b] and a half-open interval [a, b) (or (a, b]) in $\boldsymbol{R}$. A closed half-space $\boldsymbol{H}^n$ in $\boldsymbol{R}^n$, $n = 1, 2, \ldots$. A closed ball with a radius of c in $\boldsymbol{R}^n$, i.e. $\{\boldsymbol{x} \in \boldsymbol{R}^n \mid \|\boldsymbol{x}\| \leq c\}$, $n = 1, 2, \ldots$. Those sets are all typical manifolds with boundary.

Example 4.2   A compact cylindrical surface in $\boldsymbol{R}^3$ (see Fig. 4.1 in the next page). This can be seen as a product set of a circle and a closed interval.

The above examples give us some suggestions regarding general properties of manifolds with boundary.

Fig. 4.1

A closed interval in example 4.1 is obviously a compact 1-dimensional manifold with boundary and its boundary consists of two points. Indeed, it is known that in general this set and a circle in $\mathbf{R}^2$ constitute the connected component of compact 1-demensional manifolds with boundary. Thus we have the following claim.

Lemma 4.1 *The boundary of any compact 1-dimensional manifold with boundary consists of an even number of points.*

For the proof as well as the classification of compact 1-dimensional manifolds, see Guillemin and Pollack (1974), Appendix 2.

Next consider the cylinder in example 4.2, which is very suggestive. While the cylinder is itself a manifold with boundary, it is identified with a product set of a circle and a closed interval. Obviously, the boundary of the cylinder consists of a pair of circles which are, however, the manifold *without* boundary. It turns out that this observation is more general than it appears.

Proposition 4.1 *If M is a m-dimensional manifold with boundary, then ∂M is a $(m-1)$-dimensional manifold without boundary.*

Proof. For any given $x \in \partial M \subset M$, there exists a neighborhood V diffeomorphic to an open set U in $\mathbf{H}^m$ where U is written as the set $\{(x_1, \ldots, x_m) \in Y \mid x_m \geq 0,\ Y$ *is an open set in* $\mathbf{R}^m\}$. Let $\phi^{-1} : V \to U$ be the coordinate system and $(\phi_1^{-1}, \ldots, \phi_m^{-1})$ be its coordinate functions. Obviously, $\phi_m^{-1}(x') = 0$ for any $x' \in \partial M \cap V$. Since $\phi^{-1} : V \to U$ is a diffeomorphism, the restriction ϕ^{-1} on ∂V $(= \partial M \cap V)$ is also a diffeomorphism from ∂V to ∂U $(= \partial H^m \cap U)$. Thus, the restriction can be seen as a coordinate system on ∂V $(\subset \partial M)$ around x. On the other hand, ∂U is nothing but the set $\{(x_1, \ldots, x_m) \in Y \mid x_m = 0\}$ which can be regarded as an open set in $\mathbf{R}^{m-1}$. Since $x \in \partial M$ is arbitrary, our claim follows. $\qquad\square$

A remark on the tangent space of manifolds with boundary is in order. The tangent space $T_x M$ of M at $x \in \partial M$ is actually a m-dimensional vector space derived by the extension of a prameterization around x mentioned above. However, the tangent space $T_x(\partial M)$ of ∂M at $x \in \partial M$ is, by the above proposition, a $(m-1)$-dimensional vector subspace in $T_x M$ (see Fig. 4.2).

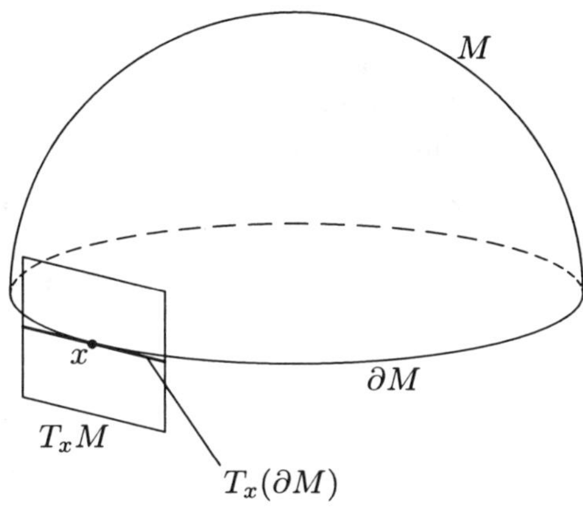

Fig. 4.2

Now return to example 4.2 and note there that one manifold without boundary (a circle) plus one manifold with boundary (a closed interval) substantially amounts to a manifold with boundary (a cylinder). This situation is generalized as follows.

Proposition 4.2 *The product of a manifold without boundary K and a manifold with boundary M forms another manifold with boundary. Moreover, we have*

$$\partial(K \times M) = K \times \partial M$$

and

$$dim(K \times M) = dimK + dimM.$$

Proof. For any point $(x, y) \in K \times M$, let $\psi : U \to K$ be a parameterization around x in K and $\phi : W \to M$ be a parameterization around y in M. Since $U \subset \mathbf{R}^k$ and $W \subset \mathbf{H}^m$ are open, $U \times W \subset \mathbf{R}^k \times \mathbf{H}^m = \mathbf{H}^{k+m}$ is open. Thus $\psi \times \phi : U \times W \to K \times M$ qualifies as a parameterization around (x, y) in $K \times M$. So we have that $dim(K \times M) = dimK + dimM$. On the other hand, it is easily seen that

$$\partial(U \times W) = \{(x_1, \ldots, x_k, x_{k+1}, \ldots, x_{k+m}) \in \boldsymbol{H}^{k+m} \mid (x_1, \ldots, x_k) \in U,$$
$$(x_{k+1}, \ldots, x_{k+m}) \in \boldsymbol{H}^m, \ x_{k+m} = 0\},$$

which is equal to $U \times \partial W$. Thus we obtain that $\partial(K \times M) = K \times \partial M$. $\square$

We finally refer to the preimage theorem on manifolds with boundary. First note that a restriction of a smooth map defined on M to ∂M can be seen as a smooth map defined on another manifold (i.e. ∂M).

Before proceeding to our goal, we provide a useful lemma.

Lemma 4.2 *Let M be a m-dimensional manifold without boundary. If a smooth map $f : M \to \boldsymbol{R}$ has 0 as a regular value, then the subset $\{x \in M | f(x) \geq 0\}$ is a manifold with boundary and its boundary is the set $\{x \in M | f(x) = 0\}$.*

Proof. The set $\{x \in M | f(x) > 0\}$ is obviously open in M, thus a submanifold of the same dimension as M. Hence, consider the set $f^{-1}(0)$. Suppose that $\bar{x} \in f^{-1}(0)$. Since $\bar{x}$ is a regular point, there exist a parametrization $\phi : W \to M$ around $\bar{x}$ such that $f \circ \phi(x_1, \ldots, x_m) - x_m$ where W is an open set in $\boldsymbol{R}^m$ and $\phi(0) = \bar{x}$ (see lemma 2.1). Thus $\phi(W) \cap \{x \in M | f(x) \geq 0\}$ is diffeomorphic to the set $\{(x_1, \ldots, x_m) \in W | x_m \geq 0\}$ which is an open set in $\boldsymbol{H}^m$. Since $\bar{x}$ is an arbitrary point of $f^{-1}(0)$, our claim follows. $\square$

It can be easily proved by this lemma that a closed ball $\{x \in \boldsymbol{R}^n | \|x\| \leq c\}$ with a radius of c in $\boldsymbol{R}^n$ is actually a manifold with boundary, for we have only to consider the map $f : \boldsymbol{R}^n \to \boldsymbol{R}$ defined by $f(x) = c - \|x\|^2$.

It is worth noting that even if M (and/or K) is a manifold with boundary, a differentiability of a map $f : M \to K$ is defined similarly to the boundaryless case. Indeed, we have only to replace $\boldsymbol{R}^m$ (and/or $\boldsymbol{R}^k$) by $\boldsymbol{H}^m$ (and/or $\boldsymbol{H}^k$) in the definition (see definition 1.3).

Now let's state the preimage theorem of manifolds with boundary version.

Theorem 4.1 *Let M be an m-dimensional manifolds with boundary and K be a $k \ (< m)$-dimensional manifolds without boundary. Suppose that for a smooth map $f : M \to K$, a point $\bar{y} \in K$ is a regular value both of f and the restriction $f|_{\partial M}$ of f to ∂M. Then the preimage $f^{-1}(\bar{y})$ is a $(m - k)$-dimensional manifolds with boundary and its boundary $\partial f^{-1}(\bar{y})$ is equal to $f^{-1}(\bar{y}) \cap \partial M$.*

Proof. For any given point $\bar{x} \in f^{-1}(\bar{y})$, there exist parametrizations around $\bar{x}$ and $\bar{y}$ such that $\psi^{-1} \circ f \circ \phi : W \to U$ is a smooth map, which we denote $\tilde{f}$, where W is an open set in $\boldsymbol{H}^m$ and U is an open set in $\boldsymbol{R}^k$. Note that $f^{-1}(\bar{y})$ is diffeomorphically represented in a neighborhood of $\bar{x}$ as $\tilde{f}^{-1}(\hat{y})$ in W where $\hat{y} = \psi^{-1}(\bar{y})$. If $\phi^{-1}(\bar{x})$ is an interior point of $\boldsymbol{H}^m$, then by taking a small W if necessary, the situation turns out to be substantially the same as theorem 2.1. Hence, we only consider the case in which $\phi^{-1}(\bar{x}) \in \partial \boldsymbol{H}^m$.

Let $\tilde{\phi} : \tilde{W} \to M$ be an extension of ϕ remarked just below definition 4.4 where $\tilde{W}$ is an open set in $\boldsymbol{R}^m$ including W. We consider $\psi^{-1} \circ f \circ \tilde{\phi} : \tilde{W} \to \boldsymbol{R}^k$, abbreviated $\tilde{f}_*$. By taking an appropriate $\tilde{W}$ we may assume that $\tilde{f}$ and $\tilde{f}_*$ are identical on $\tilde{W} \cap \boldsymbol{H}^m$. Thus we have that $\tilde{f}_*^{-1}(\hat{y}) \cap \boldsymbol{H}^m = \tilde{f}^{-1}(\hat{y}) \cap \tilde{W} = \tilde{f}^{-1}(\hat{y})$. On the other hand, by taking an appropriate W, we may presume that $\tilde{W}$ consists of only regular points since the set of regular points is open. Thus $\hat{y}$ is a regular value of $\tilde{f}_*$, so that $\tilde{f}_*^{-1}(\hat{y})$ is itself a $(m - k)$-dimensional manifold without boundary in $\boldsymbol{R}^m$.

Now pick the projection $\pi : \boldsymbol{R}^m \to \boldsymbol{R}$ defined by $\pi(x_1, \ldots, x_m) = x_m$ and consider a restriction of the projection to $\tilde{f}_*^{-1}(\hat{y})$, which we denote $\tilde{\pi}$ for simplicity. Then obviously $\tilde{f}_*^{-1}(\hat{y}) \cap \boldsymbol{H}^m$ is represented as the set $\{x \in \tilde{f}_*^{-1}(\hat{y}) | \tilde{\pi}(x) \geq 0\}$. Therefore, if 0 is a regular value of $\tilde{\pi}$, then our claim is immediate by lemma 4.2. In the following we will show that 0 is actually a regular value of $\tilde{\pi}$.

Noting that the derivative of the projection π mentioned above is the projection π itself, we should show that a restriction of the projection to the tangent space $T_x(\tilde{f}_*^{-1}(\hat{y}))$ of $\tilde{f}_*^{-1}(\hat{y})$ at any point $x \in \tilde{\pi}^{-1}(0)$ is surjective. To this end, it suffices from the construction of π to show that the tangent space $T_x(\tilde{f}_*^{-1}(\hat{y}))$ is not included in $\boldsymbol{R}^{m-1} \times 0$. Since $\bar{y}$ is a regular value of both f and the restriction $f|_{\partial M}$, x is a regular point of both $\tilde{f}$ and $\tilde{f}|_{\partial(\tilde{W} \cap \boldsymbol{H}^m)}$. However, $T_x(\tilde{W} \cap \boldsymbol{H}^m) = \partial \boldsymbol{H}^m = \boldsymbol{R}^{m-1} \times 0 \subset T_x \tilde{W} = \boldsymbol{R}^m$, so that $d\tilde{f}_x : \boldsymbol{R}^m \to \boldsymbol{R}^k$ is surjective on both $\boldsymbol{R}^m$ and $\boldsymbol{R}^{m-1} \times 0$. Thus the kernel $d\tilde{f}_x^{-1}(0)$ is not included in $\boldsymbol{R}^{m-1} \times 0$. Indeed, otherwise, then the kernel of $d\tilde{f}_x$ in $\boldsymbol{R}^m$ is equal to the kernel of $d\tilde{f}_x$ in $\boldsymbol{R}^{m-1} \times 0$, which leads to a contradiction. Recall that $\tilde{f} = \tilde{f}_*$ on $\tilde{W} \cap \boldsymbol{H}^m$, thus $d\tilde{f}_x = d(\tilde{f}_*)_x$. Since the kernel of $d(\tilde{f}_*)_x$ is , by corollary 2.1, equal to $T_x(\tilde{f}_*^{-1}(\hat{y}))$, our claim follows. $\qquad\square$

4.1.3 *Homotopy*

So far we have been concerned with properties of a single map from one manifold to another. Here we shall discuss the relation of two smooth maps having the same domain and the same range. 'Homotopy' is the most basic idea relating one map to another. Roughly speaking, two maps are said to be homotopic if one can be "deformed" into the other through one parameter. Thus, a homotopy is like a family of maps. Although homotopy is primarily defined on the basis of general topological spaces and continuous maps, we shall confine ourselves to differential topology for convenience. First we lay down the definition.

Definition 4.5 Let M, K be ordinary (boundaryless) manifolds. Let f, g be smooth maps from M to K and let $I = [0,1]$, the unit interval. Then f is smoothly homotopic to g if there is a smooth map $F : M \times I \to K$ which satisfies the conditions: $F(x,0) = f(x)$ and $F(x,1) = g(x)$ for all $x \in M$. F is called a smooth homotopy between f and g.

Intuitively, homotopy forms a smooth path from f to g in the functional space $C^\infty(M, K)$.

The relation 'f is smoothly homotopic to g' is an equivalence relation on $C^\infty(M, K)$; that is, the relation is reflexive, symmetric and transitive (for the proof, especially of transitivity, see Milnor (1969), § 4). An equivalence class of maps under the relation 'smoothly homotopic' is called a homotopy class. If f and g are smoothly homotopic, we write $f \sim g$ in the following.

It is worth noting that a smooth homotopy F between f and g is itself a smooth map from a manifold with boundary to a manifold without boundary since $M \times I$ is a manifold with boundary (see proposition 4.2).

Now we introduce a special homotopy called 'isotopy', which is also used later.

Definition 4.6 Let f, g be both diffeomorphisms from a manifold M to a manifold K. Then f is smoothly isotopic to g if there is a smooth homotopy F between f and g such that for each $t \in [0,1]$, the map $F(\cdot,t) : M \to K$ is a diffeomorphism. Then F is called a smooth isotopy between f and g.

Now that we have introduced the concept of a homotopy, we shall return to our initial issue, that is, justification of $deg_2 f$ in definition 4.2.

Recall that we were wondering if the modulo 2 residue class of the preimage is common to all regular values for a smooth map $f : M \to K$ where M and K satisfy the conditions stated earlier; that is, M is compact (and boundaryless), K is connected and $dimM = dimK$. We shall proceed step by step to the final answer.

Let f, g be smooth maps from M to K where M and K satisfy the above conditions. If f and g have a common regular value (say y), obviously $f^{-1}(y)$ and $g^{-1}(y)$ are both finite. In addition, if $f \sim g$, that is, f and g are smoothly homotopic, then we have much more.

Proposition 4.3 *Let f, g be smoothly homotopic maps from M to K where M and K satisfy the above conditions. If $y \in K$ is a regular value for both f and g, then*

$$\sharp f^{-1}(y) = \sharp g^{-1}(y) \ (mod \ 2),$$

that is, $f^{-1}(y)$ and $g^{-1}(y)$ have the same modulo 2 residue class.

Proof. First we consider the case in which y is also a regular value for a smooth homotopy F between f and g. Noting that by proposition 4.2 $\partial(M \times [0,1]) = (M \times 0) \cup (M \times 1)$, f and g forms a restriction of F to the boundary. Thus, by applying theorem 4.1, we have that $F^{-1}(y)$ is a manifold with boundary whose dimension amounts to $dim(M \times [0,1]) - dimK = m + 1 - k = 1$ (see proposition 4.2 for $dim(M \times [0,1])$) and that

$$\begin{aligned}
\partial F^{-1}(y) &= F^{-1}(y) \cap (\partial(M \times [0,1])) \\
&= F^{-1}(y) \cap ((M \times 0) \cup (M \times 1)) \\
&= (F^{-1}(y) \cap (M \times 0)) \cup (F^{-1}(y) \cap (M \times 1)) \\
&= (f^{-1}(y) \times 0) \cup (g^{-1}(y) \times 1).
\end{aligned}$$

Thus the number of elements of $\partial F^{-1}(y)$ is equal to $\sharp f^{-1}(y) + \sharp g^{-1}(y)$. Since M is compact, so is $F^{-1}(y)$. Then, by lemma 4.1, $\sharp f^{-1}(y) + \sharp g^{-1}(y)$ turns out to be even, which implies that $\sharp f^{-1}(y) = \sharp g^{-1}(y) \ (mod \ 2)$.

Next suppose that y is not a regular value for F. Since y is a regular value for f and g, there exists open neighborhood V_1 and V_2 around y such that $\sharp f^{-1}$ and $\sharp g^{-1}$ are respectively constant on V_1 and V_2 (see the proof of theorem 3.3.). Since in $V_1 \cap V_2$ we have, by Sard's theorem, a regular value (say z) for not only f and g but also F, the argument of the preceding paragraph allows us to have that $\sharp f^{-1}(z) = \sharp g^{-1}(z) \ (mod \ 2)$. Moreover, it is obvious that $\sharp f^{-1}(y) = \sharp f^{-1}(z)$ and $\sharp g^{-1}(y) = \sharp g^{-1}(z)$, so that $\sharp f^{-1}(y) = \sharp g^{-1}(y) \ (mod \ 2)$. This completes the proof. $\square$

We need another proposition, known as Homogeneity Lemma, to get to our goal.

Proposition 4.4 *Let K be a connected manifold and y, z be any interior points of K. Then there exists a diffeomorphism $h : K \to K$ that carries y to z and is smoothly isotopic to the identity map on K.*

For the proof of this proposition, see Milnor (1969), § 4.

We are now in a position to state the final proposition that gives us the answer to our question.

Proposition 4.5 *Let f be a smooth map from M to K where M and K satisfy the above conditions. If y and z are regular values of f, then we have*

$$\sharp f^{-1}(y) = \sharp f^{-1}(z) \ (mod\ 2).$$

Proof. Proposition 4.4 assures that there is a diffeomorphism $h : K \to K$ which carries y to z and is smoothly isotopic to the identity map on K. Then, the composite $h \circ f : M \to K$ is smoothly homotopic to f and has z as a regular value. Hence, by proposition 4.3, we have that $\sharp(h \circ f)^{-1}(z) = \sharp f^{-1}(z)(mod\ 2)$. However, $\sharp(h \circ f)^{-1}(z) = \sharp f^{-1}(y)$ because $(h \circ f)^{-1}(z) = f^{-1} \circ h^{-1}(z) = f^{-1}(y)$. Thus it follows that $\sharp f^{-1}(y) = \sharp f^{-1}(z) \ (mod\ 2).\square$

This proposition assures the consistency of definition 4.2. Furthermore, proposition 4.3 brings something more.

Proposition 4.6 *Let f, g be smooth maps from M to K where M and K satisfy the foregoing conditions. If $f \sim g$, then $deg_2 f = deg_2 g$.*

Proof. The intersection of the sets of regular values for f and g is, by Sard's theorem, not empty. Thus there exists a point $y \in K$ which is a regular value for both f and g. Then, by proposition 4.3, $\sharp f^{-1}(y) = \sharp g^{-1}(y) \ (mod\ 2)$, which implies that $deg_2 f = deg_2 g$. $\square$

In short, the modulo 2 degree of a smooth map depends only on the smooth homotopy class. This proposition will play a crucial role in the economical analysis.

4.2 Economical Analysis

4.2.1 Existence of Equilibria

First of all, we consider the existence of equilibria for economies in general. As is well known, the existence of equilibria for an economy has been proved in the literature under a variety of assumptions on a demand function or an underlying utility function. Hence, it seems meaningful to investigate the existence of equilibria for an economy satisfying assumption 3.1. Does an economy always have equilibria as long as assumption 3.1 is fulfilled? In fact, we are able to give an affirmative answer to this question. Let's show in the sequel how it works. Our argument is based on Aliprantis, Brown and Burkinshaw (1990), esp. theorem 1.4.8. The main tool to be used in the argument is Kakutani's fixed point theorem, which is concerned with a point-to-set map, i.e. a correspondence. The theorem is stated as follows.

Theorem 4.2 *Let C be a nonempty, compact and convex subset of $\mathbf{R}^n$. If a correspondence $\Psi : C \to C$ is closed with nonempty compact convex values, then Ψ has a fixed point, i.e. there exists an $x^* \in C$ such that $x^* \in \Psi(x^*)$ where Ψ is closed if and only if it holds for any $x \in C$ that whenever $x^i \to x$, $y^i \in \Psi(x^i)$ and $y^i \to y$, then $y \in \Psi(x)$.*

For proof, see, e.g., Border (1989) in which another important concept of the upper hem-continuity of a correspondence is also fully explained in connection with the closedness.

Now recall the demand function of consumer i. Given an economy $\omega = (\omega^1, \ldots, \omega^I) \in \mathbf{R}^{LI}_{++}$, it is written as $f^i(\mathbf{p}, \mathbf{p} \cdot \omega^i)$ for any $\mathbf{p} \in \mathbf{R}^L_{++}$, $i = 1, \ldots, I$. Note that $f^i(\mathbf{p}, \mathbf{p} \cdot \omega^i)$ is itself a vector valued function, thus it is described in component form as $(f^i_1(\mathbf{p}, \mathbf{p} \cdot \omega^i), \ldots, f^i_L(\mathbf{p}, \mathbf{p} \cdot \omega^i))$. We have made some assumptions on each f^i (see assumption 1.3) one of which allows us to restrict price vectors to S^{L-1}_{++}. First we have the following lemma.

Lemma 4.3 *Let $\{\mathbf{p}^q\}_q (= (p^q_1, \ldots, p^q_L)_q)$ be a sequence in S^{L-1}_{++} convergent to some $\mathbf{p}^0 (= (p^0_1, \ldots, p^0_L))$. If $p^0_l > 0$ for some l, then $\{f^i_l(\mathbf{p}^q, \mathbf{p}^q \cdot \omega^i)\}_q$ is a bounded sequence for any given $\omega \in \mathcal{E} (= \mathbf{R}^{LI}_{++})$, $i = 1, \ldots, I$.*

Proof. Obviously we can take some $\mathbf{r} \in \mathbf{R}^L_{++}$ such that $\mathbf{p}^q < \mathbf{r}$ for all q. Since $\lim_{q \to \infty} p^q_l = p^0_l (> 0)$, there exists some $\delta > 0$ such that $p^q_l > \delta$ for all q. Noting assumption 1.3, for any given $\omega = (\omega^1, \ldots, \omega^I) \in \mathcal{E}$ we have

$$p^q_l f^i_l(\mathbf{p}^q, \mathbf{p}^q \cdot \omega^i) \le \sum_{h=1}^{L} p^q_h f^i_h(\mathbf{p}^q, \mathbf{p}^q \cdot \omega^i) = \mathbf{p}^q \cdot f^i(\mathbf{p}^q, \mathbf{p}^q \cdot \omega^i) = \mathbf{p}^q \cdot \omega^i \le \mathbf{r} \cdot \omega^i,$$

which implies that for all q,

$$f^i_l(\mathbf{p}^q, \mathbf{p}^q \cdot \omega^i) \le \frac{\mathbf{r} \cdot \omega^i}{p^q_l} \le \frac{\mathbf{r} \cdot \omega^i}{\delta} < +\infty.$$

It is obvious from the definition of the demand function that $f_l^i(\boldsymbol{p}^q, \boldsymbol{p}^q \cdot \boldsymbol{\omega}^i) > 0$ for all q, thus our claim follows. $\qquad\square$

We now consider the aggregate excess demand function $G(\omega, \boldsymbol{p})$, which has been defined for any $(\omega, \boldsymbol{p}) \in \mathcal{E} \times S_{++}^{L-1}$ as follows.

$$G(\omega, \boldsymbol{p}) = \sum_{i=1}^{I} f^i(\boldsymbol{p}, \boldsymbol{p} \cdot \boldsymbol{\omega}^i) - \sum_{i=1}^{I} \boldsymbol{\omega}^i.$$

Hence, an equilibrium price vector $\boldsymbol{p}^*$ for an economy $\omega \in \mathcal{E}$ is obviously the price vector that satisfies that $G(\omega, \boldsymbol{p}^*) = 0$.

Under the assumptions provided before, we have the following general result concerning the existence of equilibria.

Theorem 4.3   *Under assumptions 1.3 and 3.1, there exists at least one equilibrium price vector for any economy of $\mathcal{E}$.*

Proof.   Pick any $\omega \in \mathcal{E}$ and fix it. For simplicity of the notation, we shall write in the sequel the aggregate excess demand function corresponding to the ω just as $G(\boldsymbol{p})$ which is phrased in component form as $(G_1(\boldsymbol{p}), \ldots, G_L(\boldsymbol{p}))$.

Let $\Lambda(\boldsymbol{p})$ be the set of commodity numbers which have the largest excess demand for each $\boldsymbol{p} \in S_{++}^{L-1}$. That is,

$$\Lambda(\boldsymbol{p}) = \{k \in 1, \ldots, L \mid G_k(\boldsymbol{p}) = max\{G_l(\boldsymbol{p}), \ l = 1, \ldots, L\}\}.$$

As for each $\boldsymbol{p} \in S_+^{L-1} \setminus S_{++}^{L-1} (= \partial S_{++}^{L-1})$, $\Lambda(\boldsymbol{p})$ is defined by

$$\Lambda(\boldsymbol{p}) = \{k \in \{1, \ldots, L\} \mid p_k = 0\}.$$

Thus, we have $\Lambda(\boldsymbol{p})$ on S_+^{L-1} which is obviously a compact convex set.

Then consider the correspondence $\Psi : S_+^{L-1} \to S_+^{L-1}$ which is derived from $\Lambda(\boldsymbol{p})$ as follows.

$$\Psi(\boldsymbol{p}) = \{\tilde{\boldsymbol{p}} \in S_+^{L-1} \mid \tilde{p}_k = 0, \ k \notin \Lambda(\boldsymbol{p})\}.$$

It is easily seen that Ψ is nonempty, compact and convex valued. We shall show that Ψ is also closed.

Let $\boldsymbol{p}^q \to \boldsymbol{p}^0$ in S_+^{L-1} and $\boldsymbol{x}^q \to \boldsymbol{x}^0$ where $\boldsymbol{x}^q \in \Psi(\boldsymbol{p}^q)$ for any q. We have to show that $\boldsymbol{x}^0 \in \Psi(\boldsymbol{p}^0)$ for any $\boldsymbol{p}^0 \in S_+^{L-1}$.

We classify two cases for $\boldsymbol{p}^0$.

(1) $\boldsymbol{p}^0 \in S_{++}^{L-1}$.

In this case we can assume that $\boldsymbol{p}^q$ are strictly positive for all q without loss of generality. For any $k \notin \Lambda(\boldsymbol{p}^0)$ there exists some t such that $G_k(\boldsymbol{p}^q) <$

$max\{G_l(\boldsymbol{p}^q), l = 1, \ldots, L\}$ for all $q \geq t$, thus $k \notin \Lambda(\boldsymbol{p}^q)$ for all $q \geq t$. It follows from $\boldsymbol{x}^q = (x_1^q, \ldots, x_L^q) \in \Psi(\boldsymbol{p}^q)$ that $x_k^q = 0$ for all $q \geq t$. Since $\boldsymbol{p}^q \to \boldsymbol{p}^0$ and $\lim_{q\to\infty} x_k^q = x_k^0$, we have that $x_k^0 = 0$. This holds for an arbitrary $k \notin \Lambda(\boldsymbol{p}^0)$, thus $\boldsymbol{x}^0 \in \Psi(\boldsymbol{p}^0)$.

(2) $\boldsymbol{p}^0 \in \partial S_{++}^{L-1}$.

We can assume that $\boldsymbol{p}^0 = (0, \ldots, 0, p_{r+1}, \ldots, p_L)$, $p_l > 0$, $l = r + 1, \ldots, L$, thus $\Psi(\boldsymbol{p}^0) = \{\tilde{\boldsymbol{p}} \in S_+^{L-1} \mid \tilde{p}_l = 0, \ l = r + 1, \ldots, L\}$.

First suppose that $\{\boldsymbol{p}^q\}_q$ has a subsequence in S_{++}^{L-1}. For simplicity, we denote the subsequence as $\{\boldsymbol{p}^q\}_q$ itself. Then, it follows from lemma 4.3 that the sequence $\{G_l(\boldsymbol{p}^q)\}_q$ is bounded for each $l = r + 1, \ldots, L$ while by assumption 3.1 $\|G(\boldsymbol{p}^q)\| \to +\infty$. Hence, $G_l(\boldsymbol{p}^q)$ $(l = l = r + 1, \ldots, L)$ can not be the largest excess demand for a $\boldsymbol{p}^q$ close enough to $\boldsymbol{p}^0$, which means that there exists some t such that $\Lambda(\boldsymbol{p}^q) \subseteq \{1, \ldots, r\}$ for all $q \geq t$, equivalently, $x_l^q = 0$, $l = r + 1, \ldots, L$ for all $q \geq t$. This implies that $\boldsymbol{x}^q \in \Psi(\boldsymbol{p}^0)$ for all $q \geq t$, thus we have that $\boldsymbol{x}^0 = \lim_{q\to\infty} \boldsymbol{x}^q \in \Psi(\boldsymbol{p}^0)$.

Secondly, suppose that $\{\boldsymbol{p}^q\}_q$ does not have any subsequence in S_{++}^{L-1}. In this case we can assume that $\{\boldsymbol{p}^q\}_q \subset \partial S_{++}^{L-1}$. Since $\boldsymbol{p}^q \to \boldsymbol{p}^0$, there exists some t such that $p_l^q = 0$, $l = 1, \ldots, r$ for all $q \geq t$, that is, $\Lambda(\boldsymbol{p}^q) \subseteq \{1, \ldots, r\}$ for all $q \geq t$. Since $\boldsymbol{x}^q \in \Psi(\boldsymbol{p}^q)$, $x_l^q = 0$, $l = r + 1, \ldots, L$ for all $q \geq t$, $\boldsymbol{x}^q \in \Psi(\boldsymbol{p}^0)$ for all $q \geq t$, thus $\boldsymbol{x}^0 = \lim_{q\to\infty} \boldsymbol{x}^q \in \Psi(\boldsymbol{p}^0)$.

Thus, it turns out that Ψ is nonempty, compact, convex valued *and* closed. Then, by applying Kakutani's fixed point theorem, we have some $\boldsymbol{p}^* \in S_+^{L-1}$ such that $\boldsymbol{p}^* \in \Psi(\boldsymbol{p}^*)$. It is easily seen from the constructions of Λ and Ψ that $\boldsymbol{p}^* \notin \partial S_{++}^{L-1}$, that is, $\boldsymbol{p}^* \in S_{++}^{L-1}$. Thus, $\Lambda(\boldsymbol{p}^*) = 1, \ldots, L$, which means that at $\boldsymbol{p}^*$ excess demands of all the commodities are equal. Let c be the excess demand of each commodity. Then, according to Walras' law, we have

$$c = (\sum_{l=1}^{L} p_l^*)c = \sum_{l=1}^{L} p_l^* c = \sum_{l=1}^{L} p_l^* G_l(\boldsymbol{p}^*) = \boldsymbol{p}^* G(\boldsymbol{p}^*) = 0,$$

which implies that $G(\boldsymbol{p}^*) = 0$. Thus, $\boldsymbol{p}^*$ is an equilibrium price vector. $\qquad\square$

4.2.2 *The Number of Equilibria in Regular Economies*

Under assumption 3.1, theorem 4.3 gives us a decisive conclusion as far as the existence of equilibria is concerned. Namely, *every* economy has at least one equilibrium. In contrast, the theory of regular economies has shown us that for almost all economies the set of equilibria is finite. A further consequence concerning equilibria can be deduced by applying the modulo 2 degree in the theory of regular economies. The argument provided below is based on the works of Dierker (1972, 1974), Mityagin (1972), and Balasko (1975).

Recall the characterization of regular economies provided in 3.2.4. That is, an economy $\omega \in \mathcal{E}$ is a regular economy if and only if 0 is a regular value for the map $\tilde{G}_\omega$ (see proposition 3.3). Noting that $\tilde{G}_\omega^{-1}(0)$ represents the set of equilibrium price vectors for the economy, therefore, $deg_2 \tilde{G}_\omega$ for a regular economy ω tells us if the number of equilibria is even or odd. This is the idea which we shall adopt.

There is, however, a crucial difficulty in following the proposed idea. It is due to the fact that the domain of $\tilde{G}_\omega$, i.e. S_{++}^{L-1}, is not compact, which violates condition (1) required of the domain (see 4.1.1). If the domain is not compact, then the modulo 2 degree of a map itself would not be well defined.

Thus, we give up considering $deg_2 \tilde{G}_\omega$ itself. Instead, we make use of proposition 4.3. It is true in general that the difficulty mentioned above is still a bottleneck in applying the proposition. See the figure below. Given the graphs of two smooth maps f_0 and f_1 both from $(0,1) \to \boldsymbol{R}$ as shown in the diagram, we easily see that for a common regular value 0 to those maps $\sharp f_0^{-1}(0) \ mod \ 2 \neq \sharp f_1^{-1}(0) \ mod \ 2$.

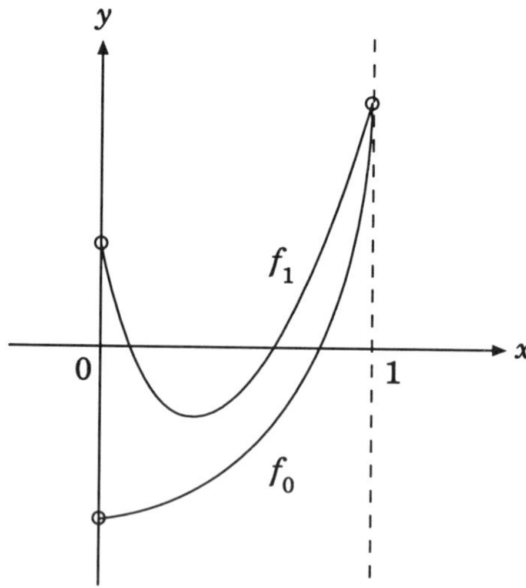

Fig. 4.3

But even if a manifold M is not compact, the proposition holds *provided for a common regular value y to f and g, $f^{-1}(y)$, $g^{-1}(y)$ and $F^{-1}(y)$ are all compact* where F is the smooth homotopy between f and g. The claim can be established in almost the same way as the proof of proposition 4.3 (so it will be left to the reader as an exercise).

We shall show that assumption 3.1 can be utilized in the modified version of proposition 4.3 provided above so as to obtain the desirable consequence concerning the number of equilibria in regular economies. For this purpose, we give a useful lemma which is concerned with a general homotopy.

Lemma 4.4 *Let M, K be ordinary (boundaryless) manifolds. Let f, g be smooth maps from M to K with the homotopy $F : M \times [0,1] \to K$. Suppose that there exists $y \in K$ such that for any $t \in [0,1]$, $F_t^{-1}(y)$ is compact in M where $F_t \equiv F(\cdot, t) : M \to K$. Then, $F^{-1}(y)$ is compact in $M \times [0,1]$.*

Proof. Consider the correspondence $\Psi : [0,1] \to M$ defined by $\Psi(t) = F_t^{-1}(y)$. Note that the graph of Ψ is nothing but $F^{-1}(y)$.

Ψ is, of course, compact valued. In addition, we shall show that Ψ is closed. Let $t^q \to t^0$ in $[0,1]$ and $x^q \to x^0$ where $x^q \in \Psi(t^q)$ for any q. Noting that $x^q \in \Psi(t^q)$ is equivalent to that $F(x^q, t^q) = y$, it follows from the continuity of F that $\lim_{q \to \infty} F(x^q, t^q) = F(x^0, t^0) = y$, which implies that $x^0 \in F_{t^0}^{-1}(y) = \Psi(t^0)$. Thus Ψ is closed at t^0. Since $t^0 \in [0,1]$ is arbitrary, Ψ is closed, which means that the graph of Ψ is closed in $M \times [0,1]$.

Pick any sequence $\{(x^q, t^q)\}_q$ in $F^{-1}(y)$. We classify two cases.

(1) $\{(x^q, t^q)\}_q$ is itself convergent.

In this case the limit point of the sequence is contained in $F^{-1}(y)$ since $F^{-1}(y)$ is closed.

(2) $\{(x^q, t^q)\}_q$ is not convergent. If so, there exists some $t \in [0,1]$ such that $\{(x^q, t^q)\}_q$ has a subsequence $\{(x^{q_n}, t^{q_n})\}_{q_n}$, $t^{q_n} = t$ for all q_n so that $\{(x^{q_n})\}_{q_n} \subset F_t^{-1}(y)$. Since $F_t^{-1}(y)$ is compact by the assumption, $\{(x^{q_n})\}_{q_n}$ has a subsequence convergent to some point in $F_t^{-1}(y)$, which implies that $\{(x^q, t^q)\}_q$ has a subsequence convergent to some point in $F^{-1}(y)$.

In view of (1) and (2), we have that $F^{-1}(y)$ is compact. $\qquad\square$

We are now in a position to state the final consequence.

Theorem 4.4 *Under assumption 3.1, every regular economy has an odd number of equilibrium price vectors.*

Proof.   For any regular economy ω, 0 is a regular value of $\tilde{G}_\omega$ (see proposition 3.3).   Under assumption 3.1, $\tilde{G}_\omega^{-1}(0)$ (the set of equilibrium price vectors for ω) is finite, thus compact.

To apply proposition 4.3, we need to figure out some tractable map with 0 as a regular value which is smoothly homotopic to $\tilde{G}_\omega$. We consider the following map $f : S_{++}^{L-1} \to \mathbf{R}^{L-1}$ as such.

$$f(p_1,\dots,p_L) = (p_1,\dots,p_{L-1}) - \left(\frac{1}{L},\dots,\frac{1}{L}\right).$$

It is easily seen that f is a smooth submersion, thus 0 is a regular value of f. Furthermore, $f^{-1}(0)$ is a singleton, thus compact. Then $\tilde{G}_\omega \sim f$. Indeed we can consider the following smooth homotopy $F : S_{++}^{L-1} \times [0,1] \to \mathbf{R}^{L-1}$ between $\tilde{G}_\omega$ and f.

$$F(\mathbf{p},t) = t\tilde{G}_\omega(\mathbf{p}) + (1-t)f(\mathbf{p}).$$

Now we shall show that for any given $t \in [0,1]$, $F_t^{-1}(0)$ is compact. First note that $F_t^{-1}(0)$ is closed by continuity of $F_t : S_{++}^{L-1} \to \mathbf{R}^{L-1}$. Pick any sequence $\{\mathbf{p}^q\}_q$ in $F_t^{-1}(0)$. Obviously $t\tilde{G}_\omega(\mathbf{p}^q) + (1-t)f(\mathbf{p}^q) = 0$ for all q. Since $\{\mathbf{p}^q\}_q$ is bounded in $\mathbf{R}^L$, thus it has a convergent subsequence in $\mathbf{R}^L$. Let the subsequence be denoted by the same notation as $\{\mathbf{p}^q\}_q$ for simplicity. Then, $\{\mathbf{p}^q\}_q$ turns out to be convergent to some point of S_{++}^{L-1}. Indeed, suppose not, then $\lim_{q\to\infty} \mathbf{p}^q \in \partial S_{++}^{L-1}$, which leads to that $\lim_{q\to\infty} \|\tilde{G}_\omega(\mathbf{p}^q)\| = +\infty$. This contradicts the condition that $t\tilde{G}_\omega(\mathbf{p}^q) + (1-t)f(\mathbf{p}^q) = 0$ for all q. Since $F_t^{-1}(0)$ is closed, the limit point of $\{\mathbf{p}^q\}_q$ is included in $F_t^{-1}(0)$. Hence we have that $F_t^{-1}(0)$ is compact.

Then, through lemma 4.4 we obtain that $F^{-1}(0)$ is compact. Thus, in view of the modified version of proposition 4.3 provided above, we have

$$\sharp\tilde{G}_\omega^{-1}(0) = \sharp f^{-1}(0) \ (mod\ 2).$$

But $f^{-1}(0)$ is a singleton, thus $\tilde{G}_\omega^{-1}(0)\ mod\ 2 = 1$. That is, the number of equilibrium price vectors for ω is odd. $\qquad\square$

Thus, it turns out that the odd number of equilibria is a generic property with respect to economies. In other words, almost all economies have the particular property concerning their equilibria.

Furthermore noting that the odd number does not include zero, the above theorem asserts that every regular economy has at least one equilibrium. That is, it can be seen as an existence theorem for equilibria as far as regular economies are concerned. Alternatively put, it is a generic existence theorem for equilibria although we have a complete existence theorem for equilibria (theorem 4.3).

Chapter 5

Stability of Equilibria in Regular Economies

In this chapter we argue another property of equilibria in regular economies called local stability. As will be stated later, there are several kinds of stability concepts used in economics. What we are concerned with is a classical one: the stability of equilibrium prices by a competitive market mechanism. Since the market mechanism is properly described by a dynamical system (differential equations system), there has been a large volume of work concerning this issue that makes use of the theory of differential equations. Here we adopt a slightly different method than such a traditional one to investgate the issue. This method was developed by Dierker (1972) and Varian (1975). To this end, we need some new concepts and tools of difnrential topology; that is, the index of a vector field and Poincaré-Hopf Theorem. Because both are complicated, we proceed step by step toward the goal. We shall see that those mathematical appliances shed light on the classical issue of the stability of competitive equilibria.

5.1 Mathematical Preliminaries

5.1.1 *Oriented Manifolds*

Here we present the concept of an orientation of a manifold which is indispensable for the degree (not the modulo 2 degree) of a smooth map defined in the next subsection.

To begin with, we shall introduce an orientation to n-dimensional Euclidean space R^n which we consider a vector space. Consider the whole set of ordered bases of R^n where an ordered basis is a basis defined by taking account of the order of its component vectors. For instance, a basis $\{b_1, b_2, b_3, \ldots, b_n\}$ is considered to be distinct from a ba-

59

sis $\{b_2, b_1, b_3, \ldots, b_n\}$ in terms of the ordered bases because the order of the first two vectors are different among them. Then, we introduce a binary relation to the set of the ordered bases as follows. Pick any two ordered bases $b(= \{b_1, \ldots, b_n\})$ and $b'(= \{b_1', \ldots, b_n'\})$. Then, as is well known, there exists a unique linear isomorphism $A : \mathbf{R}^n \to \mathbf{R}^n$ such that $b' = Ab$, which means that $b_1' = Ab_1, \ldots, b_n' = Ab_n$. Note that this linear transformation A can be represented by a nonsingular $n \times n$ matrix of coefficients. If the determinant of the matrix is positive, then b and b' are said to have the same orientation or to be equivalently oriented. If it is negative, they are said to have the opposite orientation or to be oppositely oriented. It is easily checked, through the product rule of determinants, that the binary relation of the same orientation is an equivalence relation on the set of all ordered bases and that there are exactly two equivalence classes. A choice of one of these equivalence classes to affix a positive sign is said to orient $\mathbf{R}^n$. In the process, the other class is automatically given a negative sign. The sign of the class an ordered basis b belongs to is called its orientation; thus b is either positively oriented or negatively oriented. Thus there are two possible orientations for $\mathbf{R}^n$ although it is usually oriented in such a way that the standard ordered basis $\{(1, 0, 0, \ldots, 0), (0, 1, 0, \ldots, 0), (0, 0, 1, \ldots, 0), \ldots, (0, 0, 0, \ldots, 1)\}$ is positively oriented.

Example 5.1 The orientation of $\mathbf{R}^2$: Since the standard basis $\{(1, 0), (0, 1)\}$ is positively oriented, a basis $\{(0, 1), (1, 0)\}$ is negatively oriented. Indeed, the linear transformation between them is represented by the following matrix:

$$\begin{pmatrix} 0 & 1 \\ 1 & 0 \end{pmatrix}$$

whose determinant is -1. As is similarly checked, another basis $\{(1, 0), (-1, -1)\}$ is also negatively oriented.

The argument provided above can be easily applied to a general finite-dimensional real vector space V and we obtain the concept of an orientation of V although the determination of the orientation on V is arbitrary. A comment is in order on 0-dimensional vector space. In this case the space is a singleton, so the point itself is defined to have either a positive orientation or a negative orientation. A positive orientation is usually denoted by $+1$ and a negative orientation is denoted by -1.

Now consider the relation between two oriented vector spaces in terms of an orientation. Let V be an oriented real vector space which is linear isomorphic to another oriented real vector space W. Suppose that $L : V \to W$ is an isomorphism. Pick any basis v in V, then $L(v)$ turns out to be a basis in W. If the orientation of v in V (i.e. positive or negative) is the same as the orientation of $L(v)$ in W, then we shall say that L preserves orientation. If not, L reverses orientation. This definition is independent on the choice of a basis in V since it is easily seen that whenever v and v' in V have the same orientation, so do the corresponding $L(v)$ and $L(v')$ in W.

We now turn to an orientation of a manifold. Roughly speaking, an orientation of a manifold is obtained by smoothly choosing the orientation on the tangent (vector) space at each point through the derivative of a corresponding parametrization. To be precise,

Definition 5.1 If around each point of a m-dimensional manifold M there exists a parametrization $\phi : U \to M$ such that $d\phi_u : \mathbf{R}^m \to T_{\phi(u)}M$ preserves orientation at each point u of $U(\subset \mathbf{R}^m)$, then M is orientable.

If a manifold is orientable, then the manifold together with a smooth orientation is called an oriented manifold.

Note that not all manifolds are orientable. Consider any closed loop on a manifold M. Let $\bar{x} \in M$ be a terminal point of the loop. If M is orientable, then by the definition the tangent space at any point x on the loop has the same orientation as the tangent space at a point close to x, thus the tangent space at $\bar{x}$ as a start point is equally oriented to the tangent space at $\bar{x}$ as an end point. However, if you take a closed loop on the Möbius band (see Fig. 5.1) depicted like in the figure below, then it turns out that orientations of the twofold tangent spaces at any terminal point are incompatible.

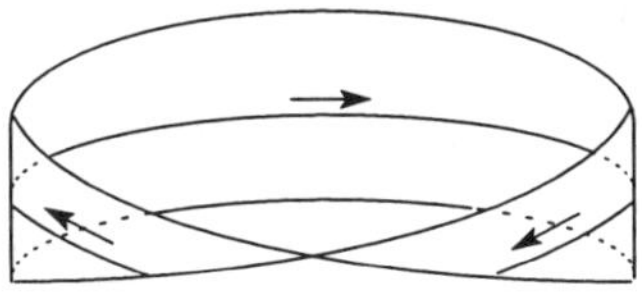

Fig. 5.1

An orientation of a manifold with boundary is our special concern. Let M be a manifold with boundary. As we have shown, the boundary ∂M is itself a manifold (without boundary) whose dimension is just one less than that of $M \setminus \partial M$. Furthermore, if M is orientable, then ∂M is oriented as follows.

First consider two tangent spaces at any point $x \in \partial M$. One is $T_x M$ and the other is $T_x(\partial M)$. Since $T_x(\partial M) \subset T_x M$ and $dim T_x(\partial M) = dim T_x M - 1$, $T_x M$ is partitioned by $T_x(\partial M)$ into two open-half spaces one of which locally approximates a neighborhood of x in M. Let this open-half space be H^+ and the other one be H^- (see Fig. 5.2).

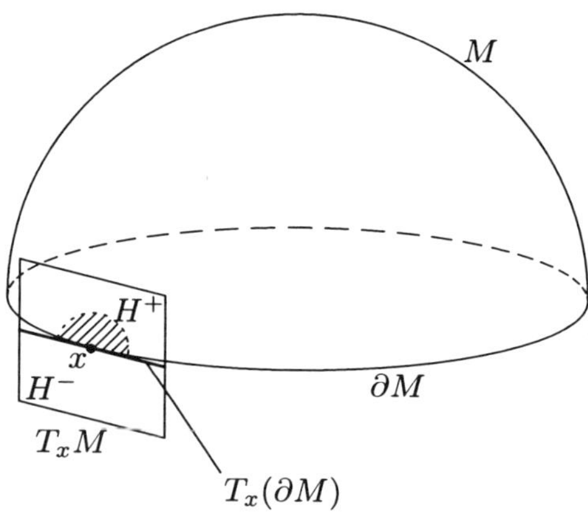

Fig. 5.2

We call a vector of $T_x M$ which belongs to H^+ (resp. H^-) an inward (resp. outward) vector. Since M is oriented, we can choose a positively oriented basis $\{v_1, v_2, \ldots, v_m\}$ for $T_x M$ in such a way that $v_2, \ldots, v_m$ all belong to $T_x(\partial M)$ and that v_1 is an outward vector. Then, obviously $\{v_2, \ldots, v_m\}$ constitutes a basis of $T_x(\partial M)$ which is defined to be positively oriented. This procedure determines an orientation for ∂M at x. Since x is arbitrary, we obtain the required orientation for ∂M.

Example 5.2   1-dimensional manifold with boundary: its boundary point

Fig. 5.3

(0-dimensional manifold) x is assigned the orientation $+1$ if a positively oriented vector in the tangent space at x is outward. Otherwise, it is assigned the orientation -1 (See Fig. 5.3). If the closed arc ab is oriented in such a way that the direction of the arrow is the positive orientation, then a boundary point a is assigned -1 and b is assigned $+1$.

Example 5.3   Homotopy space $M \times [0, 1]$ where M is a boundaryless manifold: This has two boundaries, $M \times 0$ and $M \times 1$ which are identical as a manifold. However, if $M \times [0, 1]$ is oriented, induced orientation on $M \times 0$ is opposite to the one on $M \times 1$. See Fig. 5.4. Let $\{v_1, v_2\}$ be a positively oriented basis for $M \times [0, 1]$. Then, a tangent vector v_a at a point a to $M \times 1$ which is considered to be a basis for the tangent space $T_a(M \times 1)$ is positively oriented whereas the tangent vector $v_{a'}$ at a point a' to $M \times 0$ which is also a basis for the tangent space $T_{a'}(M \times 0)$ is negatively oriented.

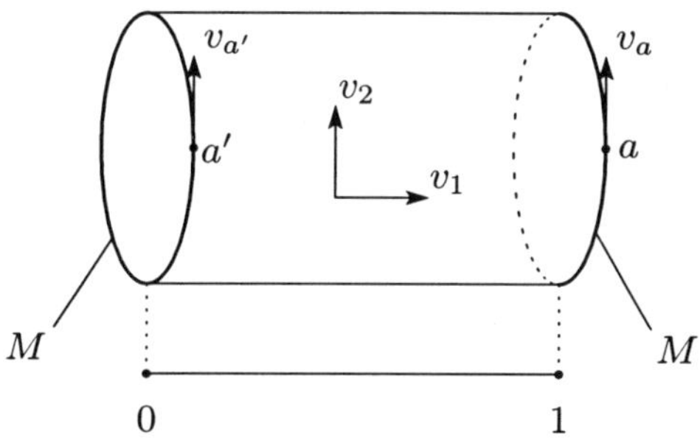

Fig. 5.4

5.1.2 *Degree of Smooth Maps*

The degree of a smooth map is an elaboration of the modulo 2 degree of a smooth map by means of orientation of relevant manifolds. Let $f : M \to K$ be a smooth map where M and K are the ordinary (boundaryless) manifolds with the same properties as those in the modulo 2 degree; that is to say, (1) M is compact, (2) K is connected and (3) $dimM = dimK$. In addition, we assume here that M and K are both oriented. Then, we can determine whether the derivative df_x of f at any *regular* point $x \in M$ preserves or reverses orientation since $df_x : T_xM \to T_{f(x)}K$ is a linear isomorphism between oriented vector spaces. So, if df_x preserves (resp. reverses) orientation, then we define the sign of df_x to be $+1$ (resp. -1).

On the analogy of the modulo 2 degree, the degree itself gives some information concerning a regular value through its preimage. As we have seen in the modulo 2 degree, for any regular value $y \in K$ its preimage $f^{-1}(y)$ forms a finite set which, of course, consists of regular points. Thus, at each point $x \in f^{-1}(y)$ we can define the sign of df_x in the way mentioned above. Then, consider the sum of those signs, that is, $\sum_{x \in f^{-1}(y)} sign\ df_x$, which we denote $sign(f; y)$. To appreciate this notion, let's take as an example a smooth map $f : \boldsymbol{R} \to \boldsymbol{R}$ whose graph is depicted in the figure below.

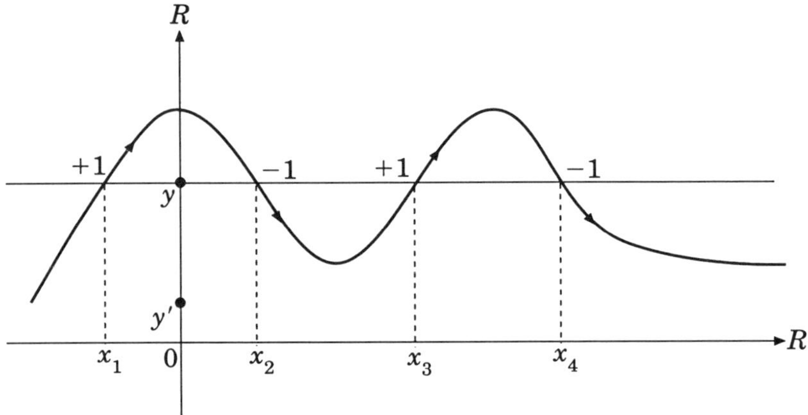

Fig. 5.5

We assume that a vector with the direction of the arrow drawn in the diagram is a positively oriented basis for both a horizontal and a vertical axis. Obviously y is a regular value and $f^{-1}(y) = \{x_1, x_2, x_3, x_4\}$. First consider the derivative df_{x_1} at x_1. By inspection, a positively oriented vector in the horizon axis is carried by df_{x_1} to a positively oriented vector in the vertical axis, so $sign\ df_{x_1} = +1$. In contrast, we can see that df_{x_2} carries a positively oriented vector in the horizon axis to a negatively oriented vector in the vertical axis, thus $sign\ df_{x_2} = -1$. We can determine $sign\ df_{x_i}$, $i = 3, 4$, in the same way to obtain that $sign(f; y) = \sum_{i=1}^{4} sign\ df_{x_i} = +1 - 1 + 1 - 1 = 0$.

In the above diagram the domain of f is not compact. But once we require that the domain be a compact (and boudaryless) manifold, then, interestingly enough, it turns out that the integer $sign(f; y)$ does not depend on the choice of regular value y. Note that for another regular value y' in the above diagram, $sign(f; y')$ is not 0 but $+1$.

Definition 5.2 Let $f : M \to K$ be a smooth map where M and K satisfy the conditions provided above. Then, the degree of f, which we denote $deg\ f$, is the integer $sign(f; y)$ for any regular value y.

We shall give a sketch of the proof that $sign(f; y)$ does not depend on the choice of regular value y. The proof proceeds in almost the same way as that in 4.1.3. That is, the key is the following lemma.

Lemma 5.1 *Let f, g be smoothly homotopic maps from M to K where M and K satisfy the above conditions. If $y \in K$ is a regular value for both f and g, then*

$$sign(f; y) = sign(g; y).$$

For the proof of this lemma, see Milnor (1969), pp. 28-29.

On the basis of this lemma, we can show that if y and z are regular values of f, then $sign(f; y) = sign(f; z)$. Indeed, there exists a diffeomorphism $h : K \to K$ that carries y to z and is isotopic to the identity. Since h preserves orientation, we have

$$deg(f; y) = deg(h \circ f; h(y))$$

because $sign\ d_x(h \circ f) = sign\ dh_y \cdot sign\ df_x$ for any $x \in f^{-1}(y)$. On the other hand, since f is homotopic to $h \circ f$, the above lemma asserts that

$$deg(h \circ f; z) = deg(f; z).$$

which leads to the required consequence.

In view of Sard's theorem, we immediately obtain the same proposition concerning the degree as proposition 4.6 regarding the modulo 2 degree. That is,

Proposition 5.1 *Let f, g be smoothly homotopic maps from M to K where M and K satisfy the above conditions. Then, $deg\ f = deg\ g$.*

Hence, the degree of a smooth map also depends only on the smooth homotopy class of the map. In other words, $deg\ f$ is a smooth homotopy invariant just like $deg_2 f$.

There is a close relation between *deg f* and *deg₂f*. That is, *deg f* is an odd (resp. even) integer if and only if $deg_2 f$ is 1 (resp. 0). This immediately follows from the fact that if $deg_2 f$ is 1 (resp. 0), $f^{-1}(y)$ consists of an odd (resp. even) number of points for any regular value y and that *deg f* is made of the sum of the sign $(+1\ or -1)$ assigned to each point of $f^{-1}(y)$.

In addition, *deg f* gives us more information concerning a behavior of f than $deg_2 f$. In view of the argument provided above, *sign df$_x$* is interpreted to identify one of the two exclusive behaviors of f at x which are observed in terms of orientation for manifolds. Since *sign df$_x$* is designated as either $+1$ or -1, the sum of those signs, i.e. *deg f*, shows that in the preimage of any regular value, the number of points where one behavior is observed for f is larger just by $\sharp|deg\ f|$ than the number of points in which the other behavior is observed for f, regardless of a magnitude of the preimage itself.

5.1.3 *Vector Fields and Index*

We now consider a specific map called a vector field which will play a crucial role in the economic analysis stated later.

Definition 5.3 A vector field v on a manifold M in $\boldsymbol{R}^n$ is a smooth map $v : M \to \boldsymbol{R}^n$ such that $v(x) \in T_x M$ for each $x \in M$.

The smoothness of a vector field is precisely as follows. Let $\boldsymbol{E}_x^1, \ldots, \boldsymbol{E}_x^m$ be the basis for $T_x M$ corresponding to a standard basis for $\boldsymbol{R}^m$ through the derivative of a parametrization around x. Note that if x is locally varied, $\boldsymbol{E}_x^i$ is a smooth map of x, $i = 1, \ldots, m$. Now $v(x)$ may be written uniquely as $v(x) = \sum_{i=1}^m \alpha^i \boldsymbol{E}_x^i$. Therefore, each coefficient α^i can be seen as a function of x. A vector field v is smooth if and only if at each point $x \in M$ these functions are all locally smooth.

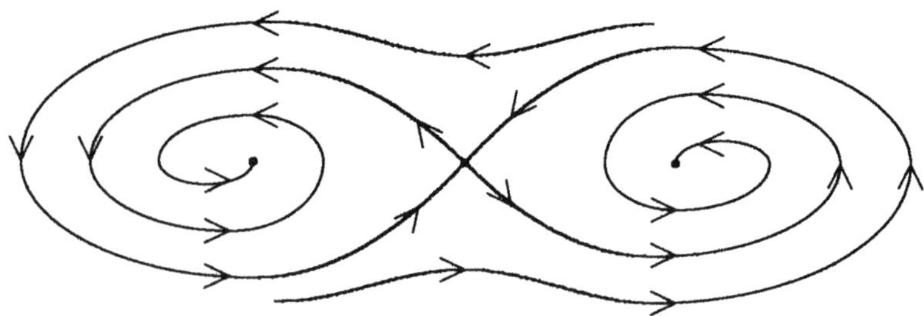

Fig. 5.6

Given a vector field on M, let's imagine that we draw flows all over M by plotting a tangent vector at each point specified by v. Then strange behaviors of flows, if any, will be found only around the points whose tangent vector is 0. With the exception of those points, we will see flows smoothly moving like in the chart depicted above.

We call the points $x \in M$ such that $v(x) = 0$ zeros of the vector field v. It is no wonder that a strange behavior of flows could occur around those zeros because a vector starting from zero may have any direction regardless of how small the magnitude of the change may be. In contrast, around the points $x \in M$ where $v(x) \neq 0$ flows are nearly constant because of the smoothness of v.

So, we try to quantify the directional change of a vector field around its zeros by means of the concept of the degree of a map. First consider a smooth vector field v defined on an open set U in $\boldsymbol{R}^n$ and assume that v has an isolated zero $z \in U$ where an isolated zero is a point around which there are no other zeros than itself. To see what happens in the directions of tangent vectors $v(x)$ around z, we confine ourselves to a small sphere $S_\epsilon(z)$ with z at the center. We may assume that z is only one zero of v in $S_\epsilon(z)$. Then, observe the direction of the tangent vector $v(x)$ at each point $x \in S_\epsilon(z)$. Since it is not the magnitude but the direction that matters for each tangent vector, we normalize the vectors to consider $v(x)/\|v(x)\|$ at each point $x \in S_\epsilon(z)$. This normalization leads to the map $\bar{v} : S_\epsilon(z) \to S^{n-1}$ defined by

$$\bar{v}(x) = \frac{v(x)}{\|v(x)\|}$$

where S^{n-1} indicates the $(n-1)$-dimensional unit sphere in $\boldsymbol{R}^n$. Obviously, $S_\epsilon(z)$ is a boudaryless manifold, S^{n-1} is connected and $dim S_\epsilon(z) = dim S^{n-1}$, thus if $S_\epsilon(z)$ and S^{n-1} are given orientation, we obtain the degree of $\bar{v}$ which is called the index of v at z, denoted by $ind_z(v)$.

To illuminate substance of the index, let's take a simple example. Suppose that a vector field v on $\boldsymbol{R}^2$ shows the flows around the origin like in the left diagram of Fig. 5.7 depicted in the next page. Since obviously the origin is a zero of v, we shall figure out $ind_0(v)$.

In the right diagram, $S_\epsilon(0)$ and S^1 are drawn which respectively constitute the domain and the range for $\bar{v}$. The arrow shows the positive orientation in each circle. First pick a regular point a of $\bar{v}$ in $S_\epsilon(0)$. We can determine whether a point in $S_\epsilon(0)$ is regular or not by inspection of the behavior of $\bar{v}$ around the point. Let $\bar{v}(a)$ be b. Then, move from a

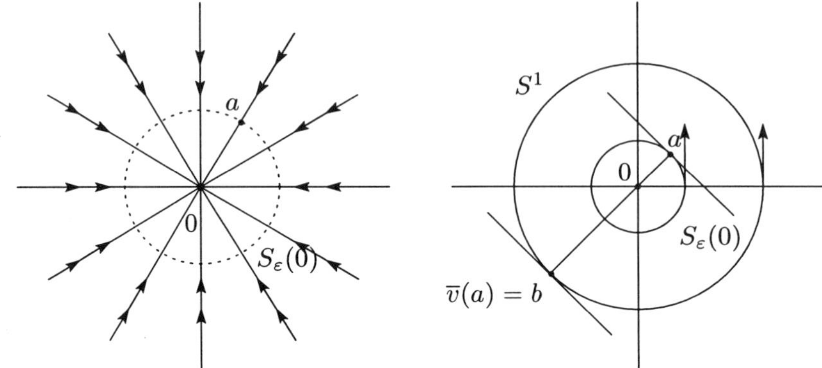

Fig. 5.7

counterclockwise around the circle and count how many times $\bar{v}(x)$ coincides with b before coming back to a, which gives us the number of regular points consisting of $v^{-1}(b)$. In the diagram we have only one regular point, i.e. a itself in $\bar{v}^{-1}(b)$. Next, to determine whether at each regular point x of $\bar{v}^{-1}(b)$ the derivative $d\bar{v}_x$ of $\bar{v}$ preserves or reverses orientation, check if $\bar{v}(x)$ coincides with b in counterclockwise movement or in clockwise movement along S^1. If the former (resp. latter) case is observed, then we have that $sign\ d\bar{v}_x = +1$ (resp. -1). In the diagram, it is immediate from inspection that $sign\ d\bar{v}_a = +1$. Finally, by summing up $sign\ d\bar{v}_x$ for all $x \in \bar{v}^{-1}(b)$, we obtain the required index of v at 0. In the diagram, obviously $ind_0(v) = +1$.

In the above argument, we implicitly assume from the beginning that $b\ (=\bar{v}(a))$ is a regular value of $\bar{v}$, which is not such a harmful treatment because through Sard's theorem almost all points of S^1 are regular values for $\bar{v}$. Indeed, the successive argument assured that b was a regular value of $\bar{v}$.

By following the procedure described above, we can easily calculate the index of each vector field whose flows are depicted in the diagram (i) $\sim$ (iii) of Fig. 5.8 in the next page where the zero in (i) is called a source, and the zero in (ii) is called a saddle.

Note that unlike the 2-dimensional case, higher dimensional cases do not admit us to rely on the geometrical treatment of the index of a vector field at its zeros. It is, in general, hard to calculate the index of a vector field in those cases.

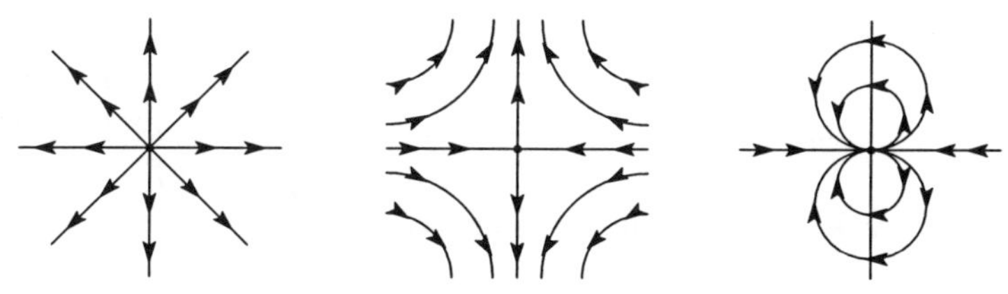

(i) source: index=+1 (ii) saddle: index=−1 (iii) index= +2

Fig. 5.8

However, if an isolated zero is a regular point for the vector field, then the index at that point can be easily obtained. Let v be a smooth vector field on an open set $U \in \mathbf{R}^m$ and $z \in U$ be an isolated zero of v that is also a regular point for v. Then, we have the following proposition.

Proposition 5.2   *The index of v at z is either $+1$ or -1 according as $\mid dv_z \mid$ is positive or negative where $\mid dv_z \mid$ is the determinant of the matrix representation of dv_z.*

Proof.   The proof is long and tedious, so that we shall only give a sketch.

(1) In general, a diffeomorphism $f : U \to \mathbf{R}^m$ is orientation preserving if and only if for every regular point $x \in U$ for f, $\mid df_x \mid > 0$.

(2) An orientation preserving diffeomorphism $f : U \to \mathbf{R}^m$ is smoothly isotopic to the identity map $i : U \to U$ (for the proof, see Milnor (1969), Chap. 6, Lemma 2).

(3) First assume that $\mid dv_z \mid > 0$, then v is orientation preserving in the neighborhood of z since v becomes a diffeomorphism there. Through an appropriate coordinate transformation we may see z as 0, thus on a neighborhood of 0 v is smoothly isotopic to the identity map.

(4) Let $\bar{i}$ be the map defined by $\bar{i}(x) = x/\|x\|$. Pick a small sphere S_0 in U that has 0 as its center. Then, $v|_{S_0} \sim \bar{v}|_{S_0}$ and $i|_{S_0} \sim \bar{i}|_{S_0}$, which implies that $\bar{v}|_{S_0} \sim \bar{i}|_{S_0}$ since $v|_{S_0} \sim i|_{S_0}$ because of $v's$ orientation preserving property.

(5) When v is orientation preserving, through homotopy invariance of the degree we have that $ind_z(v) = deg\ \bar{v}|_{S_0} = deg\ \bar{i}|_{S_0} = +1$. Thus, we obtain that if $\mid dv_z \mid > 0$, then $ind_z(v) = +1$.

(6) Secondly assume that $\mid dv_z \mid < 0$, then v reverses orientation. It is known that in general an orientation reversing diffeomorphism is smoothly isotopic to a reflection map $r_i(x_1, \ldots, x_i, \ldots, x_m) = (x_1, \ldots, -x_i, \ldots, x_m)$ for some i, thus $ind_z(v) = deg\ r_i|_{S_0} = -1$. $\qquad\square$

In view of the above proposition, we have that $ind_z v = sign| \, dv_z \, |$.

Note that the above proposition still holds even when we replace a vector field on an open set in $\boldsymbol{R}^m$ with a vector field on a manifold in $\boldsymbol{R}^m$ (for the details, see Milnor (1969), Chap. 6, Lemma 5). This fact will play a very important role in our economical analysis.

5.1.4 *Poincaré-Hopf Theorem*

A smooth vector field can present a great variety of patterns of the behavior on a manifold if it has the zeros. However, if the manifold on which a smooth vector field is defined is compact, the degree of freedom concerning behavioral patterns is restricted by some structure of the manifold. For instance, imagine that you draw a smooth vector field with the zeros on some compact surfaces, say a sphere or a torus (a surface of a donut). Then you will see that any smooth vector field on the sphere has different patterns of the behavior around the zeros than what a smooth vector field shows around its zeros on the torus. It seems like some structure of the surface has an influence on the behavior of a vector field around its zeros.

Indeed, it is known in the case of a compact oriented manifold with boundary that every smooth vector field with isolated zeros must have some behavioral property quantified by the boundary structure itself as long as the field points outward along the boundary.

Specifically, let $M \in \boldsymbol{R}^m$ be a compact m-dimensional manifold with boundary. Thus, ∂M is a compact $(m-1)$-dimensional boundaryless manifold in $\boldsymbol{R}^m$. Now consider a vector ($\in \boldsymbol{R}^m$) at any point $x \in \partial M$ that is normal to the tangent space $T_x(\partial M)$ and that points out of M. By normalizing those vectors, we have a vector uniquely determined at each point $x \in \partial M$, which is called the outward unit normal vector at x.

Definition 5.4   For a compact m-dimensional manifold with boundary $M \in \boldsymbol{R}^m$, the Gauss map $g : \partial M \to S^{m-1}$ is the map that carries each $x \in \partial M$ to the outward unit normal vector at x where S^{m-1} is the unit sphere in $\boldsymbol{R}^m$.

Proposition 5.3   *Let $M \in \boldsymbol{R}^m$ be a compact oriented m-dimensional manifold with boundary. Suppose that $v : M \to \boldsymbol{R}^m$ is a smooth vector field with isolated zeros and that v gives an outward tangent vector at each point on the boundary. Then, we have*

$$\sum_{z \in Z} ind_z(v) = deg \, g$$

where g is the Gauss map on ∂M which is endowed with the induced orientation and Z is the set of the zeros of v.

Proof. Let $z_1, \ldots, z_n$ be the zeros of v and $\mathring{B}\epsilon(z_1), \ldots, \mathring{B}\epsilon(z_n)$ be open ϵ-balls each of which has z_i as its center, $i = 1, \ldots, n$ where ϵ is sufficiently small. Let M' be the set $M - (\bigcup_{i=1}^{n}\mathring{B}\epsilon(z_i))$. Then, M' is a m-dimensional manifold with boundary. Note that its boundary consists of ∂M, $S_\epsilon(z_1), \ldots, S_\epsilon(z_n)$ where $S_\epsilon(z_i)$ is a ϵ-sphere with z_i at the center, $i = 1, \ldots, n$. Consider the map $\bar{v} : M' \to S^{m-1}$ defined by $\bar{v}(x) = v(x)/\|v(x)\|$.

In general, it has been shown that for a compact oriented manifold with boundary X and a connected oriented manifold without boundary N, the following holds. That is, if a smooth map $f : \partial X \to N$ extends to a smooth map $F : X \to N$, then $deg\, f = 0$. For the proof, see Milnor (1969), § 5, Lemma 1.

Since the restriction of $\bar{v}$ to $\partial M'$, that is, $\bar{v}|_{\partial M'} : \partial M' \to S^{m-1}$ obviously extends to $\bar{v}$, we have through the above claim that $deg\, \bar{v}|_{\partial M'} = 0$. As we noted, $\partial M' = \partial M \cup S_\epsilon(z_1) \cup \ldots \cup S_\epsilon(z_n)$ and ∂M, $S_\epsilon(z_1), \ldots, S_\epsilon(z_n)$ are disjoint with each other, so

$$deg\, \bar{v}|_{\partial M'} = deg\, \bar{v}|_{\partial M} + deg\, \bar{v}|_{S_\epsilon(z_1)} + \ldots + deg\, \bar{v}|_{S_\epsilon(z_n)}.$$

Since $\bar{v}|_{\partial M}$ is smoothly homotopic to g, $deg\, \bar{v}|_{\partial M} = deg\, g$. On the other hand, the degree of $\bar{v}|_{S_\epsilon(z_i)}$ is by definition equal to the index of v at z_i, i.e. $ind_{z_i}(v)$, except that the induced orientation on $S_\epsilon(z_i)$ as a boundary of M' is opposite to an orientation for $S_\epsilon(z_i)$ used in the definition of $ind_{z_i}(v)$. Thus, we have that $ind_{z_i}(v) = -deg\, \bar{v}|_{S_\epsilon(z_i)}, i = 1, \ldots, n$.

In view of the equation provided above, we obtain

$$deg\, g - \sum_{i=1}^{n} ind_{z_i}(v) = 0,$$

from which the required consequence immediately follows. $\qquad\square$

It is worth noting for this proposition that on one hand the global behavior of a smooth vector field with isolated zeros is characterized by its index sum, while on the other hand the structure of a manifold with boundary is quantified by the degree of the Gauss map for the manifold. Thus, the proposition asserts that the behavior of a smooth vector field flowing out of a manifold with boundary is completely restricted in terms of the index sum by the structure of the manifold, however strangely it may behave inside the manifold.

Corollary 5.1 *If a smooth vector field on the unit ball D^m in $\mathbf{R}^m$ points outward at each point of the boundary S^{m-1}, then its index sum $\sum_{z \in Z} ind_z(v)$ is $+1$.*

Proof. D^m is obviously orientable and the Gauss map for D^m is the identity map on S^{m-1}. Since the degree of the identity map is $+1$, our claim immediately follows. $\square$

Corollary 5.2 *Let $M \subset \mathbf{R}^m$ be a compact oriented m-dimensional manifold with boundary. If there exists an orientation preserving diffeomorphism between M and D^m, then the index sum of a smooth vector field on M is $+1$ as long as it has isolated zeros and points out of M along the boundary.*

Proof. Let $f : D^m \to M$ be an orientation preserving diffeomorphism between M and D^m. Note that the restriction of f to the boundary S^{m-1} is also an orientation preserving diffeomorphism between S^{m-1} and ∂M. Let g and g' be respectively the Gauss maps for D^m and M (g is actually the identity map I on S^{m-1}). Since $g' \circ f|_{S^{m-1}} : S^{m-1} \to S^{m-1}$ is smoothly homotopic to $g : S^{m-1} \to S^{m-1}$, $deg\, g' \circ f|_{S^{m-1}} = deg\, g$. However, it is easily seen that $deg\, g' = deg\, g' \circ f|_{S^{m-1}}$ because $f|_{S^{m-1}}$ is an orientation preserving diffeomorphism. Thus, $deg\, g' = deg\, g\ (= deg\, I) = +1$. $\square$

The latter corollary is useful from a practical viewpoint since we very often encounter a m-dimensional manifold diffeomorphic to D^m in many applications.

The above argument is very suggestive, but the situation to be considered is limited. What if the relevant manifold has lower dimension than m? More fundamentally, what if the manifold has no boundary at all?

The Poincaré-Hopf Theorem gives us a remarkable answer to all these questions. It says as follows.

Theorem 5.1 *Let $M \in \mathbf{R}^n$ be a m-dimensional compact oriented manifold with or without boundary. Let v be a smooth vector field on M with isolated zeros. If M has a boundary, v is required to point outward along the boundary. Then, we have*

$$\sum_{z \in Z} ind_z(v) = \chi(M)$$

where Z is the set of the zeros of v and $\chi(M)$ is the Euler number of M.

Note that the Euler number is a characteristic that represents some property of a set from the viewpoint of algebraic topology and that is a topological invariant, i.e. $\chi(M) = \chi(K)$ if M is homeomorphic to K. We omit the rigorous proof of the theorem since some knowledge about algebraic topology is required to understand it (for the proof, see Milnor (1969), § 6, or Guillemin and Pollack (1974), Chap. 3, § 5). Instead, we shall explain in the low dimensional case the reason why the behavior of a smooth vector field admitted by a compact oriented manifold is strictly limited by the Euler number that expresses a topological information about the manifold. We particularly consider a 2-dimensional sphere S^2 and a 2-dimensional disk D^2 in $\boldsymbol{R}^3$.

Let's start with a very famous theorem, called Euler's theorem, concerning convex polyhedrons.

Theorem 5.2   *Let Γ be an arbitrary convex polyhedron in $\boldsymbol{R}^3$. Let λ be the number of vertices, μ be the number of edges, and ν be the number of faces for Γ. Then, we always have*

$$\lambda - \mu + \nu = 2.$$

The Euler number is that of $\sharp vertices - \sharp edges + \sharp faces$ for an extended concept of a convex polyhedron called a simplicial complex that is composed of a finite number of 0-simplex (a point),1-simplex (a segment) and 2-simplex (a triangle).

Now consider a sphere S^2 and divide its surface into pieces of triangles (which is called triangulation) so as to obtain a convex polyhedron Γ homeomorphic to the sphere. Γ can be seen as a set consisting of a finite number of 0-simplexes $\{A_i\}$, 1-simplexes $\{a_i\}$, and 2-simplexes $\{\alpha_i\}$, that is,

$$\Gamma = \{A_1, \ldots, A_\lambda, a_1, \ldots, a_\mu, \alpha_1, \ldots, \alpha_\nu\}.$$

Through Euler's theorem, $\lambda - \mu + \nu = 2$, which does not depend on the choice of a triangulation, so we call it the Euler number of a sphere denoted by $\chi(S^2)$.

Let B_i be a center point of a_i and C_i be a barycenter of α_i. Then, construct a smooth vector field $\bar{v}$ on S^2 in such a way that it has only zeros corresponding to $\{A_1, \ldots, A_\lambda, B_1, \ldots, B_\mu, C_1, \ldots, C_\nu\}$ and that its flows are like those depicted in the figure below. It is always possible to have a vector field like this.

By consulting figure 5.8, we have

$$ind_{A_i}\bar{v} = +1, \ i = 1, \ldots, \lambda,$$
$$ind_{B_i}\bar{v} = -1, \ i = 1, \ldots, \mu,$$
$$ind_{C_i}\bar{v} = +1, \ i = 1, \ldots, \nu,$$

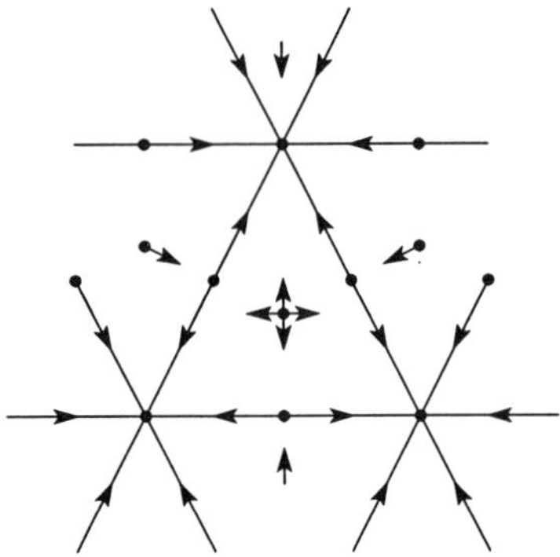

Fig. 5.9

hence, $\sum_{i=1}^{\lambda} ind_{A_i} \bar{v} + \sum_{i=1}^{\mu} ind_{B_i} \bar{v} + \sum_{i=1}^{\nu} ind_{C_i} \bar{v} = \lambda - \mu + \nu = \chi(S^2) = 2.$

Thus, we have a smooth vector field with isolated zeros on a sphere whose index sum is equal to the Euler number of the sphere.

On the other hand, it is known that on a sphere any two vector fields with isolated zeros have the same index sum. Consequently, any smooth vector field with isolated zeros defined on a sphere must have the index sum equal to the Euler number of a sphere $\chi(S^2)$ $(= 2)$.

Then, let's proceed to the case of D^2. First note that D^2 is homeomorphic to a sphere with one hole. It is known in general that the Euler number of a sphere with k holes is $\chi(S^2) - k$. Thus, the Euler number of D^2 (a sphere with one hole) is $2 - 1 = 1$.

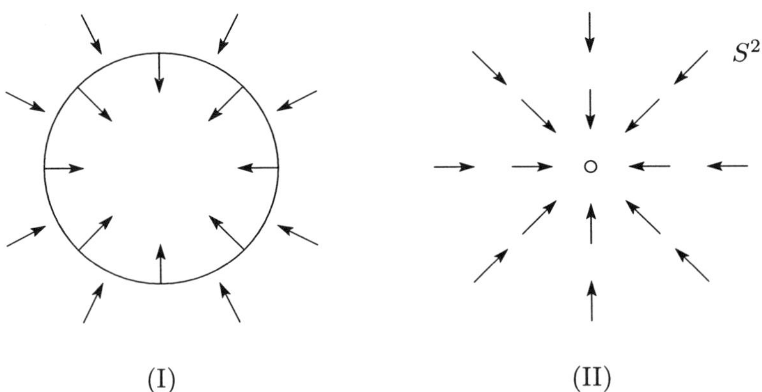

Fig. 5.10

Pick any smooth vector v on D^2 which points outward along the boundary. By diffeomorphically deforming D^2, we can identify v with the one on S^2 with one hole like that in Fig. 5.10 (I) in the previous page. Thus, for v there exists a smooth vector field v' on S^2 such that without one sink on S^2 v' would approximate v (see Fig. 5.10 (II)).

The index sum of v' is, as shown right above, equal to $\chi(S^2)$. On the other hand, the index of v' at a sink is obviously $+1$ (see Fig. 5.8). Thus, the index sum of v itself must be $\chi(S^2) - 1 = \chi(D^2)$.

For the economical analysis, we need the Euler number for the set of higher dimension. According to the generalization of the Euler number through algebraic topology, it is especially known for $n \geq 3$ that $\chi(D^n) = 1$ and that

$$
\begin{aligned}
\chi(S^n) &= 0 \quad \textit{if } n \textit{ is odd} \\
&= 1 \quad \textit{if } n \textit{ is even.}
\end{aligned}
$$

5.1.5 *Stability Conditions for Dynamical Systems*

In economics, the process of a state's evolving over time is usually described by the difference or differential equations systems. Here we shall refer to some concepts and results for ordinary differential equations systems which are necessary for our economical analysis in the next section.

We denote a state at each time t by $x(t) \in \mathbf{R}^n$. We assume that t varies in $(-\infty, +\infty)$ and x varies in an open set $U \in \mathbf{R}^n$. If the direction and the magnitude of x at each time t to change is given, then we can grasp the whole behavior of x in t. Suppose that the position of x in U determines its changing direction and magnitude. Then, we have a map $f : U \to \mathbf{R}^n$ that controls the behavioral pattern of x over time, which can be described by the following system.

$$
\dot{x} = f(x) \qquad\qquad \cdots \; (\star)
$$

where $\dot{x} = (dx_1/dt, \ldots, dx_n/dt)$. This equations system is called an autonomous first order ordinary differential equations system. If the system depends not only on the position of x but also on the time t, then we obtain the following system by substituting a map $g : U \times (-\infty, +\infty) \to \mathbf{R}^n$ for f.

$$
\dot{x} = g(x, t),
$$

which is called a nonautonomous system. We shall deal with only an autonomous system in the remainder of this section.

A solution of a differential equations system $(\star)$ is a map $x : (-\infty, +\infty) \to U$ satisfying

$$\dot{x}(t) = f(x(t)).$$

For simplicity we assume in the following that f is smooth. Then it is known that given $x(0) = x_0$, a solution of $(\star)$ uniquely exists. The condition that $x(0) = x_0$ is called an initial condition. So we could say that the process of a solution for $(\star)$ is deterministic in that once we know where x is at $t = 0$, then its entire course at all times is completely revealed.

Note that if we consider f to be a vector field on U, then the orbit of a solution for $(\star)$ can be seen as a flow generated by the vector field since the gradient vector of a solution is given by f. From this observation, we have that if the admissible set of x is not an open set but a manifold in $\boldsymbol{R}^n$, then f needs to be a smooth vector field on the manifold; that is, $f(x)$ is required to be a tangent vector at each x. Note that the argument in the remainder of this subsection still holds for that replacement.

In investigating properties of solutions for $(\star)$, a significant clue is given by a point x^* satisfying

$$f(x^*) = 0.$$

If $x(t) = x^*$, then x must remain there regardless of t since $\dot{x} = 0$, thus x^* is called an equilibrium point for $(\star)$. The notion of stability we shall be concerned with is centered on such an equilibrium point for $(\star)$.

Definition 5.5 An equilibrium point x^* for $(\star)$ is locally stable if and only if for any $\epsilon > 0$ there exists some $\delta > 0$ such that for every x_0 for which $\|x_0 - x^*\| < \delta$, the solution $x(t)$ for $(\star)$ with initial condition $x(0) = x_0$ satisfies the inequality $\|x(t) - x^*\| < \epsilon$ for all $t > 0$. If an equilibrium point is not locally stable, it is called unstable.

Definition 5.6 An equilibrium point x^* for $(\star)$ is locally asymptotically stable if and only if it is locally stable and any solution $x(t)$ in the above definition satisfies that $\lim_{t \to +\infty} x(t) = x^*$.

We can make use of the linear approximation of f around an equilibrium point x^* to see if it is locally asymptotically stable or not.

Theorem 5.3 *An equilibrium point x^* for $(\star)$ is locally asymptotically stable if all the eigenvalues of (the matrix representation of) the derivative*

df_{x^*} *of f at x^* have negative real parts. If at least one eigenvalue of df_{x^*} has a positive real part, then x^* is unstable.*

This theorem is very popular. For the proof of it, see, e.g., Smale and Hirsch (1974), Chap. 9.

In this connection, we have a notion of strict unstability as follows.

Definition 5.7 An equilibrium point x^* for $(\star)$ is locally perfectly unstable if all the eigenvalues of df_{x^*} have positive real parts.

For the above condition on the eigenvalues to be the necessary and sufficient condition, we need another notion called hyperbolicity.

Definition 5.8 An equilibrium point x^* for $(\star)$ is hyperbolic if all the eigenvalues of (the matrix representation of) the derivative df_{x^*} have nonzero real parts.

Then, the following claim is immediate.

Proposition 5.4 *Suppose that an equilibrium point x^* for $(\star)$ is hyperbolic. Then, x^* is locally asymptotically stable (resp. locally perfectly unstable) if and only if all the eigenvalues of the derivative df_{x^*} have negative (resp. positive) real parts.*

In general, there is a specific relation between the determinant of a square matrix and its eigenvalues.

Proposition 5.5 *If all the eigenvalues of an $n \times n$ matrix A have negative (resp. positive) real parts, then we have*

$$det(A) > 0 \quad if\ n\ is\ even$$
$$det(A) < 0 \quad if\ n\ is\ odd$$
$$(resp.\ det(A) > 0 \quad if\ n\ is\ odd)$$

where $det(A)$ designates the determinant of A.

Proof.   Noting that $det(A)$ is equal to the product of all the eigenvalues of A and that a conjugate of a complex eigenvalue of A is also an eigenvalue of A, the claim immediately follows. $\qquad\qquad\square$

In view of this proposition, we obtain a necessary condition for a hyperbolic equilibrium point to be locally asymptotically stable (resp. locally perfectly unstable).

Proposition 5.6 *If a hyperbolic equilibrium point x^* for $(\star)$ is locally asymptotically stable (resp. locally perfectly unstable), then we have*

$$det(df_{x^*}) > 0 \quad if \ n \ is \ even$$
$$det(df_{x^*}) < 0 \quad if \ n \ is \ odd$$
$$(resp. \ det(df_{x^*}) > 0 \quad if \ n \ is \ odd).$$

5.2 Economical Analysis

In economics, there are several concepts of stability used, depending on the analytical context for an economic system. First of all, we should touch on a concept of stability for the equilibrium. This is the earliest issue in which they have questioned whether a state, once deviated from its equilibrium, will converge to the original position or not. In this connection, there exists another stability concept called structural stability. This concept emerges when we try to investigate how a process of a state over time is qualitatively influenced by the perturbation of the data of the system.

Furthermore, from the game theoretical point of view, we should refer to the stability of a coalition in cooperative games in which some specific ideas, such as stable sets or ϕ-stability, have been devised to estimate the sustainability of a coalition consisting of different members with different interests.

What we shall treat here is the classical issue; that is the stability of general equilibrium. More specifically, we limit ourselves to the local stability of an equilibrium price vector and related topics in regular economies.

5.2.1 *Walrasian Adjustment Mechanism*

First recall the aggregate excess demand function $G : \mathcal{E} \times S_{++}^{L-1} \to \boldsymbol{R}^L$ defined by

$$G(\omega, \boldsymbol{p}) = \sum_{i=1}^{I} f^i(\boldsymbol{p}, \boldsymbol{p} \cdot \boldsymbol{\omega}^i) - \sum_{i=1}^{I} \boldsymbol{\omega}^i$$

where $\mathcal{E}$ is the space of economies that is nothing but $\boldsymbol{R}_{++}^{LI}$ and $f^i : \boldsymbol{R}_{++}^{L} \times (0, +\infty) \to \boldsymbol{R}_{+}^{L}$ is a demand function of consumer i, $i = 1, \ldots, I$.

Now consider the 'tatonnement' price adjustment process called Walrasian adjustment mechanism which is the abstraction from the workings of a competitive market. We assume that there is an 'auctioneer' in each market who adjusts supply and demand in such a way that he raises the price for excess demand and lowers it for excess supply. Agents are supposed to respond to each price and announce their supply/demand plan to the auctioneer but they are prohibited to trade until supply and demand are equal.

By considering a price vector $\boldsymbol{p}$ to be a function of time t, this adjustment process is described by the following differential equations system.

$$dp_l/dt = \lambda_l G_l(\omega, \boldsymbol{p}), \quad l = 1, \ldots, L$$

where λ_l $(l = 1, \ldots, L)$ is a positive constant called the speed of adjustment. For simplicity, we assume that $\lambda_l = 1$ $(l = 1, \ldots, L)$. Indeed, the speeds of adjustments do not play any crucial role in the following analysis.

This system, however, has a difficulty as the differential equations system. Note in the system that the admissible set of $\boldsymbol{p}$ still remains the strictly positive $(L-1)$-dimensional simplex S_{++}^{L-1}, so that $G(\omega, \boldsymbol{p})$ is not qualified as a vector field on S_{++}^{L-1}, though Walras' law enables us to have that $\boldsymbol{p} \cdot G(\omega, \boldsymbol{p}) = 0$ for any $\boldsymbol{p}$ and any $\omega \in \mathcal{E}$. Thus, it is expedient for us to adopt another normalization of prices, substituting the strictly positive $(L-1)$-dimensional *unit sphere* (denoted by just S) for S_{++}^{L-1} so that we can make $G(\omega, \boldsymbol{p})$ a vector field. As a result, we have the following differential equations system.

$$\dot{\boldsymbol{p}} = G(\omega, \boldsymbol{p}), \quad \boldsymbol{p} \in S \qquad \cdots \; (\dagger).$$

Now consider the vector field $G(\omega, \boldsymbol{p})$ on S. It turns out that for any economy ω, $G(\omega, \boldsymbol{p})$ has a specific property as follows.

Proposition 5.7   *There exists a $(L-1)$-dimensional manifold with boundary, which we denote S^*, in S such that the boundary is close enough to ∂S and that $G(\omega, \boldsymbol{p})$ points inward along the boundary for any ω.*

Proof.   In view of assumption 3.1, we have that for any given $\omega \in \mathcal{E}$ if $\boldsymbol{p}$ converges to some point $\boldsymbol{p}^0 \in \partial S$, then $\lim \|G(\omega, \boldsymbol{p})\| = +\infty$. If $p_k^0 = 0$ and $p_i^0 > 0 (i \neq k)$, then through lemma 4.3 $\lim_{\boldsymbol{p} \to \boldsymbol{p}^0} G_i(\omega, \boldsymbol{p}) = +\infty$ since $G_i(\omega, \boldsymbol{p})$ is bounded from below. Noting that $G(\omega, \cdot)$ is continuous, there hence exists a $(L-1)$-dimensional manifold with boundary in S such that the boundary is close enough to ∂S and that for any $\boldsymbol{p}$ in the boundary $G_{i^*}(\omega, \boldsymbol{p}) > 0$ where $p_{i^*} = min_i p_i$, which implies that the vector field $G(\omega, \boldsymbol{p})$ points inward along the boundary. $\qquad \Box$

According to the proposition, the aggregate excess *supply* function $-G(\omega, \boldsymbol{p})$ for an economy ω turns out to be a smooth vector field on S^*

that points *outward* along the boundary. We abbreviate it with $H_\omega(p)$ on S^* and consider the following differential equations system for an economy $\omega \in \mathcal{E}$ instead of (†).

$$\dot{p} = H_\omega(p), \quad p \in S^* \qquad \cdots \ (*).$$

Note that for any economy $\omega \in \mathcal{E}$, $H_\omega(p) = 0$ if and only if $G(\omega, p) = 0$.

5.2.2 *Stability of Equilibrium Prices in Regular Economies*

Here we consider local stability of equilibrium prices in regular economies. As we have seen regular economies have many characteristics, among which we particularly note the following two properties. One is that under assumption 3.1 each regular economy has a finite number of equilibrium price vectors (see Theorem 3.2). The other is that the vector field $G_\omega(p)$ on S has 0 as its regular value for each regular economy ω, which is derived from proposition 3.3.

The former observation allows us to use the Poincaré-Hopf Theorem to obtain the following lemma.

Lemma 5.2 *Under assumption 3.1, for any regular economy ω there exists a $(L-1)$-dimensional manifold with boundary in S such that the sum of the indices at zeros of the vector field H_ω is $+1$ on the manifold.*

Proof. Noting that in general the set $\{p \mid H_\omega = 0\}$ is nothing but the set of equilibrium price vectors for an economy $\omega \in \mathcal{E}$, zeros of H_ω is finite for a regular economy ω under assumption 3.1. Thus, for any given regular economy ω, we may choose a $(L-1)$-dimensional manifold with boundary S^* in S that includes all zeros of H_ω and that allows the vector field H_ω to point outward along its boundary (see proposition 5.7). Hence, through the Poincaré-Hopf Theorem, the sum of the indices at zeros of the vector field H_ω is equal to the Euler number of S^*, which is $+1$ since S^* is homeomorphic to a $(L-1)$-dimensional disk D^{L-1}. $\square$

On the other hand, we may obtain another lemma through the latter observation.

Lemma 5.3 *Under assumption 3.1, for an equilibrium price vector p^* of a regular economy ω we have*

$$ind_{p^*}(H_\omega) = +1 \quad if \ |dH_{\omega,p^*}| > 0$$
$$ind_{p^*}(H_\omega) = -1 \quad if \ |dH_{\omega,p^*}| < 0.$$

Proof. It immediately follows from the definition of H_ω that p is a regular point for H_ω if and only if it is a regular point for G_ω. Since an equilibrium price vector p^* of a regular economy ω is a regular point for G_ω, so is p^* for H_ω. Thus, through proposition 5.2 (precisely a remark under the proposition), our claim immediately follows. $\square$

These lemmas enable us to obtain some consequences concerning local stability of equilibrium price vectors for a regular economy. As we shall see, they are closely related to the uniqueness of the equilibrium.

Theorem 5.4 *Under assumption 3.1, if there are more than two equilibrium price vectors for a regular economy, then not all of them are locally asymptotically stable as long as they are hyperbolic.*

Proof. By the definition of H_ω, at any regular point p for H_ω we have

$$|dH_{\omega,p}| = |d(-G_\omega)p| = (-1)^{L-1}|dG_{\omega,p}|.$$

Let $p^* \in S^*$ be an arbitrary equilibrium price vector for a regular economy ω where S^* is the $(L-1)$-dimensional manifold with boundary in S considered in lemma 5.3. If p^* is hyperbolic and locally asymptotically stable, then through proposition 5.6 we have that

$$|dG_{\omega,p^*}| > 0 \quad if \ L-1 \ is \ even$$
$$|dG_{\omega,p^*}| < 0 \quad if \ L-1 \ is \ odd.$$

Thus, if $L-1$ is even, then $|dH_{\omega,p^*}| > 0$, which implies through lemma 5.4 that $ind_{p^*}(H_\omega) = +1$. On the other hand, if $L-1$ is odd, we also have that $|dH_{\omega,p^*}| > 0$, thus $ind_{p^*}(H_\omega) = +1$. Therefore, the index of H_ω at any equilibrium price vector is always $+1$. Suppose that there are more than two equilibrium price vectors for ω. Then the sum of the indices at all those vectors must be more than $+2$, which contradicts lemma 5.3. $\square$

By considering a contrapositive of the above theorem, we obtain the following claim concerning the uniqueness of the equilibrium for a regular economy.

Corollary 5.3 *Under assumption 3.1, if all equilibrium price vectors for a regular economy are hyperbolic and locally asymptotically stable, then actually there exists a unique equilibrium price vector.*

From the viewpoint of unstability, we obtain the following.

Theorem 5.5 *Suppose that L is odd. Then, under assumption 3.1, if there are more than two equilibrium price vectors for a regular economy, not all of them are locally perfectly unstable.*

Proof. Let p^* be an equilibrium price vector for a regular economy ω that is locally perfectly unstable. Then by the proposition 5.6, we have that $|dG_{\omega,p^*}| > 0$. Thus, if L is odd, then $|dH_{\omega,p^*}| > 0$, which means by lemma 5.4 that the index of H_ω at p^* is $+1$. Therefore, if all the equilibrium price vectors are locally perfectly unstable, the sum of the indices at all those vectors must be more than $+2$, which contradicts lemma 5.3. $\square$

A contrapositive of the above theorem gives us another condition for the uniqueness of the equilibrium for a regular economy.

Corollary 5.4 *Suppose that L is odd. Then, under assumption 3.1, if all equilibrium price vectors for a regular economy are locally perfectly unstable, actually there exists a unique equilibrium price vector.*

Finally we refer to the case in which L is even.

Theorem 5.6 *Suppose that L is even. Then, under assumption 3.1, not all equilibrium price vectors for a regular economy are locally perfectly unstable whether the equilibrium set is plural or not.*

Proof. Let p^* be an equilibrium price vector for a regular economy ω that is locally perfectly unstable. Then, $|dG_{\omega,p^*}| > 0$. Thus, if L is even, $|dH_{\omega,p^*}| < 0$, which means by lemma 5.4 that the index of H_ω at p^* is -1. Therefore, if all equilibrium price vectors are locally perfectly unstable, the sum of the indices at all those vectors must be negative, which contradicts lemma 5.3. $\square$

This theorem immediately leads us to the following claim.

Corollary 5.5 *Suppose that L is even. Then, if a regular economy has a unique equilibrium price vector under assumption 3.1, it is not perfectly unstable.*

Scarf has shown an example in which there exists a unique perfectly unstable equilibrium in a three goods economy model (Scarf (1960)). The above and the previous corollaries provide the analytical basis for his example.

Part 2

Transversality and Regular Economies

Chapter 6

Space of Utility Functions

Here we extend the space of economies while we still remain in a pure exchange economy model. Up to this point, we have assumed that there is only one parameter that specifies an economy, i.e. initial endowments among the agents. This assumption is, of course, very restrictive. As we have noticed before (1.2.2), there is another very important factor that specifies an economy, that is, the demand attitude of each consumer. So far, a consumer's demand attitude has been implicitly assumed to be represented by its demand function. It is, however, worth noting that a consumer's demand behavior itself should be properly attributed to its specific behavioral criterion; that is, maximization of its utility. Therefore, we shall adopt consumers' utility functions instead of their demand functions to specify an economy. The space of economies, then, should include this primitive factor as well as the initial endowments. In this chapter, we first introduce a particular topology called Whitney topology to the general functional spaces. Then we consider the admissible set of the utility functions. Our admissible set consists of those which are very weakly restricted, so that we need a different equilibrium notion (called extended equilibrium) than the usual one. We, however, show that the set of utility functions in question forms an open set in the Whitney topology.

6.1 Mathematical Preliminaries

Our goal in this section is to introduce some topologies into a functional space. For the sake of simplicity, a function to be considered here is limited to a smooth map from $\boldsymbol{R}^m$ to $\boldsymbol{R}^n$. Thus , we solely deal with the space $C^\infty(\boldsymbol{R}^m, \boldsymbol{R}^n)$. However, our argument provided below is easily extended to the case of a differentiable map between two manifolds.

6.1.1 *Jet Spaces*

An efficient way to introduce some topology into $C^\infty(\boldsymbol{R}^m, \boldsymbol{R}^n)$ is to make use of an equivalence class called a jet in $C^\infty(\boldsymbol{R}^m, \boldsymbol{R}^n)$. As we shall see, it turns out that the space derived by classifying $C^\infty(\boldsymbol{R}^m, \boldsymbol{R}^n)$ through jets, which is called the jet space, has a very simple structure but provides necessary informations to topologize $C^\infty(\boldsymbol{R}^m, \boldsymbol{R}^n)$.

A jet is defined by the following equivalence relation. Let f, g be two maps in $C^\infty(\boldsymbol{R}^m, \boldsymbol{R}^n)$ and $\bar{x}$ be a point of $\boldsymbol{R}^m$. If $f(\bar{x}) = g(\bar{x})$ and all the partial derivatives at $\bar{x}$ up to r-th order are equal between f and g, then we write it as $f \sim_r g$ at $\bar{x}$. It is easily seen that this relation is an equivalence relation. An equivalence class represented by $f \in C^\infty(\boldsymbol{R}^m, \boldsymbol{R}^n)$ according to this relation is called the r-jet of f at $\bar{x}$, which is denoted by $j^r f(\bar{x})$. In particular, the whole set of the equivalence classes for all the maps carrying 0 to 0 is written by $J^r(m, n)$.

To begin with, let's consider the structure of $J^r(m, n)$. It is obvious that $J^r(m, n) = J^r(m, 1) \times \ldots \times J^r(m, 1)$, which is the n-product of $J^r(m, 1)$; thus we have only to think of $J^r(m, 1)$. Pick an element out of $J^r(m, 1)$ and denote it by $j^r f(0)$. Then, consider Taylor's series about 0 generated by $f : \boldsymbol{R}^m \to \boldsymbol{R}$, i.e.

$$f(x) = \sum_{0 \leq \|\alpha\| \leq r} \frac{x^\alpha}{\alpha!} \frac{\partial^{\|\alpha\|} f}{\partial x^\alpha}(0) + R(x)$$

where $\alpha = (\alpha_1, \ldots, \alpha_m), \alpha_i : integer, i = 1, \ldots, m$ and $\|\alpha\| = \alpha_1 + \ldots + \alpha_m$. Thus, $f \sim_r g$ at 0 if and only if their Taylor's series up to r-th order are equal with each other. Accordingly, $j^r f(0)$ itself can be represented by the coefficients of Taylor polynomial up to r-th order as follows.

$$\frac{1}{\alpha!} \frac{\partial^{\|\alpha\|} f}{\partial x^\alpha}(0), \quad 1 \leq \|\alpha\| \leq r.$$

Conversely, an allocation of coefficients for the polynomial of degree r in m variables without a constant term determines a jet. It is easily seen that there is one to one correspondence between those allocations and $J^r(m, 1)$. Since such an allocation always consists of $_{m+r}C_r - 1$ real numbers, $J^r(m, 1)$ can be seen as equipotent to $\boldsymbol{R}^H$ where $H =_{m+r} C_r - 1$. Therefore, $J^r(m, n)$ is equipotent to $\boldsymbol{R}^{nH}$, which implies that we can identify $J^r(m, n)$ with $\boldsymbol{R}^{nH}$.

Now pick any point $(x, y) \in \boldsymbol{R}^m \times \boldsymbol{R}^n$. Let $J^r(\boldsymbol{R}^m, \boldsymbol{R}^n)_{(x,y)}$ be the set of equivalent classes, which is derived by the relation "$\sim_r$ at x", for the maps carrying x to y in which x is called a source and y called a target.

Definition 6.1 The disjoint union $\bigcup_{(x,y)\in \boldsymbol{R}^m \times \boldsymbol{R}^n} J^r(\boldsymbol{R}^m, \boldsymbol{R}^n)_{(x,y)}$ is called the r-jet space on $\boldsymbol{R}^m \times \boldsymbol{R}^n$ and is denoted by $J^r(\boldsymbol{R}^m, \boldsymbol{R}^n)$.

Proposition 6.1 $J^r(\boldsymbol{R}^m, \boldsymbol{R}^n)$ *is equipotent to* $\boldsymbol{R}^m \times \boldsymbol{R}^n \times J^r(m, n)$.

Proof. For any $(\bar{x}, \bar{y}) \in \boldsymbol{R}^m \times \boldsymbol{R}^n$, consider the following coordinate transformations $\varphi_{\bar{x}} : \boldsymbol{R}^m \to \boldsymbol{R}^m$, $v_{\bar{y}} : \boldsymbol{R}^n \to \boldsymbol{R}^n$ given by

$$\varphi_{\bar{x}}(x) = (x_1 + \bar{x}_1, \ldots, x_m + \bar{x}_m)$$
$$v_{\bar{y}}(y) = (y_1 - \bar{y}_1, \ldots, y_n - \bar{y}_n).$$

Then, the map $\Psi : J^r(\boldsymbol{R}^m, \boldsymbol{R}^n) \to \boldsymbol{R}^m \times \boldsymbol{R}^n \times J^r(m, n)$ defined by

$$\Psi(j^r f(\bar{x})) = (\bar{x}, \bar{y} = f(\bar{x}), j^r(v_{\bar{y}} \circ f \circ \varphi_{\bar{x}})(0))$$

is easily proved to be a bijection. $\qquad\square$

Through this proposition, we can identify the r-jet space $J^r(\boldsymbol{R}^m, \boldsymbol{R}^n)$ with $\boldsymbol{R}^m \times \boldsymbol{R}^n \times \boldsymbol{R}^{nH}$. Furthermore, by considering a projection $\pi :$ $J^r(\boldsymbol{R}^m, \boldsymbol{R}^n) \to \boldsymbol{R}^m \times \boldsymbol{R}^n$ defined by $\pi(j^r f(x)) = (x, f(x))$, a triple $(J^r(\boldsymbol{R}^m, \boldsymbol{R}^n), \pi, \boldsymbol{R}^m \times \boldsymbol{R}^n)$ turns out to be a fibre bundle with fibre $J^r(m, n)$, so that $J^r(\boldsymbol{R}^m, \boldsymbol{R}^n)$ is often called the r-jet bundle.

Definition 6.2 For any map $f \in C^\infty(\boldsymbol{R}^m, \boldsymbol{R}^n)$, the map $j^r f : \boldsymbol{R}^m \to J^r(\boldsymbol{R}^m, \boldsymbol{R}^n)$ which carries $x \in \boldsymbol{R}^m$ to $j^r f(x)$ (the r-jet of f at x) is called the r-jet extension of f.

Noting the above proposition, the r-jet extension of f can be represented in component form as follows. That is, for $f = (f_1, \ldots, f_n) \in C^\infty(\boldsymbol{R}^m, \boldsymbol{R}^n)$ we have

$$j^r f : \boldsymbol{R}^m \to \boldsymbol{R}^m \times \boldsymbol{R}^n \times J^r(m, n)$$
$$j^r f(x) = (x, f(x), (\frac{\partial^{\|\alpha\|} f_i}{\partial x^\alpha}(x))_{1 \le \|\alpha\| \le r, 1 \le i \le n}).$$

Through this observation, we immediately obtain the following claim.

Proposition 6.2 *The r-jet extension of $f \in C^\infty(\boldsymbol{R}^m, \boldsymbol{R}^n)$ is itself C^∞ class.*

Proof. Since $f \in C^\infty(\boldsymbol{R}^m, \boldsymbol{R}^n)$, $(\frac{\partial^{\|\alpha\|} f_i}{\partial x^\alpha}(x))_{1 \le \|\alpha\| \le r, 1 \le i \le n}$ are all C^∞ class. $\qquad\square$

Note that if r is 0 then the image $j^0 f(\boldsymbol{R}^m)$ of the 0-jet extension of f is the graph of f since $j^0 f(x) = (x, f(x))$.

6.1.2   *Compact Open Topology*

Since we may presume that the r-jet space $J^r(\boldsymbol{R}^m, \boldsymbol{R}^n)$ is nothing but $\boldsymbol{R}^m \times \boldsymbol{R}^n \times \boldsymbol{R}^{nH}$, it allows a metric derived from the Euclidean norm. We denote the metric given to $J^r(\boldsymbol{R}^m, \boldsymbol{R}^n)$ by $d(\cdot, \cdot)$.

The basic idea provided below to topologize $C^\infty(\boldsymbol{R}^m, \boldsymbol{R}^n)$, roughly speaking, consists in determining how close f is to g by evaluating the distance of their r-jets on some subset of $\boldsymbol{R}^m$. To be precise, let f be an arbitrary map in $C^\infty(\boldsymbol{R}^m, \boldsymbol{R}^n)$ and δ be a continuous map from $\boldsymbol{R}^m$ to $\boldsymbol{R}_+$. Then, consider for a positive real number k the following set $B_{\delta,k}(f)$.

$$B_{\delta,k}(f)$$

$$= \{g \in C^\infty(\boldsymbol{R}^m, \boldsymbol{R}^n) \mid d(j^r(x), j^r g(x)) < \delta(x), \ x \in \boldsymbol{R}^m \ s.t. \ \|x\| \le k\}$$

It can be easily shown that the family of the sets $B_{\delta,k}(f)$ parameterized by δ and k forms a fundamental system of neighborhoods at f, thus specifying a topology.

Definition 6.3   The topology with $B_{\delta,k}(f)$ as a neighborhood basis at each f is called the compact open C^r topology for $C^\infty(\boldsymbol{R}^m, \boldsymbol{R}^n)$.

Intuitively, all the maps in $B_{\delta,k}(f)$ are close to f in the sense that their first r-th partial derivatives are δ-close to f on some compact set of $\boldsymbol{R}^m$.

The compact open C^r topology for $C^\infty(\boldsymbol{R}^m, \boldsymbol{R}^n)$ can also be defined by a basis in place of a neighborhood basis as follows. Let K be a compact subset of $\boldsymbol{R}^m$ and U be an open subset of $J^r(\boldsymbol{R}^m, \boldsymbol{R}^n)$ $(= \boldsymbol{R}^m \times \boldsymbol{R}^n \times \boldsymbol{R}^{nH})$. Then denote by $M(K, U)$ the set

$$\{f \in C^\infty(\boldsymbol{R}^m, \boldsymbol{R}^n) \mid j^r f(K) \subseteq U\}.$$

It is easily seen that the family $\{M(K, U)\}_{(K,U)}$ of the sets $M(K, U)$ parameterized by K and U form a basis for a topology on $C^\infty(\boldsymbol{R}^m, \boldsymbol{R}^n)$; that is, the family of subsets of $C^\infty(\boldsymbol{R}^m, \boldsymbol{R}^n)$ consisting of $\emptyset$, $C^\infty(\boldsymbol{R}^m, \boldsymbol{R}^n)$ itself and all unions of members of $\{M(K, U)\}_{(K,U)}$ is qualified as a topology on $C^\infty(\boldsymbol{R}^m, \boldsymbol{R}^n)$. Indeed, this topology is equivalent to the compact open C^r topology defined above (for proof of the equivalence, see Golubitsky and Guillemin (1973), p. 43).

Note that if a subset of $C^\infty(\boldsymbol{R}^m, \boldsymbol{R}^n)$ is open for the compact open C^r topology, so is it for the compact open C^l topology $(l \ge r)$. In fact, consider the map $\pi_r^l : \boldsymbol{R}^m \times \boldsymbol{R}^n \times J^l(m, n) \to \boldsymbol{R}^m \times \boldsymbol{R}^n \times J^r(m, n)$ given by $\pi_r^l(j^l f(a)) = j^r f(a)$. Then for any compact subset $K \subset \boldsymbol{R}^m$ and any open subset $U \subset J^r(\boldsymbol{R}^m, \boldsymbol{R}^n)$, obviously $M(K, U) = M(K, (\pi_r^l)^{-1}(U))$ in which the former is open for the compact open C^r topology whereas the latter is open for the compact open C^l topology since $(\pi_r^l)^{-1}(U)$ is open because of continuity of π_r^l.

Let U_r be the family of all open subsets of $C^\infty(\boldsymbol{R}^m, \boldsymbol{R}^n)$ in the compact open C^r topology. Then, the compact open C^∞ topology on $C^\infty(\boldsymbol{R}^m, \boldsymbol{R}^n)$ is the topology whose basis is $U = \bigcup_{r=0}^{\infty} U_r$. This is a well-defined basis since, as is shown above, $U_r \subset U_l$ when $r \leq l$. Needless to say, if a subset of $C^\infty(\boldsymbol{R}^m, \boldsymbol{R}^n)$ is open for the compact open C^r topology, so is it for the compact open C^∞ topology. The compact open C^∞ topology (and also the compact open C^r topology) is very tractable. Indeed, it can be shown that it has a complete metric and a countable base. However, it is weak as a topology in that it only considers the closeness of two points (maps) on a compact set; alternatively put, it does not control the behavior of a map "at infinity". That is why it is often called the weak topology on $C^\infty(\boldsymbol{R}^m, \boldsymbol{R}^n)$.

6.1.3 *Whitney Topology*

We can naturally induce a stronger topology on $C^\infty(\boldsymbol{R}^m, \boldsymbol{R}^n)$ from the compact open C^r topology in such a way that we remove the restriction of compactness from the latter. More specifically, instead of $B_{\delta,k}(f)$ consider the following.

$$B_\delta(f) = \{g \in C^\infty(\boldsymbol{R}^m, \boldsymbol{R}^n) \mid d(j^r(x), j^r g(x)) < \delta(x), \forall x \in \boldsymbol{R}^m\}$$

Then, as before, we can construct a topology with the family of the sets $B_\delta(f)$ parameterized by δ as a fundamental system of neighborhoods at f.

Definition 6.4 The topology with $B_\delta(f)$ as a neighborhood basis at each f is called the Whitney C^r topology for $C^\infty(\boldsymbol{R}^m, \boldsymbol{R}^n)$.

Thus, according to this topology, a map g is in a neighborhood of a map f if and only if all of the first r partial derivatives of g are δ-close to f over the whole domain $(\boldsymbol{R}^m)$. In other words, this topology does control the behavior of a map "at infinity". Therefore this is often called the strong topology $C^\infty(\boldsymbol{R}^m, \boldsymbol{R}^n)$.

As in the compact open C^r topology, it is also possible to construct the Whitney C^r topology through a basis. That is, for an open subset U of $J^r(\boldsymbol{R}^m, \boldsymbol{R}^n)$ $(= \boldsymbol{R}^m \times \boldsymbol{R}^n \times \boldsymbol{R}^{nH})$ consider the following set $M(U)$.

$$M(U) = \{f \in C^\infty(\boldsymbol{R}^m, \boldsymbol{R}^n) \mid j^r f(\boldsymbol{R}^m) \subseteq U\}.$$

Note that $M(U) \cap M(V) = M(U \cap V)$.

Then the family of sets $\{M(U)\}_U$ form a basis for a topology which is equivalent to the Whitney C^r topology defined above (for proof of the equivalence of those topologies, see Golubitsky and Guillemin (1973), p. 43).

Let W_r be the family of all open subsets of $C^\infty(\boldsymbol{R}^m, \boldsymbol{R}^n)$ in the Whitney C^r topology. Then it is easily shown, as in the compact open C^r topology, that $W_r \subset W_l$ whenever $r \leq l$. Thus, we can construct another topology on $C^\infty(\boldsymbol{R}^m, \boldsymbol{R}^n)$ with $W = \bigcup_{r=0}^{\infty} W_r$ as a basis, which is called the Whitney C^∞ topology. If a subset of $C^\infty(\boldsymbol{R}^m, \boldsymbol{R}^n)$ is open for the Whitney C^r topology, then obviously so is it for the Whitney C^∞ topology.

From the viewpoint of applicability, the Whitney C^r (or C^∞) topology is not necessarily tractable since it is not metrizable and in fact does not satisfy the first axiom of countability. It is too strong for those properties. However, it does have one nice feature.

Definition 6.5   A topological space X is a Baire space if the intersection of each countable family of open dense sets in X is dense.

In general, the countable intersection of open dense sets is called a residual set. Thus, we can say that a Baire space is a topological space in which every residual set is dense.

Proposition 6.3   *The function space $C^\infty(\boldsymbol{R}^m, \boldsymbol{R}^n)$ is a Baire space in the Whitney C^r (and C^∞) topology.*

For proof of this proposition, e.g. see Hirsch (1976), Chap. 2, § 4.

Given the Whitney C^r (C^∞) topology, we can determine the continuity of various maps between two functional spaces. In particular, we give the two propositions for further argument. To this end, let $C^\infty(\boldsymbol{R}^m, \boldsymbol{R}^n)^s$ be the s-product of $C^\infty(\boldsymbol{R}^m, \boldsymbol{R}^n)$.

Proposition 6.4   *Let $\theta : C^\infty(\boldsymbol{R}^m, \boldsymbol{R}^n)^s \to C^\infty(\boldsymbol{R}^{ms}, \boldsymbol{R}^{ns})$ be the map given by*

$$\theta(f_1, \ldots, f_s) = (f_1 \times \ldots \times f_s).$$

Then θ is continuous in the Whitney C^r (C^∞) topology where $(f_1 \times \ldots \times f_s)(x_1, \ldots, x_s) = (f_1(x_1), \ldots, f_s(x_s))$.

For proof of this proposition, see Golubitsky and Guillemin (1974), pp. 49-50.

For the other proposition, recall the r-jet extension of $f \in C^\infty(\boldsymbol{R}^m, \boldsymbol{R}^n)$, which can be seen as the map from $\boldsymbol{R}^m$ to $\boldsymbol{R}^m \times \boldsymbol{R}^n \times J^r(m, n)$. Thus, we newly consider the functional space $C^\infty(\mathbf{R}^m, \mathbf{R}^m \times \mathbf{R}^n \times J^r(m,n))$. Then we have

Proposition 6.5 *Let j^r be the map from $C^\infty(\mathbf{R}^m, \mathbf{R}^n)$ to $C^\infty(\mathbf{R}^m, \mathbf{R}^m \times \mathbf{R}^n \times J^r(m,n))$ given by $j^r(f) = j^r f$. Then j^r is continuous in the Whitney C^r (C^∞) topology.*

For proof of this proposition, see Golubitsky and Guillemin (1974), pp. 46-48.

6.2 Economical Analysis

It is true that the demand behavior of each consumer is directly expressed by its demand function, but what basically determines the propensity of each consumer to demand is its preference over various goods. It is well known that a consumer's preference over goods is represented by an appropriate utility function though some assumptions regarding the preference are required to that end (see Debreu (1959, 1972)). Hence, we accept each consumer's utility function as a primitive concept to describe its demand behavior. Our argument in this and subsequent chapters is derived from the works of Smale (1974a, 1974b, 1974c, 1974d), who first achieved a successful introduction of utility functions to the theory of regular economies.

6.2.1 *Utility Functions and Demand Functions*

We first refer to the relation between the utility functions and the demand functions from the analytical viewpoint. It is obvious that the utility function is more primitive than the demand function; thus we consider the derivation of the demand function given the utility function. Pick a representative consumer and let its consumption set, wealth and utility function be respectively C, w and u. For the sake of simplicity, we assume that

    (1) $C = \mathbf{R}^L_{++}$

    (2) $w \in \mathbf{R}_{++}$

    (3) $u \in C^\infty(\mathbf{R}^L_{++}, \mathbf{R})$.

    Given a price vector $p \in \mathbf{R}^L_{++}$, its demand function $f : \mathbf{R}^L_{++} \times \mathbf{R}_{++} \to \mathbf{R}^L_{++}$ is defined as follows.

$$f(p, w) = arg\ max\{u(x) \mid p \cdot x \leq w,\ x \in \mathbf{R}^L_{++}\}.$$

It is, however, worth noting that we are not always able to obtain a well-defined demand function through this definition. In order for the demand function to make sense, we need some assumptions on the underlying utility function. Among others, the following assumptions are important.

Assumption 6.1   Boundary condition: For any $x \in R_{++}^L$, $Cl\{x' \in R_{++}^L \mid u(x') \geq u(x)\} \subset R_{++}^L$ where $Cl(A)$ means the closure of the set A in R^L.

Assumption 6.2   Monotonicity: $u(x) > u(y)$ for $x \geq y$ and $x \neq y$.

Assumption 6.3   Strict quasi-concavity: $u(\lambda x + (1 - \lambda)y) > u(y)$ for $\lambda \in (0,1)$ and $u(x) \geq u(y)$.

Proposition 6.6   *Under assumptions 6.1 $\sim$ 6.3, the demand function is well-defined and, moreover, continuous in p ($\in R_{++}^L$) and w ($\in R_{++}$).*

Proof.   For any given p ($\in R_{++}^L$) and w ($\in R_{++}$), there exists some y ($\in R_{++}^L$) such that $p \cdot y = w$. Let $u(y)$ be $\bar{u}$ and consider the following two sets.

$$A = \{x \in R_+^L \mid u(x) \geq \bar{u}\},$$
$$B = \{x \in R_+^L \mid p \cdot x \leq w\}.$$

It is easily seen that $A \cap B$ is a non-empty compact set and that, through assumption 6.1, it is contained in R_{++}^L. According to Weierstrass' theorem, there exists a maximizing element of u on $A \cap B$, which obviously constitutes a solution to the following problem.

$$\max_{x} \quad u(x)$$
$$s.t. \ \ p \cdot x \leq w.$$

In other words, that element certainly forms a demand vector for (p, w), which we denote x^*. Through assumption 6.2, x^* should satisfy that $p \cdot x^* = w$. On the other hand, assumption 6.1 assures that $x^* \in R_{++}^L$. Furthermore, through assumption 6.3, x^* is uniquely determined. Since (p, w) is arbitrarily taken, we have the well-defined demand function $f :$ $R_{++}^L \times R_{++} \to R_{++}^L$.

It remains to be shown that f is continuous in p ($\in R_{++}^L$) and w ($\in R_{++}$). For any given $(p^0, w^0) \in R_{++}^L \times R_{++}$, pick any sequence $\{p^n, w^n\}_n$ in $R_{++}^L \times R_{++}$ which converges to (p^0, w^0). Put $x^0 = f(p^0, w^0)$ and $x^n = f(p^n, w^n)$ for each n. Obviously, $x^0 \in R_{++}^L$ and $x^n \in R_{++}^L$ for all n. Here we distinguish two cases for the u.

(1) u can be continuously extended onto $\boldsymbol{R}_+^L$.

Let the extended u be $\tilde{u}$. In this case we may apply the argument provided by Malinvaud (1977, 2.6) to $\tilde{u}$ to show that $\lim_{n\to\infty} \boldsymbol{x}^n = \boldsymbol{x}^0$, that is, f is continuous at $(\boldsymbol{p}^0, w^0)$.

(2) u can not be continuously extended onto $\boldsymbol{R}_+^L$.

Note that in (2), through assumption 6.2 and assumption 6.3, u becomes $-\infty$ on $\partial\boldsymbol{R}_+^L$. It is trivial that the sequence $\{\boldsymbol{x}^n\}_n$ has a convergent sub-sequence in $\boldsymbol{R}_+^L$. Indeed, there exists a (sufficiently large) $\bar{w}$ and a number $\bar{n}$ such that all $\boldsymbol{x}^n, n \geq \bar{n}$, are included in the set $\{\boldsymbol{x} \in \boldsymbol{R}_+^L \mid \boldsymbol{p}^0 \cdot \boldsymbol{x} \leq \bar{w}\}$ which is obviously compact. Let the limit of the convergent sub-sequence be $\boldsymbol{x}'$ ($\in \boldsymbol{R}_+^L$). We again classify two cases for $\boldsymbol{x}'$. First, if $\boldsymbol{x}' \in \boldsymbol{R}_{++}^L$, then we may adopt similar procedures to those in (1) to see that $\boldsymbol{x}' = \boldsymbol{x}^0$, i.e. f is continuous at $(\boldsymbol{p}^0, w^0)$. Secondly, if $\boldsymbol{x}' \in \partial\boldsymbol{R}_+^L$, then we have a contradiction as follows. For a sufficiently large n there exists some $\hat{w}$ ($\in \boldsymbol{R}_{++}$) such that the set $\{\boldsymbol{x} \in \boldsymbol{R}_+^L \mid \boldsymbol{p}^0 \cdot \boldsymbol{x} \leq \hat{w}\}$ is a proper subset of the set $\{\boldsymbol{x} \in \boldsymbol{R}_+^L \mid \boldsymbol{p}^n \cdot \boldsymbol{x} \leq w^n\}$. Since the former set $\{\boldsymbol{x} \in \boldsymbol{R}_+^L \mid \boldsymbol{p}^0 \cdot \boldsymbol{x} \leq \hat{w}\}$ is non-empty, we may choose some strictly positive vector $\hat{\boldsymbol{x}}$ from it. Then, according to the definition of u, $u(\hat{\boldsymbol{x}})$ is finitely determined, thus put $\hat{u} = u(\hat{\boldsymbol{x}})$. As we have noted above, $\lim_{n\to\infty} u(\boldsymbol{x}^n) = -\infty$. Hence we obtain that $u(\boldsymbol{x}^n) < \hat{u}$ for a sufficiently large n, which contradicts the fact that $\boldsymbol{x}^n = f(\boldsymbol{p}^n, w^n)$. Consequently we have that $\boldsymbol{x}' \notin \partial\boldsymbol{R}_+^L$. $\qquad\square$

It is easily seen that the derived demand function $\boldsymbol{x} = f(\boldsymbol{p}, w)$ also satisfies (1) homogeneity of degree 0 with respect to $\boldsymbol{p}$ and w, and (2) $\boldsymbol{p} \cdot f(\boldsymbol{p}, w) = w$ for any $\boldsymbol{p}$ ($\in \boldsymbol{R}_{++}^L$) and w ($\in \boldsymbol{R}_{++}$).

In previous chapters, we have been using differentiable demand functions. Thus, we should refer to the conditions for the utility function to guarantee the differentiability of the demand function.

Assumption 6.4 Strong quasi-concavity: $\boldsymbol{z}^t \cdot U_{\boldsymbol{xx}} \cdot \boldsymbol{z} < 0$ for every element of $\{\boldsymbol{z} \in \boldsymbol{R}^L \mid u_{\boldsymbol{x}} \cdot \boldsymbol{z} = 0, \, \boldsymbol{z} \neq 0\}$,

where $u_{\boldsymbol{x}}$ is the gradient vector of u at $\boldsymbol{x}$ and $U_{\boldsymbol{xx}}$ is the $m \times m$ Hessian matrix of u at $\boldsymbol{x}$.

Lemma 6.1 *If the utility function u is strongly quasi-concave as well as monotone increasing (assumption 6.2), then the following matrix called the bordered Hessian matrix of u is non-singular.*

$$\begin{pmatrix} U_{\boldsymbol{xx}} & u_{\boldsymbol{x}} \\ u_{\boldsymbol{x}}^t & 0 \end{pmatrix},$$

where the superscript 't' of u_x indicates the transpose.

Proof. Let the above matrix be H. Suppose that H is singular. Then, the column vectors of H are linearly dependent, thus there exists a non-zero $L+1$-vector $(z_1, \ldots, z_L, r)$ such that $U_{xx} \cdot z + r u_x = 0$ and $u_x \cdot z = 0$ where $z = (z_1, \ldots, z_L)$. If $z = 0, r \neq 0$, then the first equation provided above leads to that $r u_x = 0$, which contradicts assumption 6.2. If $z \neq 0$, then premultiplying the first equation by z^t (with the consideration of the second equation) would result in $z^t \cdot U_{xx} \cdot z = 0, u_x \cdot z = 0, z \neq 0$, which contradicts the strong quasi-concavity of u. Thus H is non-singular. $\qquad \square$

Proposition 6.7 *If the utility function satisfies assumptions 6.1, 6.2 and 6.4, then the demand function is differentiable in p ($\in R_{++}^L$) and w ($\in R_{++}$).*

Proof. Note that the strong quasi-concavity implies the strict quasi-concavity since the latter is equivalent to the following condition.

$$z^t \cdot U_{xx} \cdot z \leq 0 \ \text{for every element of} \ \{z \in R^L \mid u_x \cdot z = 0\}.$$

Thus, through the previous proposition, we have the well-defined demand function, the value of which corresponding to any p ($\in R_{++}^L$) and w ($\in R_{++}$) is obviously given as the solution of the following maximization problem.

$$\max_{x} \quad u(x)$$
$$s.t. \ \ p \cdot x = w.$$

The first order conditions for the solution are

$$u_x - \lambda p = 0, \ w - p \cdot x = 0,$$

where λ is a Lagrange multiplier. Note that $\lambda > 0$ because of assumption 1 and strict positiveness of p.

If the matrix

$$\begin{pmatrix} U_{xx} & p \\ p^t & 0 \end{pmatrix}$$

is non-singular, the Implicit Function Theorem assures that the above first order conditions yield the unique functions $x_i(p, w)$, $i = 1, \ldots, L$, $\lambda(p, w)$ which are all differentiable. Since $u_x = \lambda p$, the above matrix is non-singular if and only if the bordered Hessian matrix of u is non-singular. Accordingly, through lemma 6.1, our claim follows. $\qquad \square$

6.2.2 *Admissible Utility Functions and the Space of Economies*

It is worth noting that if we directly depend on one's utility function instead of its demand function, then we could take into account a much more variety of its demand behavior. Indeed, as we have shown in 6.2.1, the demand function that has been usually used in the literature is very restrictive in that it is only generated by a special form of utility function. We are going to allow a very wide variety of utility functions so that we can cover the behavior that is not based on a demand function.

All we assume on the utility function of a consumer is monotonicity as well as differentiability. Thus, an economy is defined as follows.

Definition 6.6 An economy consists of $\{(u^i),(\omega^i)\}_i$ where u^i is the utility function of consumer i $(i=1,\ldots,I)$ which satisfies
  (1) $u^i \in C^\infty(\boldsymbol{R}^L_{++},\boldsymbol{R})$
  (2) $du^i_{\boldsymbol{x}} > 0$ for all $\boldsymbol{x} \in \boldsymbol{R}^L_{++}$
and ω^i is the initial endowment vector of consumer i which is an element of $\boldsymbol{R}^L_{++}$.

Note that the so-called demand function of a consumer may not be well-defined in our economy because of a lack of any concavity.

Let's consider the properties of the space of our admissible utility functions from the viewpoint of the Whitney topology. That is, given the Whitney C^∞ topology to $C^\infty(\boldsymbol{R}^L_{++},\boldsymbol{R})$, investigate the topological structure of the following set.

$$U = \{u \in C^\infty(\boldsymbol{R}^L_{++},\boldsymbol{R}) \mid du_{\boldsymbol{x}} > 0 \ for \ all \ \boldsymbol{x} \in \boldsymbol{R}^L_{++}\}.$$

As for this set, we have a desirable consequence as follows.

Proposition 6.8 *U is open in the Whitney C^∞ topology.*

Proof. It suffices to show that U is open in the Whitney C^1 topology. Consider the following set U.

$$U = \{(a_1,\ldots,a_L,b,c_1,\ldots,c_L) \in J^1(\boldsymbol{R}^L_{++},\boldsymbol{R}) \mid c_l > 0, \ l = 1,\ldots,L\}$$

where $J^1(\boldsymbol{R}^L_{++},\boldsymbol{R})$ is the 1-jet bundle which is substantially equal to $\boldsymbol{R}^L_{++} \times \boldsymbol{R} \times \boldsymbol{R}^L$ as shown before. Thus, U is obviously open in $J^1(\boldsymbol{R}^L_{++},\boldsymbol{R})$. On the other hand, it is easily seen that

$$U = \{f \in C^\infty(\boldsymbol{R}^L_{++},\boldsymbol{R}) \mid j^1 f(\boldsymbol{R}^L_{++}) \subset U\}.$$

Hence, according to the argument in 6.1.3, we immediately obtain the desired consequence. $\qquad\square$

We can also obtain an interesting result concerning the set of strongly quasi-concave utility functions. Let $\tilde{U}$ be the following set.

$$\tilde{U} = \{f \in C^\infty(\boldsymbol{R}^L_{++}, \boldsymbol{R}) \mid f \text{ is strongly quasi} - \text{concave}\}.$$

Proposition 6.9 $\quad \tilde{U}$ *is open in the Whitney* C^∞ *topology.*

Proof. We are going to show that $\tilde{U}$ is open in the Whitney C^2 topology, which implies our claim.

Let $(\boldsymbol{a}, b, \boldsymbol{c})$ be a representative element of $J^2(\boldsymbol{R}^L_{++}, \boldsymbol{R})$ where

$$\boldsymbol{a} = (a_1, \ldots, a_L),$$

$$\boldsymbol{c} = (c_1, \ldots, c_L, c_{11}, c_{12}, \ldots, c_{1L}, c_{22}, c_{23}, \ldots, c_{2L}, c_{33}, c_{34}, \ldots, c_{3L}, \ldots, c_{LL}),$$

since $J^2(\boldsymbol{R}^L_{++}, \boldsymbol{R})$ is equal to $\boldsymbol{R}^L_{++} \times \boldsymbol{R} \times \boldsymbol{R}^H$ in which $H = L(L+3)/2$. Consider the map $\tau : \boldsymbol{R}^L_{++} \times \boldsymbol{R} \times \boldsymbol{R}^H \to \boldsymbol{R}^L_{++} \times \boldsymbol{R} \times \boldsymbol{R}$ given by

$$\tau(\boldsymbol{a}, b, \boldsymbol{c}) = (\boldsymbol{a}, b, det(C))$$

where C is the matrix defined as follows

$$\begin{pmatrix} c_{11} & c_{12} & \cdots & c_{1L} & c_1 \\ c_{12} & c_{22} & \cdots & c_{2L} & c_2 \\ \vdots & \vdots & \ddots & \vdots & \vdots \\ c_{1L} & c_{2L} & \cdots & c_{LL} & c_L \\ c_1 & c_2 & \cdots & c_L & 0 \end{pmatrix}.$$

It is obvious that τ is continuous. Then, choose the set Z in $\boldsymbol{R}^L_{++} \times \boldsymbol{R} \times \boldsymbol{R}$ given by

$$Z = \boldsymbol{R}^L_{++} \times \boldsymbol{R} \times ((-\infty, 0) \cup (0, +\infty))$$

which is obviously open in the ambient space, thus $\tau^{-1}(Z)$ is also open in $\boldsymbol{R}^L_{++} \times \boldsymbol{R} \times \boldsymbol{R}^H$. However, it is easily seen that according to the definition of the strong quasi-concavity, $\tilde{U}$ is represented by the following set

$$\{f \in C^\infty(\boldsymbol{R}^L_{++}, \boldsymbol{R}) \mid j^2 f(\boldsymbol{R}^L_{++}) \subset \tau^{-1}(Z)\}$$

which is open in the Whitney C^2 topology as we have noted in 6.1.3. $\qquad\square$

Since the utility function which can generate the differentiable demand function should be included in the open set $U \cap \tilde{U}$, confining ourselves to U would really cover the demand behaviors of each consumer beyond the scope of the demand function.

Finally, we formally state the altered space of economies. Since we have determined to accept U as the set of admissible utility functions for each consumer, the space of economies grows from $\boldsymbol{R}_{++}^{LI}$ to be $U^I \times \boldsymbol{R}_{++}^{LI}$ in which U^I is the I-product of U. To avoid the confusion of notation, we denote this new space by $\hat{\mathcal{E}}$ in the following.

6.2.3 Extended Equilibrium

Here we consider an equilibrium state for a given economy $(u^i, \omega^i)_i \in \hat{\mathcal{E}}$. Since we still r emain in a pure exchange model, each consumer behaves as a price taker. As for the prices, we retain assumption 1.1, i.e. $\boldsymbol{p} \in \boldsymbol{R}_{++}^L$.

Up to chapter 6, we have considered a characteristic describing an equilibrium state to be only a price vector. However, when using utility functions previously provided in place of demand functions, it is appropriate for us to substitute $((\boldsymbol{x}^i)_i, \boldsymbol{p})$ for $\boldsymbol{p}$ alone. This is because our utility functions do not necessarily yield a unique demand vector for each consumer associated with any given prices.

Definition 6.7 An equilibrium state (or simply an equilibrium) for a given economy $(u^i, \omega^i)_i$ is a pair $((\boldsymbol{x}^i)_i, \boldsymbol{p})$ such that
 (1) $\boldsymbol{x}^i$ is a solution for the following problem, $i = 1, \ldots, I$

$$\max_{\boldsymbol{x}^i} \quad u^i(\boldsymbol{x}^i)$$
$$s.t. \quad \boldsymbol{p} \cdot \boldsymbol{x}^i \leq \boldsymbol{p} \cdot \omega^i$$

 (2) $\sum_i^I \boldsymbol{x}^i = \sum_i^I \omega^i$.

It follows from the conditions in the definition that the normalization is allowed, so that we may restrict $\boldsymbol{p}$ to the strictly positive $L-1$-dimensional unit sphere S.

Since u^i $(i = 1, \ldots, I)$ is monotone increasing, the budget constraint for consumer i is represented as an equality rather than inequality, thus an equilibrium should satisfy the following conditions.

$$du_{\boldsymbol{x}^i}^i - \lambda^i \boldsymbol{p} = 0, \ \boldsymbol{p} \cdot \boldsymbol{x}^i - \boldsymbol{p} \cdot \omega^i = 0, \quad i = 1, \ldots, I$$

where λ^i is a Lagrange multiplier and $du^i_{\boldsymbol{x}^i}$ should be interpreted as a vector-representation of the derivative of u^i at $\boldsymbol{x}^i$ (thus substantially equal to the gradient vector of u^i at $\boldsymbol{x}^i$).

Here we consider the set of $((\boldsymbol{x}^i)_i, \boldsymbol{p}) \in \boldsymbol{R}^{LI}_{++} \times S$ fulfilling the conditions stated above, which is not equal to the set of equilibria itself but, obviously, contains it. We purposely focus on this set an element of which is called an extended equilibrium (Smale (1974a)).

Noting that $\boldsymbol{p}$ is confined to S, an extended equilibrium is then defined as follows.

Definition 6.8   An extended equilibrium for a given economy $(u^i, \boldsymbol{\omega}^i)_i$ is a pair $((\boldsymbol{x}^i)_i, \boldsymbol{p})$ satisfying

     (1) $du^i_{\boldsymbol{x}^i}/\|du^i_{\boldsymbol{x}^i}\| = \boldsymbol{p}, \quad i = 1, \ldots, I$
     (2) $\boldsymbol{p} \cdot \boldsymbol{x}^i = \boldsymbol{p} \cdot \boldsymbol{\omega}^i, \quad i = 1, \ldots, I$
     (3) $\sum_i^I \boldsymbol{x}^i = \sum_i^I \boldsymbol{\omega}^i.$

We denote the set of extended equilibria for $(u^i, \boldsymbol{\omega}^i)_i$ by $E_{ex}((u^i, \boldsymbol{\omega}^i)_i)$ in the following. We are concerned with $E_{ex}((u^i, \boldsymbol{\omega}^i)_i)$ because it gives us useful informations about the set of true equilibria.

Chapter 7

Transversality and Regular Economies

In this chapter we will concentrate on transversality, which is a naturally extended concept of regularity (specifically regular points and regular values) provided in the previous chapters.

Up to this point, we have grasped regular economies solely on the basis of regular values of a smooth map. Accordingly there is a good prospect that the notion of transversality will expand the scope of regular economies. In fact, we broadened the space of economies so as to include utility functions with a stretch of the concept of equilibrium states in the preceding chapter. In these circumstances, it is difficult to stipulate regular economies in connection with regular values. Transversality, however, allows us to determine regular economies easily and naturally. In this chapter we shall show how it goes, following the mathematical exposition of transversality.

7.1 Mathematical Preliminaries

7.1.1 *Geometrical Meaning of Transversality*

To grasp the image of transversality, it is convenient to start with the geometrical relation between two manifolds. Let's look at the situations depicted in the figure of the next page where the ambient space is considered R^3.

Though $X \cap Y \neq \emptyset$ in both situations, geometrically there is a difference between them. In (i), X is tangent to Y whereas X is crossing Y in (ii). Transversality is solely concerned with the latter case. That is, we say 'X and Y are transversal in (ii) but not in (i).'

To obtain the precise definition of the transversality, we should resort to the tangent spaces at an intersection point for X and Y. In fact, it is

99

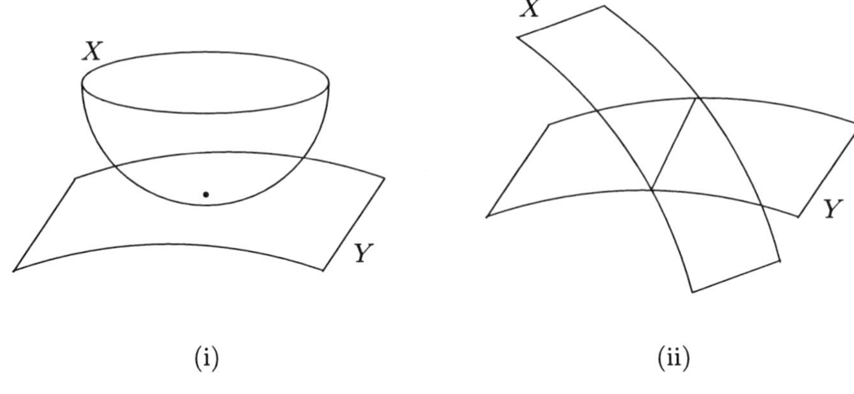

Fig. 7.1

easily seen that at any point in $X \cap Y$ the two tangent spaces for X and Y 'span' the ambient space $\boldsymbol{R}^3$ in (ii) but not in (i). From this observation, we have the following general definition of the trasversality for manifolds.

Definition 7.1   Let X and Y be two manifolds in $\boldsymbol{R}^n$. Then, X and Y are said to be transversal (or intersect transversely) if at each point $x \in X \cap Y$ we have

$$T_x X + T_x Y = \boldsymbol{R}^n.$$

Note that if $X \cap Y = \emptyset$ then X and Y are logically qualified to be transversal since the premise is not met. Thus we may say that if we arbitrarily put any two objects in space we would typically have the transversal relation for that pair. Furthermore, even if the pair is not transversal, we would be able to make them transversal by a sufficiently small perturbation. In contrast, to be noticed, if the pair is trasversal a small perturbation will not change the position of the transversality for those objects. In this sense, the transversality can be said to be a typical and stable geometrical relation for the manifolds.

It is obvious that the above argument holds for any two submanifolds in an ambient manifold. That is, two manifold $M, K \subset X$ are said to be transversal if at each point $x \in M \cap K$

$$T_x M + T_x K = T_x X.$$

Finally we give a significant remark on the transversality. It is worth noting that the definition requires "spanning" of the ambient space with two tangent spaces. Hence, even if two curves are crossing with each other in $\boldsymbol{R}^3$, they cannot be transversal. They are transversal only if they are disjoint.

7.1.2 *Transversality with Maps*

There is another (particularly important) notion of transversality involving smooth maps, which is closely related to the transversality provided above.

Let's look at the picture in the following figure where (a part of) the graph of a smooth map $f : \boldsymbol{R}^2 \to \boldsymbol{R}$ and a horizontal plane through the point $\{a\}$ in the vertical axis are depicted.

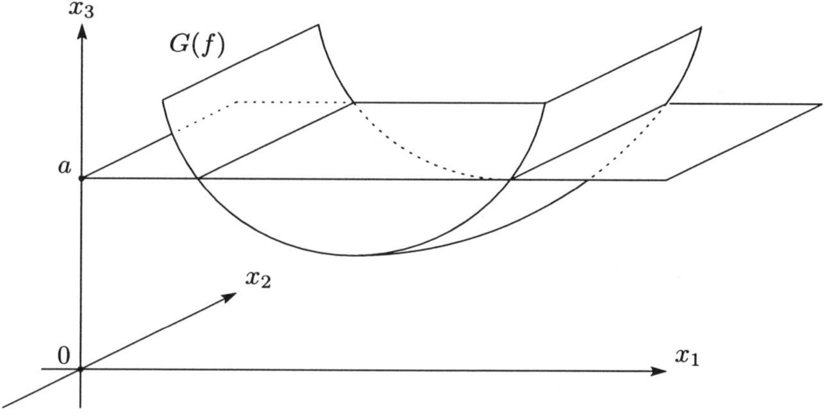

Fig. 7.2

It is easily seen by inspection that those geometrical objects are transversal in $\boldsymbol{R}^3$. We consider generalizing this picture. First note that in general the graph of a smooth map $f : M \to K$, where M and K are manifolds with m and k dimensions respectively, constitutes a submanifold in $M \times K$. In fact, there exists a smooth map $\tilde{f} : U \to V$, where U is an open set of $\boldsymbol{R}^m$ and V also an open set of $\boldsymbol{R}^k$, such that the graph of f can be locally identified with the set $\{(x, y) \in U \times V \mid y = \tilde{f}(x),\ x \in U\}$ denoted Γ. Then the map $F : U \to \boldsymbol{R}^{m+k}$ defined by $F(x) = (x, \tilde{f}(x))$ is a diffeomorphism from U onto Γ, thus qualified as a local parametrization.

On the other hand, from a point in $\boldsymbol{R}$ ($\{a\}$ in Fig. 7.2) we abstract a submanifold in K. Let Q be a submanifold in K. Obviously $M \times Q$ itself forms a submanifold in $M \times K$.

Thus we are naturally led to consider the transversality of those two geometrical objects (the graph of f and $M \times Q$) in $M \times K$.

Definition 7.2 Let $f : M \to K$ be a smooth map and Q be a submanifold of K. Then, if the graph of f and $M \times Q$ are transversal in $M \times K$, f is said to be transversal to Q (or intersect Q transversely).

In the following we denote the graph of f by $G(f)$.

As for the transversality with maps, there is another definition equivalent to the above one.

Definition 7.3 Let $f : M \to K$ be a smooth map and Q be a submanifold of K. Then if for any point $\{x\} \in f^{-1}(Q)$

$$df_x(T_x M) + T_{f(x)}Q = T_{f(x)}K,$$

f is said to be transversal to Q (or intersect Q transversely).

Note that if $f^{-1}(Q) = \emptyset$, f is transversal to Q.

This definition is less intuitive but technically more tractable than the previous one, thus more frequently used in application.

Before proceeding, let's show the equivalence between those two definitions. First for any point $\{x\} \in f^{-1}(Q)$ we have

$$G(df_x) = T_{(x,f(x))}G(f)$$

where $G(df_x)$ is the graph of the derivative of f at x, i.e. the set $\{(v, w) \in T_x M \times T_{f(x)}K \mid w = df_x(v)\}$. In fact, consider the map $F : M \to G(f)$ defined by $F(x) = (x, f(x))$, then noting that F is a diffeomorphism and that $dF_x = (I, df_x)$ where I designates an identity map, we obtain

$$\begin{aligned}
T_{(x,f(x))}G(f) &= dF_x(T_x M) \\
&= (I, df_x)(v), \quad v \in T_x M \\
&= (v, df_x(v)), \quad v \in T_x M \\
&= G(df_x) \\
&= T_x M \times df_x(T_x M).
\end{aligned}$$

Now, if $G(f)$ and $M \times Q$ are transversal in $M \times K$, then we have

$$T_{(x,f(x))}G(f) + T_{(x,f(x))}(M \times Q) = T_{(x,f(x))}(M \times K),$$

which can be, through the above observation, rephrased as follows.

$$T_x M \times df_x(T_x M) + T_x M \times T_{f(x)}Q = T_x M \times T_{f(x)}K$$

which leads to the desired equation

$$df_x(T_xM) + T_{f(x)}Q = T_{f(x)}K.$$

Conversely, by premultiplying T_xM by both sides of the above equation, we can obtain the transversality of $G(f)$ and $M \times Q$. Our claim is proved.

Now suppose that we take a single point $\{\bar{y}\}$ as a submanifold in K. If f is transversal to $\{\bar{y}\}$, then definition 7.3 asserts that $\bar{y}$ is a regular value of f. In fact, noting that $T_{\bar{y}}\{\bar{y}\} = 0$, the transversality of f to $\{\bar{y}\}$ is equivalent to that $df_x(T_xM) = T_{\bar{y}}K$ for any $x \in f^{-1}(\bar{y})$, which substantially says that $\bar{y}$ is a regular value of f. In this sense, the transversality with smooth maps can be seen as a broad notion that has been evolved out of the regularity of smooth maps.

7.1.3 *Generalization of Preimage Theorem*

Recall that the preimage $f^{-1}(\bar{y})$ of a regular value $\bar{y} \in K$ for $f : M \to K$ constitutes a submanifold of M (see theorem 2.1). Then, on the basis of the above argument, we might conjecture that a similar result holds for the transversality with smooth maps. In fact, we have the following claim.

Theorem 7.1 *If a smooth map $f : M \to K$ is transversal to a submanifold Q in K and $f^{-1}(Q)$ is nonempty, then $f^{-1}(Q)$ is a submanifold in M with* codim $f^{-1}(Q) = $ codim Q *and for any $x \in f^{-1}(Q)$, $df_x(T_x f^{-1}(Q)) = T_{f(x)}Q$.*

Proof. Let $dim\,M$ be m, $dim K$ be k and $dim\,Q$ be q. It is sufficient to check the claim locally, thus choose an arbitrary point $a \in f^{-1}(Q)$ and investigate the structure of a neighborhood of this point. Set $b = f(a)$.

Since Q is a submanifold of K, there exists an open neighborhood $W \in K$ around b and a coordinate system $\varphi\ (= (\varphi_1, \ldots, \varphi_k)) : W \to \mathbf{R}^k$ such that $y \in W \cap Q$ if and only if $\varphi_1(y) = \ldots = \varphi_{k-q}(y) = 0$ (see example 1.4). Set $\bar{\varphi} = (\varphi_1, \ldots, \varphi_{k-q}) : W \to \mathbf{R}^{k-q}$. Obviously $\bar{\varphi}^{-1}(0) = W \cap Q$. Let $f^{-1}(W)$ be V. V is an open neighborhood in M around a, satisfying that $f^{-1}(Q) \cap V = f^{-1} \circ \bar{\varphi}^{-1}(0) = (\bar{\varphi} \circ f)^{-1}(0)$. Our concern is with the structure of $f^{-1}(Q) \cap V$. Select any point $x \in f^{-1}(Q) \cap V$ and consider the derivative of $\bar{\varphi} \circ f$ at x. We show under the transversality that the derivative $d(\bar{\varphi} \circ f)_x : T_xM \to \mathbf{R}^{k-q}$ is surjective. To this end, first note that since $\bar{\varphi}(y) = 0$ for any $y \in Q$, $d\bar{\varphi}_{f(x)}(T_{f(x)}Q) = 0$. In addition, obviously $d\bar{\varphi}_{f(x)}(T_{f(x)}K) = \mathbf{R}^{k-q}$.

Now suppose that f is transversal to Q. Then we have that

$$df_x(T_xM) + T_{f(x)}Q = T_{f(x)}K.$$

Applying $d\bar{\varphi}_{f(x)}$ to both sides of this equation, we obtain

$$d\bar{\varphi}_{f(x)}(df_x(T_xM) + T_{f(x)}Q) = \boldsymbol{R}^{k-q}.$$

Since $\bar{\varphi}^{-1}(0) = W \cap Q$, $d\bar{\varphi}_{f(x)}(T_{f(x)}Q) = 0$, which turns the above equation into the following one.

$$d\bar{\varphi}_{f(x)}(df_x(T_xM)) = \boldsymbol{R}^{k-q}$$

which implies that $d(\bar{\varphi} \circ f)_x : T_xM \to \boldsymbol{R}^{k-q}$ is surjective.

Since x is an arbitrary point of $(\bar{\varphi} \circ f)^{-1}(0)$, 0 is a regular value of $\bar{\varphi} \circ f$. Thus, through the preimage theorem, $(\bar{\varphi} \circ f)^{-1}(0)$ $(= f^{-1}(Q) \cap V)$ is a submanifold in M whose dimension is $m - (k - q)$, thus its codimension is $k - q$ which is equal to *codim Q*.

It remains to be shown that for any $x \in f^{-1}(Q)$, $df_x(T_xf^{-1}(Q)) = T_{f(x)}Q$. As we noticed, $d\bar{\varphi}_{f(x)}(T_{f(x)}Q) = 0$, which leads to that

$$d\bar{\varphi}^{-1}_{f(x)}(0) = T_{f(x)}Q.$$

On the other hand, since $(\bar{\varphi} \circ f)^{-1}(0) = f^{-1}(Q) \cap V$, we have that

$$d(\bar{\varphi} \circ f)_x(T_xf^{-1}(Q)) = 0.$$

Thus, applying $d\bar{\varphi}^{-1}_{f(x)}$ to both sides of this equation, we obtain the desired consequence. $\qquad\square$

It is worth noting that the preimage theorem (theorem 2.1) can be seen as a special case of this theorem. This theorem also yields the following interesting claim.

Corollary 7.1 *Let M and K be the two manifolds in $\boldsymbol{R}^n$. Let dim M be m and dim K be k. If M and K are transversal, then $M \cap K$ is either an empty set or a $m + k - n$-dimensional manifold in $\boldsymbol{R}^n$.*

Proof. Let $i : M \to \boldsymbol{R}^n$ be the inclusion map. Then, it is easily seen that the transversality of M and K is equivalent to the transversality of i to K. Therefore, through the above theorem, $i^{-1}(K)$ $(= M \cap K)$ is a submanifold of M (thus a manifold in $\boldsymbol{R}^n$) whose codimension is $n - k$, hence *dim $M \cap K = m + k - n$*. $\qquad\square$

Note that in the situation of the corollary we have that

$$codim\ (M \cap K) = codim\ M + codim\ K$$

if $M \cap K \neq \emptyset$. It follows from this corollary that if $m + k - n < 0$, then the transversality of M and K implies that $M \cap K = \emptyset$. Needless to say, this corollary holds for any two submanifolds not in $\boldsymbol{R}^n$ but in any ambient manifold.

7.2 Economical Analysis

7.2.1 *Transversality and Regular Economies*

Here we try to formulate regular economies under the altered space of economies. There are two difficulties in doing our job. One is the existence of the functional space (the space of utility functions) in our economy space. A functional space is not a manifold, thus we are not allowed to apply the familiar differential calculus on it. The other is a stretch of the notion of equilibrium states; that is, an extended equilibrium. We are unable to use usual demand functions to characterize those equilibria. To cope with these difficulties, we are required to adopt a different way than what has been used so far. Transversality is just what we need to get through this crisis.

To show how transversality works, first recall the specific characterization of regular economies described in 3.2.4. We can summarize the characterization as follows.

First construct a family of maps $F : E \times M \to K$ parameterized by economies of E where M is considered the space consisting of conceivable states of economies. This family of maps is required to have a specific property; that is, the preimage $F^{-1}(\bar{y})$ of a particular value $\bar{y} \in K$ should form the set of the pairs $\{(an\ economy\ e, equilibria\ of\ e)\}$. Then a regular economy is shown to be the economy e in which $F_e : M \to K$ has $\bar{y}$ as a regular value where $F(e, x) = F_e(x)$. It is worth noting here that we can say that $F_e : M \to K$ *is transversal to* $\bar{y}$ instead of saying that F_e has $\bar{y}$ as a regular value.

We are going to formalize regular economies under our extended economies by making use of this characterization.

For this purpose, we first specify the space of economies and the space of states. The former is, of course, $\hat{\mathcal{E}}\ (=\ U^I \times \boldsymbol{R}_{++}^{LI})$. As for the latter, since an equilibrium state is represented not by a price vector alone but a pair of consumption allocation *and* a price vector in our extended economy (see 6.2.3), we have to consider $\boldsymbol{R}_{++}^{LI} \times S$ where S designates the strictly positive $L-1$-dimensional unit sphere in $\boldsymbol{R}^{L}$.

Then we need to construct an appropriate family of maps parameterized by economies. Considering the specification of extended equilibria described in definition 6, we can properly devise the following one as such a family of maps.

$$F : \hat{\mathcal{E}} \times \boldsymbol{R}_{++}^{LI} \times S \to S^{I+1} \times \boldsymbol{R}^{I-1} \times \boldsymbol{R}^{L}$$

$$F(\{u^i, \boldsymbol{\omega}^i\}_i, (\boldsymbol{x}^i)_i, \boldsymbol{p}) = (du_{\boldsymbol{x}^1}^1/\|du_{\boldsymbol{x}^1}^1\|, \ldots, du_{\boldsymbol{x}^I}^I/\|du_{\boldsymbol{x}^I}^I\|, \boldsymbol{p},$$
$$\boldsymbol{p} \cdot \boldsymbol{x}^1 - \boldsymbol{p} \cdot \boldsymbol{\omega}^1, \ldots, \boldsymbol{p} \cdot \boldsymbol{x}^{I-1} - \boldsymbol{p} \cdot \boldsymbol{\omega}^{I-1},$$
$$\sum_i^I \boldsymbol{x}^i - \sum_i^I \boldsymbol{\omega}^i).$$

This family of maps F has a desirable property in the following sense.

Let Δ be the diagonal set of S^{I+1}; that is, $\Delta = \{(\boldsymbol{s}_1, \ldots, \boldsymbol{s}_{I+1}) \in S^{I+1} \mid \boldsymbol{s}_1 = \ldots = \boldsymbol{s}_{I+1}\}$. Then it is easily seen that the preimage $F^{-1}(\Delta \times 0)$ of $\Delta \times 0$, where $0 \in \boldsymbol{R}^{I-1+L}$, constitutes the set of the pairs $\{(an\ economy, corresponding\ extended\ equilibria)\}$. Note that the budget constraint of the last agent (I-th consumer) is disregarded in the map because through Walras' law it is automatically met.

For simplicity, we write $u = (u^1, \ldots, u^I), \omega = (\boldsymbol{\omega}^1, \ldots, \boldsymbol{\omega}^I)$ and $x = (\boldsymbol{x}^1, \ldots, \boldsymbol{x}^I)$ in the following. Thus we are allowed to write $F(u, \omega, x, \boldsymbol{p}) = F_{(u,\omega)}(x, \boldsymbol{p})$ as usual.

Considering that Δ forms a $L-1$ dimensional submanifold in S^{I+1}, we finally obtain the desired formulation of regular economies in our extended framework.

Definition 7.4 An economy (u, ω) is said to be a regular economy if $F_{(u,\omega)} : \boldsymbol{R}_{++}^{LI} \times S \to S^{I+1} \times \boldsymbol{R}^{I-1} \times \boldsymbol{R}^{L}$ is *transversal* to $\Delta \times 0$.

7.2.2 *Properties of Regular Economies*

As we have noticed before, in the theory of regular economies, we are mainly concerned with two points. One is a specific structure of the equilibrium set of a regular economy and the other is a specific position that regular economies occupy in the space of economies. As for the former, we can immediately give the answer.

Theorem 7.2 *The set of extended equilibria for each regular economy is locally unique.*

Proof. Note that the set of extended equilibria $E_{ex}(u,\omega)$ for an economy (u,ω) is equal to $F_{(u,\omega)}^{-1}(\Delta\times 0)$ where $F_{(u,\omega)}$ is the map provided in definition 7.4. Since $F_{(u,\omega)}$ is transverasal to $\Delta\times 0$ for any regular economy (u,ω), theorem 7.1 assures that $F_{(u,\omega)}^{-1}(\Delta\times 0)$ is a submanifold in $R_{++}^{LI}\times S$ and that *codim* $F_{(u,\omega)}^{-1}(\Delta\times 0) = codim\ \Delta\times 0$. Thus *dim* $F_{(u,\omega)}^{-1}(\Delta\times 0) = dim\ (R_{++}^{LI}\times S) - dim\ (S^{I+1}\times R^{I-1}\times R^L) + dim\ (\Delta\times 0) = LI + L - 1 - (L-1)(I+1) - I + 1 - L + L - 1 = 0$, which implies that $E_{ex}(u,\omega)$ is a 0-dimensional submanifold, i.e. a discrete set in $R_{++}^{LI}\times S$. Consequently the claim follows. $\qquad\square$

Note that the set of extended equilibria can be empty. To assure the existence of extended equilibria, we need more assumptions on the utility function of each consumer. We shall refer to this issue later (see chapter 9).

Since the set of extended equilibria contains the set of true equilibria, we can say through the above theorem that the set of true equilibria, if any, is also locally unique.

We now turn to the second issue; that is, a specific position that regular economies occupy in the space of economies. This one is, however, less tractable. It is because the functional space stands in the way.

Recall again the argument in 3.2.4 which motivated us to formulate regular economies in our new setting. It is worth noting that the family of maps $F : E \times M \to K$ (abstract form) provided there can not only characterize regular economies but also play a crucial role in determining the position of regular economies in the space of economies. Specifically, if F itself is *smooth*, lemma 3.1 assures density of the set of regular economies.

Therefore, on this analogy, if our newly devised family of maps $F : \hat{\mathcal{E}} \times R_{++}^{LI} \times S \to S^{I+1} \times R^{I-1} \times R^L$ is *smooth*, we might as well anticipate obtaining the same (desired) outcome in the new setting. However, it is not successful because of the existence of the functional space U^I in the space of economies $\hat{\mathcal{E}}$. In fact, since a functional space is not a manifold, we cannot conceive differentiability of a map defined on it.

Fortunately, we have an appropriate way to cope with this difficulty. It is based on a specific theorem called Thom transversality theorem which we shall address in the next chapter.

Chapter 8

Transversality Theorems and Regular Economies

Our task in this chapter is to investigate a specific position that regular economies occupy in the space of economies in our enlarged framework. The key for our move is, as we have suggested at the end of the preceding chapter, the transversality of the family of maps $F : \hat{\mathcal{E}} \times \boldsymbol{R}_{++}^{LI} \times S \to S^{I+1} \times \boldsymbol{R}^{I-1} \times \boldsymbol{R}^{L}$ to the submanifold $\Delta \times 0$. It is worth noting about this family of maps that the parametric space $\hat{\mathcal{E}}$ consists of two different types of components; that is, a functional space (U^I) and a usual manifold ($\boldsymbol{R}_{++}^{LI}$).

Therefore, in Mathematical Preliminaries of this chapter, we shall present two kinds of transversality theorems. One is based on a family of maps only involving a usual manifold as its parametric space, and the other is based on the one that only carries a functional space as its parametric space. The former is called the basic transversality lemma or, simply the transversality theorem, while the latter is known as the Thom transversality theorem.

By combining these two theorems, we succeed in obtaining a definite outcome concerning the position of regular economies in the enlarged space of economies, which will be shown in our economical analysis.

8.1 Mathematical Preliminaries

8.1.1 *Transversality Theorem*

We begin with a family of maps with a usual manifold as its parametric space, which is nothing but a smooth family of maps already defined in 3.1.3 (definition 3.3). Let a smooth map $F : P \times M \to K$ be a smooth family of maps where M, K and P are all manifolds. Recall that if F has a regular value (say, $\bar{y}$), then the subset of P yielding $\bar{y}$ possesses a special structure (see lemma 3.3). When considering the transversality of maps to be a generalization of the regularity of maps, we might as well expect that some propositions concerning the latter can also be valid for the former. In fact, this is the case for our present matter. That is, the above claim can carry over to the case in which F is transversal to a submanifold in K. In the following, we write $F(p, x) = F_p(x)$ as we have done before.

Lemma 8.1 *Let $F : P \times M \to K$ be a smooth family of maps and Q be a submanifold in K. If F is transversal to Q, then the set*

$$\{p \in P \mid F_p : M \to K \text{ is transversal to } Q\}$$

is equal to the set

$$\{p \in P \mid p \text{ is a regular value of } \pi|_{F^{-1}(Q)}\}$$

where $\pi|_{F^{-1}(Q)}$ is a restriction of the projection $\pi : P \times M \to P$ to $F^{-1}(Q)$.

Proof. We can prove this claim in almost the same way as the proof of lemma 3.3. Since F is transversal to Q, for any $(p, x) \in F^{-1}(Q)$ we have

$$dF_{(p,x)}(T_{(p,x)}(P \times x)) + dF_{(p,x)}(T_{(p,x)}(p \times M)) + T_{F(p,x)}Q$$
$$= T_{F(p,x)}K, \qquad (8.1)$$
$$dF_{(p,x)}(T_{(p,x)}(F^{-1}(Q))) = T_{F(p,x)}Q. \qquad (8.2)$$

Set $P_1 = \{p \in P \mid F_p : M \to K \text{ is transversal to } Q\}$ and $P_2 = \{p \in P \mid p \text{ is a regular value of } \pi|_{F^{-1}(Q)}\}$.

Suppose that $p \in P_1$, then for any $x \in F_p^{-1}(Q)$ we have

$$dF_{p,x}(T_x M) + T_{F_p(x)}Q = T_{F_p(x)}K.$$

Since $dF_{p,x}(T_x M) = dF_{(p,x)}(T_{(p,x)}(p \times M))$, (8.1) and (8.2) yield that

$$dF_{(p,x)}(T_{(p,x)}(P \times x)) \subset dF_{(p,x)}(T_{(p,x)}(p \times M)) + dF_{(p,x)}(T_{(p,x)}(F^{-1}(Q))),$$

hence

$$T_{(p,x)}(P \times x) \subset T_{(p,x)}(p \times M) + T_{(p,x)}(F^{-1}(Q)). \qquad (8.3)$$

Then, consider the derivative $d\pi_{(p,x)} : T_{(p,x)}(P \times M) \to T_p P$ of the projection $\pi : P \times M \to P$ at any $(p, x) \in P \times M$. It is obvious that

$$d\pi_{(p,x)}(T_{(p,x)}(p \times M) + T_{(p,x)}(F^{-1}(Q))) = d\pi_{(p,x)}(T_{(p,x)}(F^{-1}(Q)))$$

and

$$d\pi_{(p,x)}(T_{(p,x)}(P \times x)) = T_p P.$$

Therefore, applying $d\pi_{(p,x)}$ to both sides of (8.3), we have

$$T_p P \subset d\pi_{(p,x)}(T_{(p,x)}(F^{-1}(Q))),$$

which means that the derivative of the restriction $\pi|_{F^{-1}(y)}$ at (p, x) is surjective; that is, p is a regular value of $\pi|_{F^{-1}(Q)}$. Since we can inversely follow this reasoning, the lemma is proved. $\qquad\square$

This lemma immediately yields the following theorem, which is called the basic transversality lemma (Gibson (1979), 2.2) or, simply, the transversality theorem (Guillemin and Pollack (1974), 2.3).

Theorem 8.1 *Let $F : P \times M \to K$ be a smooth family of maps and Q be a submanifold in K. If F is transversal to Q, then the set*

$$\{p \in P \mid F_p : M \to K \text{ is transversal to } Q\}$$

is dense in P.

Proof. Since the set in question is, through the above lemma, equal to the set

$$\{p \in P \mid p \text{ is a regular value of } \pi|_{F^{-1}(Q)}\}$$

which is dense in P according to Sard's theorem. $\qquad\square$

It is quite advisable to see the figure in the next page to intuitively understand this theorem.

In the diagram, the graph of a smooth map $F : P \times M \to K$ is depicted. Here we consider a single point $\{a\} \in K$ to be a submanifold in K. Then the transversality of F and $\{a\}$ implies that $G(F)$ (the graph of F) intersects the horizontal plane through $\{a\}$ transversely. This is just what the figure shows. On the other hand, to see whether F_p is transversal to $\{a\}$, set a screen at each point p on P-axis parallel to $M - K$ coordinate hyperplane and determine whether the slice of $G(F)$ at the screen intersects the horizontal line through $\{a\}$ transversely on the screen. The theorem asserts that the set of points accompanying those screens on which the slice is not transversal to the horizontal line has Lebesgue measure zero in P. In fact, we distinguish only one point $\bar{p}$ as such in the diagram.

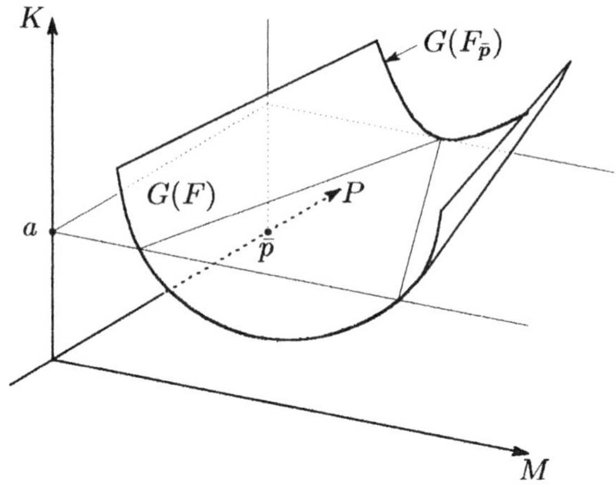

Fig. 8.1

8.1.2 *Thom Transversality Theorem*

In this subsection, we state the Thom transversality theorem, which is concerned with the simultaneous behavior of a whole family of maps. This theorem is based on the following fundamental lemma.

Lemma 8.2 *Let M, N and P be manifolds and $Q \subset N$ be a submanifold of N. Let G be a topological space and j be a map from G to $C^\infty(M, N)$. Suppose that for each $g \in G$ there exists $p_0 \in P$ and a continuous map $\varphi : P \to G$ such that $\varphi(p_0) = g$ and a map $\Phi : P \times M \to N$ defined by $\Phi(p, x) = j(\varphi(p))(x)$ is smooth and transversal to Q. Then the set*

$$\{g \in G \mid j(g) \text{ is transversal to } Q\}$$

is dense in G.

Proof. Set $Z = \{\, g \in G \mid j(g) \text{ is transversal to } Q\}$. The key for proof consists in lemma 8.1. Fix any $g \in G$. Note that the map $\Phi : P \times M \to N$ corresponding to g is actually a smooth family of maps, thus through lemma 8.1, the set

$$\{p \in P \mid j(\varphi(p)) \text{ is transversal to } Q\}$$

is equal to the set

$$\{p \in P \mid p \text{ is a regular value of } \pi|_{\Phi^{-1}(Q)}\}$$

where $\pi|_{\Phi^{-1}(Q)}$ is a restriction of the projection $\pi : P \times M \to P$ to $\Phi^{-1}(Q)$.

Then consider any open neighborhood $U(g)$ of g in G. Since φ is continuous, $\varphi^{-1}(U(g))$ is an open neighborhood of p_0 in P. Since the set of regular values of $\pi|_{\Phi^{-1}(Q)}$ is, by Sard's theorem, dense in P, there exists some regular value p of $\pi|_{\Phi^{-1}(Q)}$ in $\varphi^{-1}(U(g))$. For such a p, through the above observation, $j(\varphi(p))$ is transversal to Q. Thus, $\varphi(p) \in U(g) \cap Z$, which implies that Z is dense in G since g is arbitrarily chosen. $\square$

This lemma has very rich applicability. In fact, if G is equal to P and φ is the identity map, then this lemma yields the transversality theorem provided in the preceding subsection. Furthermore, it is worth noting that the G in the lemma is only required to be a topological space. Thus we are allowed to choose a functional space with Whitney (or compact open) topology as such. The Thom transversality theorem is induced according to this way of thinking.

Before stating the theorem, we need to review jet spaces. For simplicity, we consider the functional space $C^\infty(\boldsymbol{R}^m, \boldsymbol{R}^k)$. Then the r-jet space on $\boldsymbol{R}^m \times \boldsymbol{R}^k$ denoted by $J^r(\boldsymbol{R}^m, \boldsymbol{R}^k)$ is defined as the disjoint union $\bigcup_{(x,y)\in\boldsymbol{R}^m\times\boldsymbol{R}^k} J^r(\boldsymbol{R}^m, \boldsymbol{R}^k)_{(x,y)}$ where an equivalent class $J^r(\boldsymbol{R}^m, \boldsymbol{R}^k)_{(x,y)}$ consists of all the maps in $C^\infty(\boldsymbol{R}^m, \boldsymbol{R}^k)$ which carry x to y and have the same partial derivatives at x up to r-th order (see definition 6.1). Recall that $J^r(\boldsymbol{R}^m, \boldsymbol{R}^k)$ is identified with $\boldsymbol{R}^m \times \boldsymbol{R}^k \times J^r(m, k)$ where $J^r(m, k)$ is substantially equal to $\boldsymbol{R}^q$ where $q = k(_{m+r}C_r - 1)$ (see proposition 6.1). Thus $J^r(\boldsymbol{R}^m, \boldsymbol{R}^k)$ itself is considered to be a manifold.

In this connection, there is another important concept; that is, the r-jet extension j^r, which associates each map $f \in C^\infty(\boldsymbol{R}^m, \boldsymbol{R}^k)$ with the map $j^r f : \boldsymbol{R}^m \to J^r(\boldsymbol{R}^m, \boldsymbol{R}^k)$ that carries $x \in \boldsymbol{R}^m$ to $j^r f(x)$ (the r-jet of f at x). We should point out that the above arguments hold for the case in which $\boldsymbol{R}^m$ and $\boldsymbol{R}^k$ are respectively replaced by M (m-dimensional manifold) and K (k-dimensional manifold).

Now we are in a position to state the Thom transversality theorem. First we deal with the case in which the functional space is given the compact open C^∞ topology.

Theorem 8.2 *Let M, K be manifolds and Q be a submanifold of the r-jet space $J^r(M, K)$. Then the set*

$$\{f \in C^\infty(M, K) \mid j^r f : M \to J^r(M, K) \ (the \ r-jet \ extension \ of \ f)$$
$$is \ transversal \ to \ Q\}$$

is dense in $C^\infty(M, K)$ in the compact open C^∞ topology.

Proof.   We may confine ourselves to the case in which $M = \boldsymbol{R}^m$ and $K = \boldsymbol{R}^k$ without loss of generality.

Set $M = \boldsymbol{R}^m$, $N = J^r(\boldsymbol{R}^m, \boldsymbol{R}^k)$, $G = C^\infty(\boldsymbol{R}^m, \boldsymbol{R}^k)$ and $j = j^r$ in lemma 8.2. As for P in the lemma, we may choose the set of polynomial maps $P(m, k; r)$ from $\boldsymbol{R}^m$ to $\boldsymbol{R}^k$ up to degree r, which constitutes a manifold identified with $\boldsymbol{R}^l$ where $l = {}_{k_{m+r}}C_r$. Then for any given $f \in C^\infty(\boldsymbol{R}^m, \boldsymbol{R}^k)$, set $p_0 = 0 \in P(m, k; r)$ and define $\varphi : P(m, k; r) \to C^\infty(\boldsymbol{R}^m, \boldsymbol{R}^k)$ as follows.

$$\varphi(p)(x) = p(x) + f(x).$$

It is easily seen that φ is continuous in the compact open C^∞ topology. Furthermore, the map $\Phi : P(m, k; r) \times \boldsymbol{R}^m \to J^r(\boldsymbol{R}^m, \boldsymbol{R}^k)$ defined by $\Phi(p, x) = j(\varphi(p))(x) = j^r(p + f)(x)$ is smooth, and moreover, a submersion because for fixed x the map substantially represents an affine transformation of p. Thus Φ is transversal to Q, which immediately leads to the desired consequence according to lemma 8.2. $\square$

We can also obtain the same theorem for the case in which the functional space is given the Whitney C^∞ topology. To prove this, we can follow the same method as above *with one exception.* The trouble is that the map φ chosen in the above proof is *not* continuous in the Whitney C^∞ topology. In fact, even if $p \to p^*$, $p(x) + f(x)$ can be indefinitely far away from $p^*(x) + f(x)$ at infinity of x. Therefore we need to modify the map φ, which necessarily requires other considerations. Consequently the full proof is tedious, thus we only give a sketch of it.

Theorem 8.3   *Let M, K be manifolds and Q be a submanifold of the r-jet space $J^r(M, K)$. Then the set*

$$\{f \in C^\infty(M, K) \mid j^r f : M \to J^r(M, K) \ (the \ r - jet \ extension \ of \ f)$$
$$is \ transversal \ to \ Q\}$$

is dense in $C^\infty(M, K)$ in the Whitney C^∞ topology.

Proof.   Here is a sketch of the proof. As before, we may concentrate on the case in which $M = \boldsymbol{R}^m$ and $K = \boldsymbol{R}^k$. The point of proof consists in the use of lemma 8.2 along with the Baire property of $C^\infty(\boldsymbol{R}^m, \boldsymbol{R}^k)$ in the Whitney C^∞ topology.

To begin with, set $Z = \{f \in C^\infty(\boldsymbol{R}^m, \boldsymbol{R}^k) \mid j^r f \text{ is transversal to } Q\}$.

(1) First observe that there exists a countable compact covering $\{K_j\}$ of Q; that is, $Q = \cup_{j=1}^\infty K_j$, where K_j is compact in $J^r(\boldsymbol{R}^m, \boldsymbol{R}^k)$ for

each j. This is because $J^r(\boldsymbol{R}^m, \boldsymbol{R}^k)$ is, after all, considered to be a finite dimensional Euclidean space.

(2) Set $Z_j = \{f \in C^\infty(\boldsymbol{R}^m, \boldsymbol{R}^k) \mid j^r f$ *is transversal to* Q *on* $K_j\}$ where '$j^r f$ is transversal to Q on K_j' means that

$$dj^r f_x(\boldsymbol{R}^m) + T_{j^r f(x)} Q = T_{j^r f(x)}(J^r(\boldsymbol{R}^m, \boldsymbol{R}^k))$$

for all x for which $j^r f(x) \in Q$. Note that $Z = \bigcap_{j=1}^\infty Z_j$.

(3) We show that Z_j is open and dense in $C^\infty(\boldsymbol{R}^m, \boldsymbol{R}^k)$ in the Whitney C^∞ topology for all j. First, to show the openness of Z_j, consider the set $\tilde{Z}_j$ defined as follows.

$$\{g \in C^\infty(\boldsymbol{R}^m, J^r(\boldsymbol{R}^m, \boldsymbol{R}^k)) \mid g \text{ is transversal to } Q \text{ on } K_j\}.$$

In general, we have that for any two manifolds X, Y and a submanifold $W \subset Y$, if W is closed in Y, then the set

$$\{f \in C^\infty(X, Y) \mid f \text{ is transversal to } W\}$$

is open in $C^\infty(X, Y)$ in the Whitney C^∞ topology (see Golubitsky and Guillemin (1973), Chap II, proposition 4.5).

Since K_j is closed and contained in Q, this claim can be easily applied to show that $\tilde{Z}_j$ is open. Obviously $Z_j = (j^r)^{-1}(\tilde{Z}_j)$, which implies that Z_j is open since the map $j^r : C^\infty(\boldsymbol{R}^m, \boldsymbol{R}^k) \to C^\infty(\boldsymbol{R}^m, J^r(\boldsymbol{R}^m, \boldsymbol{R}^k))$ is continuous in the Whitney C^∞ topology (see proposition 6.5).

(4) Secondly we show the density of Z_j. To this end, first consider the projection $\pi : J^r(\boldsymbol{R}^m, \boldsymbol{R}^k) \to \boldsymbol{R}^m$ and take $\pi(K_j)$ which is obviously compact in $\boldsymbol{R}^m$. Then there exists a smooth map $\rho_j : \boldsymbol{R}^m \to \boldsymbol{R}$ such that $\rho_j(x) = 1$ for all x in a neighborhood of $\pi(K_j)$ and that $\rho_j(x) = 0$ for all x outside a compact subset including $\pi(K_j)$. Define the map $\varphi_j : P(m, k; r) \to C^\infty(\boldsymbol{R}^m, \boldsymbol{R}^k)$ as follows.

$$\varphi_j(p)(x) = \rho_j(x)p(x) + f(x).$$

Then it is easily seen that φ_j is continuous in the Whitney C^∞ topology. Thus, lemma 8.2 is readily adapted to show that Z_j is dense in $C^\infty(\boldsymbol{R}^m, \boldsymbol{R}^k)$ in the Whitney C^∞ topology.

(5) Since $C^\infty(\boldsymbol{R}^m, \boldsymbol{R}^n)$ is a Baire space in the Whitney C^∞ topology (see proposition 6.3), we obtain that $Z \ (= \bigcap_{j=1}^\infty Z_j)$ is dense in $C^\infty(\boldsymbol{R}^m, \boldsymbol{R}^n)$ in the Whitney C^∞ topology. $\qquad\square$

The Thom transversality theorem can be seen from a viewpoint of a family of maps as follows.

Let's consider j^r to be a family of maps parameterized by a smooth map; that is, $j^r : C^\infty(M, K) \times M \to J^r(M, K)$ which carries (f, x) to $j^r f(x)$. For convenience we write $j_f^r(x)$ in place of $j^r f(x)$. Then, the theorem says that for almost all f, $j_f^r : M \to J^r(M, K)$ is transversal to a submanifold Q in K. It is worth noting that in contrast to the transversality theorem provided in the preceding subsection, this claim holds without any condition for the family of maps j^r (although the continuity of j^r is assured (see proposition 6.5)). This observation is particularly suggestive when we consider the following consequence derived from the Thom transversality theorem, which is often called the elementary transversality theorem.

Corollary 8.1   *Let M, K be manifolds and Q be a submanifold of K. Then the set*

$$\{f \in C^\infty(M, K) \mid f \text{ is transversal to } Q\}$$

is dense in $C^\infty(M, K)$ in both the compact C^∞ topology and the Whitney C^∞ topology.

Proof.   Let r be 0 and Q be $M \times Q$ in the Thom transversality theorem. Then the theorem immediately leads to the claim. $\square$

Note that if Q is closed, then the set in the corollary is also open (see (3) in the proof of theorem 8.3).

This corollary generalizes the transversality theorem in the preceding subsection in the sense that the former is concerned with all smooth maps, whereas the latter is only concerned with parameterized smooth maps; thus, the claim of the latter is inferable from the former.

Finally a remark from the viewpoint of application is in order. As is shown through the above arguments, the Thom transversality theorem (theorems 8.2 and 8.3) is basically a special case of the fundamental lemma (lemma 8.2), which is, however, just the reason that the theorem is important for our practical purposes. To be precise, the theorem is useful for our economical analysis not only because it is concerned with a family of maps accompanying a functional space as its parametric space, but also because the family of maps in the theorem involves the derivatives of a parametric function. We shall see the meaning of this statement in 8.2 (esp. 8.2.2).

8.1.3 *Some Modifications of Transversality Theorems*

Before proceeding to our economical analysis, we need to partly modify the above theorems for the application. This is because we are required to consider multiple parameters at a time when considering the trade among many agents.

To begin with, we are concerned with the case in which each parameter is an element of each manifold.

Let's consider s parameters $p_1, \ldots, p_s$ each of which belongs to each manifold P_i $(i = 1, \ldots, s)$ and specifies a smooth map from M to K denoted by f_{p_i} $(i = 1, \ldots, s)$. Then we obtain the following claim similar to theorem 8.1 (the transversality theorem).

Proposition 8.1 *Let M^s, $\prod_{i=1}^{s} P_i$ and K^s be s-products of M, P_i and K respectively. Let Q be a submanifold of K^s. If a smooth map $F : \prod_{i=1}^{s} P_i \times M^s \to K^s$ defined by*

$$F(p_1, \ldots, p_s, x_1, \ldots, x_s) = (f_{p_1}(x_1), \ldots, f_{p_s}(x_s))$$

is transversal to Q, then the set

$$\{(p_1, \ldots, p_s) \in \prod_{i=1}^{s} P_i \mid f_{p_1} \times \ldots \times f_{p_s} : M^s \to K^s \text{ is transversal to } Q\}$$

is dense in $\prod_{i=1}^{s} P_i$ where $f_{p_1} \times \ldots \times f_{p_s} : M^s \to K^s$ is defined by $f_{p_1} \times \ldots \times f_{p_s}(x_1, \ldots, x_s) = (f_{p_1}(x_1), \ldots, f_{p_s}(x_s))$.

Proof. For simplicity, we write $\boldsymbol{p} = (p_1, \ldots, p_s)$, $\boldsymbol{x} = (x_1, \ldots, x_s)$ and $F\boldsymbol{p}(\boldsymbol{x}) = F(\boldsymbol{p}, \boldsymbol{x})$. Obviously $F\boldsymbol{p} = f_{p_1} \times \ldots \times f_{p_s}$.

As for the smooth map F, we have

$$dF_{(\boldsymbol{p},\boldsymbol{x})}(T_{(\boldsymbol{p},\boldsymbol{x})}(\prod_{i=1}^{s} P_i \times M^s)) = dF_{(\boldsymbol{p},\boldsymbol{x})}(\prod_{i=1}^{s} T_{(p_i,x_i)}(P_i \times x_i))$$
$$+ dF_{(\boldsymbol{p},\boldsymbol{x})}(\prod_{i=1}^{s} T_{(p_i,x_i)}(p_i \times M)).$$

On the other hand, regarding $F\boldsymbol{p}$, we obtain

$$dF\boldsymbol{p},\boldsymbol{x}(T\boldsymbol{x}M^s) = dF_{(\boldsymbol{p},\boldsymbol{x})}(\prod_{i=1}^{s} T_{(p_i,x_i)}(p_i \times M)).$$

Here we consider the projection $\pi : \prod_{i=1}^{s} P_i \times M^s \to \prod_{i=1}^{s} P_i$. Then obviously we have

$$d\pi_{(\boldsymbol{p},\boldsymbol{x})}(\prod_{i=1}^{s} T_{(p_i,x_i)}(p_i \times M) + T_{(\boldsymbol{p},\boldsymbol{x})}(F^{-1}(Q))) = d\pi_{(\boldsymbol{p},\boldsymbol{x})}(T_{(\boldsymbol{p},\boldsymbol{x})}(F^{-1}(Q))).$$

Noting those observations, we are allowed to follow the same way as in lemma 7.1 to show that the set

$$\{(p_1,\ldots,p_s) \in \prod_{i=1}^{s} P_i \mid f_{p_1} \times \ldots \times f_{p_s} : M^s \to K^s \text{ is transversal to } Q\}$$

is equal to the set

$$\{(p_1,\ldots,p_s) \in \prod_{i=1}^{s} P_i \mid (p_1,\ldots,p_s) \text{ is a regular value of } \pi|_{F^{-1}(Q)}\}.$$

Hence, through Sard's theorem, we obtain the desired result. $\square$

Secondly, we consider the case in which the parameter consists of multiple smooth functions. Specifically, we try to substitute $C^\infty(M,K)^s$ for $C^\infty(M,K)$ in the Thom transversality theorem where $C^\infty(M,K)^s$ designates the s-product of $C^\infty(M,K)$. To this end, let $J^r(M,K)^s$ be the s-product of $J^r(M,K)$ and j_s^r be the map from $C^\infty(M,K)^s$ to $C^\infty(M^s, J^r(M,K)^s)$ defined by $j_s^r(f_1,\ldots,f_s)(x_1,\ldots,x_s) = (j^r f_1(x_1),\ldots,j^r f_s(x_s))$. Then we have the following claim.

Proposition 8.2 *Let M, K be manifolds and Q be a submanifold of $J^r(M,K)^s$. Then the set*

$$\{(f_1,\ldots,f_s) \in C^\infty(M,K)^s \mid j_s^r(f_1,\ldots,f_s) : M^s \to J^r(M,K)^s$$
$$\text{is transversal to } Q\}$$

is dense in $C^\infty(M,K)^s$ in both the compact open C^∞ topology and the Whitney C^∞ topology.

Proof. We shall only prove the claim in the case of the compact open C^∞ topology. As for the Whitney C^∞ topology, we can follow a similar procedure to the one provided in the proof of theorem 8.3.

We deal with the case in which $M = \boldsymbol{R}^m$ and $K = \boldsymbol{R}^k$ as usual.

Set $M = \boldsymbol{R}^{ms}$, $N = J^r(\boldsymbol{R}^m, \boldsymbol{R}^k)^s$, $G = C^\infty(\boldsymbol{R}^m, \boldsymbol{R}^k)^s$, $j = j_s^r$ and $P = P(m,k;r)^s$ in lemma 8.2 where $P = P(m,k;r)^s$ is the s-product of the set of polynomial maps $P(m,k;r)$ from $\boldsymbol{R}^m$ to $\boldsymbol{R}^k$ up to degree r. For any given $(f_1, \ldots, f_s) \in C^\infty(\boldsymbol{R}^m, \boldsymbol{R}^k)^s$, set $p_0 = 0 \in P(m, k; r)^s$ and define the map $\varphi : P = P(m, k; r)^s \to C^\infty(\boldsymbol{R}^m, \boldsymbol{R}^k)^s$ as follows.

$$\varphi(p_1, \ldots, p_s)(x_1, \ldots, x_s) = (p_1(x_1) + f_1(x_1), \ldots, p_s(x_s) + f_s(x_s)),$$

which is obviously continuous in the compact open C^∞ topology. Then the map $\Phi : P(m, k; r)^s \times \boldsymbol{R}^{ms} \to J^r(\boldsymbol{R}^m, \boldsymbol{R}^k)^s$ defined by $\Phi(p_1, \ldots, p_s, x_1, \ldots, x_s) = j(\varphi(p_1, \ldots, p_s))(x_1, \ldots, x_s) = (j^r(p_1 + f_1)(x_1), \ldots, j^r(p_s + f_s)(x_s))$ is smooth, and moreover, a submersion, thus lemma 8.2 immediately yields the desired outcome. $\qquad\square$

8.2 Economical Analysis

Now recall our economical issue declared in 7.2.1. In our enlarged framework, an economy consists of two components; that is, all agents' utility functions $(u^1, \ldots, u^I)$ denoted by u and all agents' initial endowments $(\omega^1, \ldots, \omega^I)$ denoted by ω. An economy (u, ω) is said to be a regular economy if $F_{(u,\omega)} : \boldsymbol{R}_{++}^{LI} \times S \to S^{I+1} \times \boldsymbol{R}^{I-1} \times \boldsymbol{R}^L$ is transversal to $\Delta \times 0$ where the map $F_{(u,\omega)}$ is defined by

$$\begin{aligned}
F_{(u,\omega)}((\boldsymbol{x}^i)_i, \boldsymbol{p}) = (\,&du_{\boldsymbol{x}^1}^1 / \|du_{\boldsymbol{x}^1}^1\|, \ldots, du_{\boldsymbol{x}^I}^I / \|du_{\boldsymbol{x}^I}^I\|, \boldsymbol{p}, \\
&\boldsymbol{p} \cdot \boldsymbol{x}^1 - \boldsymbol{p} \cdot \boldsymbol{\omega}^1, \ldots, \boldsymbol{p} \cdot \boldsymbol{x}^{I-1} - \boldsymbol{p} \cdot \boldsymbol{\omega}^{I-1}, \\
&\sum_i^I \boldsymbol{x}^i - \sum_i^I \boldsymbol{\omega}^i)
\end{aligned}$$

and $\Delta = \{(\boldsymbol{s}_1, \ldots, \boldsymbol{s}_{I+1}) \in S^{I+1} \mid \boldsymbol{s}_1 = \ldots = \boldsymbol{s}_{I+1}\}$ (see definition 7.4). Note that for each economy the set of extended equilibria (including all the true equilibria) is represented by the preimage $F^{-1}(\Delta \times 0)$ of $\Delta \times 0$, where $0 \in \boldsymbol{R}^{I-1+L}$. As we have shown, if an economy is regular, then the preimage $F^{-1}(\Delta \times 0)$ is a 0 dimensional manifold, thus the set of extended equilibria is locally unique (see theorem 7.2).

Our task here is to investigate the position regular economies occupy in the space of economies. We shall take two steps toward the goal.

8.2.1 *The Transversality Theorem and Regular Economies*

We will take two parametric spaces one by one.

First fix u of $F_{(u,\omega)}$ and only consider ω. Then $F_{(u,\omega)}$ can be seen to be a smooth family of maps with ω as a parameter, which we denote $\hat{F}_\omega$ in the following. In this case, our task is to investigate to what extent ω can be qualified as a regular economy. More specifically, we have to determine how many ω's can make $\hat{F}_\omega$ transversal to $\Delta \times 0$. Since ω consists of I vectors (i.e. $\omega^1, \ldots, \omega^I$), we are allowed to rely on proposition 8.1 in order to cope with this problem. For convenience, we write $\hat{F}(\omega, (\boldsymbol{x}^i)_i, \boldsymbol{p})$ in place of $\hat{F}_\omega((\boldsymbol{x}^i)_i, \boldsymbol{p})$, thus $\hat{F}$ is literally a smooth family of maps from $\boldsymbol{R}_{++}^{LI} \times \boldsymbol{R}_{++}^{LI} \times S$ to $S^{I+1} \times \boldsymbol{R}^{I-1} \times \boldsymbol{R}^L$.

However, in view of the construction of $\hat{F}$, we would not be able to use proposition 8.1 successfully without any condition on a given u. In fact, it is not hard to specify u so as to violate the proposition.

In order to consider an appropriate condition on u, let's extract the relevant part to u from $\hat{F}$ and construct the map $v_u : \boldsymbol{R}_{++}^{LI} \to S^I$ as follows.

$$v_u(\boldsymbol{x}^1, \ldots, \boldsymbol{x}^I) = (du_{\boldsymbol{x}^1}^1/\|du_{\boldsymbol{x}^1}^1\|, \ldots, du_{\boldsymbol{x}^I}^I/\|du_{\boldsymbol{x}^I}^I\|).$$

Since our original issue is the transversality of $\hat{F}$ to $\Delta \times 0$, we are properly inspired to consider the relation of v_u to $\hat{\Delta}$ where $\hat{\Delta}$ is the diagonal set of S^I. In this connection, we impose the following assumption on a given u.

Assumption 8.1 For a given u, the map v_u is transversal to $\hat{\Delta}$.

Let's consider the map $\tilde{v}_u : \boldsymbol{R}_{++}^{LI} \times S \to S^{I+1}$ given by $\tilde{v}_u(x, \boldsymbol{p}) = (v_u(x), \boldsymbol{p})$. For this map that can be seen as an expanded form of v_u, we have the following claim.

Lemma 8.3 *If u satisfies assumption 8.1, then $\tilde{v}_u$ is transversal to Δ in S^{I+1}.*

Proof. For simplicity, we set $x = (\boldsymbol{x}^1, \ldots, \boldsymbol{x}^I)$ in the following.

According to the definition of the transversality, we shall show that for any point $(x, \boldsymbol{p}) \in \tilde{v}_u^{-1}(\Delta)$

$$(dv_{u,x} \times I)(T_{(x,\boldsymbol{p})}(\boldsymbol{R}_{++}^{LI}) \times T_{\boldsymbol{p}}S) + T_y\Delta = T_{v_u(x)}S^I \times T_{\boldsymbol{p}}S$$

where I designates the identity map as usual and $y = \tilde{v}_u(x, \boldsymbol{p})$.

Set $V = \{\boldsymbol{x} \in \boldsymbol{R}^L \mid x_1 + \ldots + x_L = 0\}$. We may consider V to be a tangent space to S, which can be commonly used at every point of S. It suffices to show that

$$T_{v_u(x)}S^I \times T_{\boldsymbol{p}}S \subset (dv_{u,x} \times I)(T_{(x,\boldsymbol{p})}(\boldsymbol{R}_{++}^{LI}) \times T_{\boldsymbol{p}}S) + T_y\Delta.$$

Pick an arbitrary point $(s^1, \ldots, s^{I+1}) \in T_{v_u(x)} S^I \times T_{\boldsymbol{p}} S$. Since v_u is transversal to $\hat{\Delta}$, there exists $(\boldsymbol{c}^1, \ldots, \boldsymbol{c}^I) \in \boldsymbol{R}^{LI}$ and $\boldsymbol{a} \in V$ such that $dv_{u,x}(\boldsymbol{c}^1, \ldots, \boldsymbol{c}^I) + (\boldsymbol{a}, \ldots, \boldsymbol{a}) = (\boldsymbol{s}^1, \ldots, \boldsymbol{s}^I)$ where $(\boldsymbol{a}, \ldots, \boldsymbol{a})$ denotes I-sets of $\boldsymbol{a}$. Note that $T_{(x,\boldsymbol{p})}(\boldsymbol{R}_{++}^{LI}) = \boldsymbol{R}^{LI}$ and that $(\boldsymbol{a}, \ldots, \boldsymbol{a}) \in T_{v_u(x)}\hat{\Delta}$. Set $\boldsymbol{b} = \boldsymbol{s}^{I+1} - \boldsymbol{a}$. Obviously $\boldsymbol{b} \in V$, thus $\boldsymbol{b}$ can be considered an element of $T_{\boldsymbol{p}} S$. Then we have

$$dv_{u,x}(\boldsymbol{c}^1, \ldots, \boldsymbol{c}^I) \times I(\boldsymbol{b}) + (\boldsymbol{a}, \ldots, \boldsymbol{a}) \times \boldsymbol{a} = (\boldsymbol{s}^1, \ldots, \boldsymbol{s}^I) \times \boldsymbol{s}^{I+1}.$$

Since $(\boldsymbol{s}^1, \ldots, \boldsymbol{s}^{I+1})$ is arbitrarily chosen, the lemma is proved. $\qquad\square$

Proposition 8.3 *If u satisfies assumption 8.1, then for almost all ω's in $\boldsymbol{R}_{++}^{LI}$, (u, ω) is a regular economy.*

Proof. It suffices for us to show that $\hat{F}$ is transversal to $\Delta \times 0$. In fact, if this is the case, then proposition 8.1 immediately leads to the claim.

Let $(\bar{\omega}, \bar{x}, \bar{\boldsymbol{p}})$ be an arbitrary element of $\hat{F}^{-1}(\Delta \times 0)$. We should show that the following equation holds for $(\bar{\omega}, \bar{x}, \bar{\boldsymbol{p}})$.

$$d\hat{F}_{(\bar{\omega}, \bar{x}, \bar{\boldsymbol{p}})}(T_{\bar{\omega}}(\boldsymbol{R}_{++}^{LI}) \times T_{\bar{x}}(\boldsymbol{R}_{++}^{LI}) \times T_{\bar{\boldsymbol{p}}} S) + T_{\hat{F}(\bar{\omega}, \bar{x}, \bar{\boldsymbol{p}})}(\Delta \times 0)$$
$$= T_{\hat{F}(\bar{\omega}, \bar{x}, \bar{\boldsymbol{p}})}(S^{I+1} \times \boldsymbol{R}^{I-1} \times \boldsymbol{R}^L). \qquad \cdots (*)$$

Let $\mu : \boldsymbol{R}_{++}^{LI} \times \boldsymbol{R}_{++}^{LI} \times S \to \boldsymbol{R}^{I-1} \times \boldsymbol{R}^L$ be the map given by

$$\mu(\omega, x, \boldsymbol{p}) = \boldsymbol{p} \cdot \boldsymbol{x}^{I-1} - \boldsymbol{p} \cdot \boldsymbol{\omega}^{I-1} \sum_i^I \boldsymbol{x}^i - \sum_i^I \boldsymbol{\omega}^i.$$

Then we have that $\hat{F}(\omega, x, \boldsymbol{p}) = (\tilde{v}_u(x, \boldsymbol{p}), \mu(\omega, x, \boldsymbol{p}))$ and that $d\hat{F}_{(\omega, x, \boldsymbol{p})} = (d\tilde{v}_{u,(x,\boldsymbol{p})}, d\mu_{(\omega, x, \boldsymbol{p})})$. Under assumption 8.1, lemma 8.3 assures that

$$d\tilde{v}_{u,(\bar{x}, \bar{\boldsymbol{p}})}(T_{\bar{x}}(\boldsymbol{R}_{++}^{LI}) \times T_{\bar{\boldsymbol{p}}} S) + T_{\bar{y}}\Delta = T_{\bar{y}} S^{I+1}$$

where $\bar{y} = \tilde{v}_u(\bar{x}, \bar{\boldsymbol{p}})$. Thus, in order to show the validity of equation $(*)$, we have only to establish the following equation.

$$d\mu_{(\bar{\omega}, \bar{x}, \bar{\boldsymbol{p}})}(T_{\bar{\omega}}(\boldsymbol{R}_{++}^{LI}) \times T_{\bar{x}}(\boldsymbol{R}_{++}^{LI}) \times T_{\bar{\boldsymbol{p}}} S) = T_{\mu(\bar{\omega}, \bar{x}, \bar{\boldsymbol{p}})}(\boldsymbol{R}^{I-1} \times \boldsymbol{R}^L).$$

Note that $T_{\mu(\bar{\omega}, \bar{x}, \bar{\boldsymbol{p}})}(\boldsymbol{R}^{I-1} \times \boldsymbol{R}^L) = \boldsymbol{R}^{I-1} \times \boldsymbol{R}^L$.

The part of the derivative $d\mu_{(\bar{\omega},\bar{x},\bar{p})}$ relevant to $T_{\bar{\omega}}(\boldsymbol{R}_{++}^{LI})$ $(= \boldsymbol{R}^{LI})$ can be, by computation, represented by the following $(I - 1 + L) \times LI$ matrix.

$$
\left(
\begin{array}{ccccccccccc|c}
-p_1 & \cdots & -p_L & 0 & \cdots & \cdots & \cdots & \cdots & \cdots & & 0 & \\
0 & \cdots & 0 & -p_1 & \cdots & -p_L & 0 & \cdots & \cdots & & 0 & \mathcal{O} \\
\vdots & \vdots & \vdots & \vdots & \vdots & \vdots & \ddots & \vdots & \vdots & & \vdots & \\
0 & \cdots & \cdots & \cdots & \cdots & \cdots & 0 & -p_1 & \cdots & & -p_L & \\
\hline
\multicolumn{3}{c}{-\mathcal{I}} & \multicolumn{3}{c}{-\mathcal{I}} & \multicolumn{3}{c}{\cdots} & \multicolumn{2}{c|}{-\mathcal{I}} & -\mathcal{I}
\end{array}
\right)
$$

where $\mathcal{O}$ indicates a $(I - 1) \times L$ null matrix and $\mathcal{I}$ designates the identity matrix of order L.

It is easily seen that we can take the following square matrix of $(I - 1 + L)$-order out of the above one.

$$
\left(
\begin{array}{cccc|c}
-p_1 & 0 & \cdots & 0 & \\
0 & -p_1 & \cdots & 0 & \mathcal{O} \\
\vdots & \vdots & \ddots & \vdots & \\
0 & \cdots & \cdots & -p_1 & \\
\hline
-1 & -1 & \cdots & -1 & \\
0 & 0 & \cdots & 0 & -\mathcal{I} \\
\vdots & \vdots & \ddots & \vdots & \\
0 & 0 & \cdots & 0 &
\end{array}
\right)
$$

which is obviously nonsingular. Thus the derivative $d\mu_{(\bar{\omega},\bar{x},\bar{p})}$ is surjective, which completes the proof. $\square$

8.2.2   *Thom Transversality Theorem and Regular Economies*

Now we are in the final stage. It remains to be shown to what extent u as a parameter can contribute to the generation of a regular economy. Proposition 8.3 tells us that it depends on whether or not the map v_u is transversal to $\hat{\Delta}$.

Therefore, it turns out that our central issue is how many u's can make v_u transversal to $\hat{\Delta}$. To deal with this problem, we are allowed to rely on the Thom transversality theorem. Before proceeding, however, some preliminary lemmas should be prepared for our successful use of the theorem.

Lemma 8.4   *A smooth map $g : R_{++}^{LI} \to S^I$ given by*

$$g(x^1, \ldots, x^I) = (x^1/\|x^1\|, \ldots, x^I/\|x^I\|)$$

is a submersion.

Proof.   This claim is trivial since it can be easily seen from computation that the map $\tilde{g} : R_{++}^L \to S$ given by $\tilde{g}(x) = x/\|x\|$ is a submersion. $\square$

Lemma 8.5   *Let X, Y and Z be manifolds and $W \subset Z$ be a submanifold of Z. Let $f : X \to Y$ and $h : Y \to Z$ be smooth maps. Suppose that h is a submersion. Then, if f is transversal to $h^{-1}(W)$, $h \circ f$ is transversal to W.*

Proof.   First note that $h^{-1}(W)$ is a submanifold of Y because of the transversality of h to W. Since f is transversal to $h^{-1}(W)$, for any $x \in (h \circ f)^{-1}(W)$ we have

$$df_x(T_x X) + T_{f(x)}(h^{-1}(W)) = T_{f(x)} Y. \tag{8.4}$$

On the other hand, $f(x)$ belongs to $h^{-1}(W)$ for this x, thus we also have

$$dh_{f(x)}(T_{f(x)} Y) + T_{h \circ f(x)} W = T_{h \circ f(x)} Z \tag{8.5}$$

and

$$dh_{f(x)}(T_{f(x)}(h^{-1}(W))) = T_{h \circ f(x)} W. \tag{8.6}$$

Applying $dh_{f(x)}$ to both sides of (8.4) leads to

$$dh_{f(x)} \circ df_x(T_x X) + dh_{f(x)}(T_{f(x)}(h^{-1}(W))) = dh_{f(x)}(T_{f(x)} Y),$$

which turns out through (8.6) to

$$dh_{f(x)} \circ df_x(T_x X) + T_{h \circ f(x)} W = dh_{f(x)}(T_{f(x)} Y).$$

Adding $T_{h \circ f(x)} W$ to both sides of this equation and noting (8.5), we have

$$dh_{f(x)} \circ df_x(T_x X) + T_{h \circ f(x)} W = T_{h \circ f(x)} Z,$$

which implies that $h \circ f$ is transversal to W since $x \in (h \circ f)^{-1}(W)$ is arbitrarily chosen. $\square$

Now we turn to the application of the Thom transversality theorem. Recall that it is the transversality of v_u to $\hat{\Delta}$ that matters. Since v_u only involves first order derivatives of $u^i : R_{++}^L \to R$ $(i = 1, \ldots, I)$, we properly consider the 1-jet space $J^1(R_{++}^L, R)$.

Note that in our context the parametric space consists of I-product of U; that is, $C^\infty(\boldsymbol{R}^L_{++}, \boldsymbol{R})^I$. Thus, in view of the Thom transversality theorem (esp. proposition 8.2), the key map to be considered is as follows.

$$j^1_I : C^\infty(\boldsymbol{R}^L_{++}, \boldsymbol{R})^I \to C^\infty(\boldsymbol{R}^{LI}_{++}, J^1(\boldsymbol{R}^L_{++}, \boldsymbol{R})^I)$$
$$j^1_I(u^1, \ldots, u^I)(\boldsymbol{x}^1, \ldots, \boldsymbol{x}^I) = (j^1 u^1(\boldsymbol{x}^1), \ldots, j^1 u^I(\boldsymbol{x}^I)).$$

In fact, we are able to illuminate the structure of the set of u that yields the transversality of v_u to $\hat{\Delta}$ by making use of the map j^1_I.

Proposition 8.4   *There exists a dense set in U^I such that for any u in the dense set v_u is transversal to $\hat{\Delta}$.*

Proof.   First note that a representative element of $J^1(\boldsymbol{R}^L_{++}, \boldsymbol{R})^I$ can be written by $(\boldsymbol{x}^1, y^1, \boldsymbol{z}^1, \ldots, \boldsymbol{x}^I, y^I, \boldsymbol{z}^I)$. Let $\eta : J^1(\boldsymbol{R}^L_{++}, \boldsymbol{R})^I \to S^I$ be the map given by

$$\eta(\boldsymbol{x}^1, y^1, \boldsymbol{z}^1, \ldots, \boldsymbol{x}^I, y^I, \boldsymbol{z}^I) = (\boldsymbol{z}^1/\|\boldsymbol{z}^1\|, \ldots, \boldsymbol{z}^I/\|\boldsymbol{z}^I\|).$$

Then, it is easily seen that v_u is equal to $\eta \circ j^1_I(u)$ for each $u \in C^\infty(\boldsymbol{R}^L_{++}, \boldsymbol{R})^I$. Thus, in order to see if v_u is transversal to $\hat{\Delta}$, we have only to check whether $\eta \circ j^1_I(u)$ is transversal to $\hat{\Delta}$ or not.

Since lemma 8.4 assures that η is a submersion, $\eta^{-1}(\hat{\Delta})$ is a submanifold of $J^1(\boldsymbol{R}^L_{++}, \boldsymbol{R})^I$. Hence, if $j^1_I(u)$ is transversal to $\eta^{-1}(\hat{\Delta})$, then, through lemma 8.5, $\eta \circ j^1_I(u)$ is transversal to $\hat{\Delta}$. Applying proposition 8.2, we have that the set of u making $j^1_I(u)$ transversal to $\hat{\Delta}$ is dense in $C^\infty(\boldsymbol{R}^L_{++}, \boldsymbol{R})^I$, which immediately leads to the desired conclusion. $\square$

Combining proposition 8.3 with 8.4, we reach the final statement.

Theorem 8.4   *There exists a dense set in U^I such that any u in the dense set goes hand in hand with almost all ω's in $\boldsymbol{R}^{LI}_{++}$ to form a regular economy.*

Proof.   Considering proposition 8.3, 8.4 and assumption 8.1, the claim is trivial. $\square$

According to the theorem, it turns out that however diverse both utility functions and initial endowments may be among the agents, in almost all cases we have a regular economy as along as each agent's utility function is monotone.

Chapter 9

The Number of Extended Equilibria in Regular Economies

So far we have shown that for almost all economies, the set of extended equilibria is locally unique. It is, however, worth noting that we have never referred to the finiteness of those equilibria or, more fundamentally, their existence. In this chapter, we discuss those subjects. In order to deal with this issue, we adopt a similar method to the one provided in 4.2.2. That is, we turn our attention to the modulo 2 residue class of extended equilibria so as to make use of a useful mathematical appliance to attain some fruitful consequences concerning the existence as well as the number of those equilibria.

To this end, we need a specific mathematical notion called the modulo 2 intersection number on which we give an adequate exposition in Mathematical Preliminaries. In order to apply our mathematical tools to the economical issue in question, however, some differential version of the boundary conditions proves to be necessary for utility functions.

9.1 Mathematical Preliminaries

9.1.1 *Modulo 2 Intersection Number*

The modulo 2 intersection number is the notion obtained by adjusting the modulo 2 degree to the transversality setting.

To begin with, recall how the modulo 2 degree has been given. Let M, K be manifolds and $f : M \to K$ be a smooth map. If M is compact and $dim\ M = dim\ K$, then the preimage of a regular value for f constitutes a finite set, the modulo 2 residue class of which is called the modulo 2 degree of f (see 4.1.1).

The extension of the modulo 2 degree to the case in which a submanifold takes the place of a regular value results in the modulo 2 intersection number. Note that a regular value can be seen as a special submanifold; that is, a 0-dimensional submanifold to which f is transversal.

To be precise, let Q be a closed submanifold of K. If f is transversal to Q and $dim\ M + dim\ Q = dim\ K$, then, through theorem 7.1, $f^{-1}(Q)$ is a closed 0-dimensional submanifold of M, thus a finite set. This yields the modulo 2 intersection number of f.

Definition 9.1 Let M, K be manifolds and Q be a closed submanifold of K. Let $f : M \to K$ be a smooth map. Suppose that M, K, Q and f satisfy the following conditions.

(1) M is compact.

(2) $dim\ M + dim\ Q = dim\ K$.

(3) f is trasversal to Q.

Then, the modulo 2 residue class of $f^{-1}(Q)$ is said to be the modulo 2 intersection number of f with Q, which is denoted by $I_2(f,\ Q)$.

Note that the definition allows the case in which $f^{-1}(Q)$ is empty. For such a case, $I_2(f,\ Q) = 0$.

It can easily be seen that for any two submanifolds Q, Q' of equal dimension, it does not necessarily hold that $I_2(f,\ Q) = I_2(f,\ Q')$ even if f is transversal to both submanifolds (imagine the case in which $I_2(f,\ Q) = \emptyset$ and $I_2(f,\ Q') \neq \emptyset$). Therefore, unlike the modulo 2 degree of f, the modulo 2 intersection number of f depends on a relevant submanifold. However, the other important property of the modulo 2 degree of f, that is, homotopy invariance (see proposition 4.3) does hold for the modulo 2 intersection number of f, which is crucial to our argument concerning the number of extended equilibria in regular economies. Thus, we shall provide the rigorous proof of the homotopy invariance in the following.

9.1.2 *Manifolds with Boundary and Transversality*

As we have seen in chapter 4, homotopy involves a manifold with boundary. This fact requires us to consider the transversality of a map in the setting involving a manifold with boundary. More specifically, our interest is in how the transversality version of the preimage theorem (theorem 7.1) and the transversality theorem (theorem 8.1) are altered when we allow a manifold with boundary. For simplicity of notation, if f is a map of X to Y and X is a manifold with boundary, we denote the restriction of f to the boundary ∂X by $\partial f : \partial X \to Y$ in the following.

We begin with the transversality version of the preimage theorem.

Theorem 9.1   *Let M, K be manifolds and Q be a submanifold of K where only M has boundary. Let $f : M \to K$ be a smooth map. Suppose that f is transversal to Q and that $\partial f : \partial M \to K$ is also transversal to Q. Then the preimage $f^{-1}(Q)$ is a manifold with boundary satisfying*

(1) $\partial(f^{-1}(Q)) = f^{-1}(Q) \cap \partial M$,

(2) codim $f^{-1}(Q)$ = codim Q.

Proof.   Let $dim\ M = m$, $dim\ K = k$ and $dim\ Q = q$. Considering theorem 7.1, we have only to focus on $f^{-1}(Q) \cap \partial M$. Choose any point x from $f^{-1}(Q) \cap \partial M$ and consider its neighborhood in $f^{-1}(Q)$. We may represent the neighborhood by $(\varphi \circ f)^{-1}(0)$ where φ is a submersion of a neighborhood around $f(x)$ in K to $\mathbf{R}^{k-q}$ (see the proof of theorem 7.1 where we denoted the submersion by $\bar{\varphi}$).

Let $\phi : U \to M$ be a parameterization around x where U is an open subset in H^m. Obviously $\phi^{-1}(x) \in \partial U \subset \partial H^m$. Then $(\varphi \circ f)^{-1}(0)$ is substitutable for $(\varphi \circ f \circ \phi)^{-1}(0)$ since we are only concerned with the topological structure of $(\varphi \circ f)^{-1}(0)$. Set $h = \varphi \circ f \circ \phi$.

Since h is obviously smooth, we may extend h to $\tilde{U}$ that is an open subset in $\mathbf{R}^m$ including U. Let the extension of h be $\tilde{h}$. Since f is transversal to Q, 0 is a regular value for $\tilde{h}$. Thus $\tilde{h}^{-1}(0)$ is a boundaryless manifold in $\mathbf{R}^m$, which we denote Z. Obviously $h^{-1}(0) = Z \cap H^m$. We shall show that $h^{-1}(0)$ is actually a manifold with boundary.

Let $\pi : \mathbf{R}^m \to \mathbf{R}$ be the projection given by $\pi(x_1, \ldots, x_m) = x_m$. Then we have

$$Z \cap H^m = \{x \in Z \mid \pi(z) \geq 0\}.$$

Let the restriction of π to Z be $\bar{\pi}$. Note that $\bar{\pi}^{-1}(0) = Z \cap \partial H^m$. Considering lemma 4.2, all we have to do is to show that $\bar{\pi}$ has 0 as a regular value.

Suppose that 0 is not a regular value for $\bar{\pi}$. Then there exists $z \in \bar{\pi}^{-1}(0)$ such that $d\bar{\pi}_z = 0$. Thus $d\bar{\pi}_z(T_z Z) = 0$. Noting that $T_z Z$ is a vector subspace in $\mathbf{R}^m$ and that $d\bar{\pi}_z = \pi$, the fact that $d\bar{\pi}_z(T_z Z) = 0$ implies that the last coordinate of every element of $T_z Z$ is 0; thus we obtain that $T_z Z \subset T_z(\partial H^m)$.

On the other hand, $T_z Z$ is the kernel of $d\tilde{h}_z$ since $Z = \tilde{h}^{-1}(0)$. Thus $T_z Z$ is also the kernel of dh_z. Obviously $z \in \partial U$; thus $d(\partial h)_z$ is conceivable. Note that $d(\partial h)_z$ is the restriction of dh_z to $T_z(\partial H^m)$ since ∂h is nothing but the restriction of h to ∂U $(\subset \partial H^m)$. As we have shown, $T_z Z$, which is equal to the kernel of dh_z, is included in $T_z(\partial H^m)$ and the kernel of $d(\partial h)_z$ is identical with the kernel of dh_z. Recall that both f and ∂f are transversal to Q. Thus both h and ∂h have 0 as a regular value. Noting that $h(z) = \partial h(z) = 0$ and that $dim\ T_z(\partial H^m) = m - 1$, the dimension of $Ker(dh_z)$ is $m - (k - q)$ whereas the dimension of $Ker(d(\partial h)_z)$ is $m - 1 - (k - q)$, which contradicts the above claim.

Thus we have that $h^{-1}(0)$ is a manifold with boundary, which implies that $f^{-1}(Q)$ is a manifold with boundary.

In addition, the foregoing arguments show that the boundary of $h^{-1}(0)$ is the intersection of $h^{-1}(0)$ with ∂U, which implies that $\partial(f^{-1}(Q)) = f^{-1}(Q) \cap \partial M$.

The other condition concerning the codimensions is trivial. $\qquad\square$

Note that a submanifold Q in the theorem is required to be boundary-less. If Q is a submanifold with boundary, the condition (1) in the theorem does not necessarily hold.

Now we turn to the transversality theorem involving a manifold with boundary.

Theorem 9.2 *Let $F : P \times M \to K$ be a smooth family of maps and Q be a submanifold in K where only M has boundary. If both F and ∂F are transversal to Q, then for almost all $p \in P$, both F_p and ∂F_p are transversal to Q.*

Proof. Let $W = F^{-1}(Q)$. Since $P \times M$ is a manifold with boundary, we obtain, by theorem 9.1, that W is a manifold with boundary and that $\partial W = W \cap \partial(P \times M)$. Let $\pi : P \times M \to P$ be the projection and $\tilde{\pi} : W \to P$ be the restriction of π to W. Then, we can apply substantially the same reasoning as the one provided in the proof of lemma 8.1 to show that whenever $p \in P$ is a regular value for $\tilde{\pi}$, F_p is transversal to Q and that whenever $p \in P$ is a regular value for $\partial\tilde{\pi} : \partial W \to P$, ∂F_p is transversal to Q. Since Sard's theorem assures that almost all $p \in P$ is a regular value for both π and $\tilde{\pi}$, the theorem is proved. $\qquad\square$

9.1.3 *Homotopy Invariance of the Modulo 2 Intersection Number*

Here we shall show the homotopy invariance of the modulo 2 intersection number. However, we need some lemmas to reach this goal.

Lemma 9.1 *Let M, K be manifolds and Q be a submanifold of K where only M has boundary. Then, for any smooth map $f : M \to K$, there exists a map $g : M \to K$ smoothly homotopic to f such that both g and ∂g are transversal to Q.*

Proof. Let $\boldsymbol{R}^l$ be the ambient Euclidean space of K. It is known that for K there exists a smooth positive function $\epsilon : K \to \boldsymbol{R}_{++}$ such that each point $w \in K^\epsilon$ has a unique closest point in K where K^ϵ is defined as the set $\{w \in \boldsymbol{R}^l \mid \|w - y\| < \epsilon(y) \ for \ some \ y \in K\}$. Moreover, the map that carries $w \in K^\epsilon$ to the closest point is a submersion, which we denote $\rho : K^\epsilon \to K$ (see Guillemin and Pollack (1974), Chap. 2, § 3, ϵ-neighborhood theorem).

Let B be the unit open ball in $\boldsymbol{R}^l$ and consider the map $F : M \times B \to K$ given by

$$F(x, b) = \rho(f(x) + \epsilon(f(x))b).$$

This map smoothly transfers each point $f(x)$ perturbed by $\epsilon(f(x))b$ into K. It is easily seen that for any given $x \in M$, $F(x, \cdot) : B \to K$ is a submersion. Thus, both F and ∂F are transversal to Q. Therefore, through theorem 9.2, for almost all $b \in B$, both F_b and ∂F_b are transversal to Q. Then, considering the map $H : M \times I \to K$ given by $H(x, t) = F(x, tb)$ for any b, F_b turns out to be smoothly homotopic to f. $\qquad\square$

Let M be a manifold with boundary. Since ∂M is a closed subset of M, there exists a neighborhood U of ∂M in M and a smooth function $\gamma : M \to [0, 1]$ such that

$$\gamma(x) = 0 \quad if \ x \in \partial M$$
$$0 < \gamma(x) < 1 \quad if \ x \in U \setminus \partial M$$
$$\gamma(x) = 1 \quad if \ x \notin U.$$

Such a function is easily constructed by means of a bump function (for a bump function, see Hirsch (1976), 2.2).

Lemma 9.2 *Let M, K be manifolds and Q be a submanifold of K where only M has boundary. Let $f : M \to K$ be a smooth map. If $\partial f : \partial M \to K$ is transversal to Q, then there exists a map $g : M \to K$ smoothly homotopic to f such that both g and ∂g are transversal to Q and that $g = f$ on ∂M.*

Proof. Let $\tau : M \to [0, 1]$ be a smooth function given by $\tau = \gamma^2$ where γ is the function just provided above. Let $\boldsymbol{R}^l$ be the ambient Euclidean space of K and B be the unit open ball in $\boldsymbol{R}^l$.

Consider the map $G : M \times B \to K$ given by $G(x, b) = F(x, \tau(x)b)$ where F is the map defined in the proof of lemma 9.1. We shall show that both G and ∂G are transversal to Q. We only deal with, however, the transversality of G to Q since the same reasoning is applicable for the other case.

Pick any point $(\bar{x}, \bar{b}) \in G^{-1}(Q)$ and separate the two cases as follows.

(1) $\tau(\bar{x}) \neq 0$: In this case, the map $F(\bar{x}, \tau(\bar{x})b)$ is easily shown to be a submersion with respect to b. Thus G is transversal to Q at $(\bar{x}, \bar{b})$.

(2) $\tau(\bar{x}) = 0$: In this case, $\bar{x} \in \partial M$. Thus at such a point f is transversal to Q. On the other hand, by the definition of τ, we have that $\gamma(x) = 0$ if and only if $\tau(x) = 0$ and that $d\tau_x = 2\gamma(x)d\gamma_x$. Thus $d\tau_{\bar{x}} = 0$. Then, noting that $F(x, 0) = f(x)$ since the map $\rho : K^\epsilon \to K$ turns out to be the identity map when restricted to K, it follows by computation that $dG_{(\bar{x}, \bar{b})} = df_{\bar{x}}$. Therefore, G is transversal to Q at $(\bar{x}, \bar{b})$.

Since $(\bar{x}, \bar{b})$ is arbitrarily chosen out of $G^{-1}(Q)$, we obtain that G is transversal to Q.

Then, through theorem 9.2, for almost all $b \in B$, both G_b and ∂G_b are transversal to Q. Thus, choose such a b and set $g = G_b$, which is the desired map. Indeed, $g(x) = f(x)$ if $x \in \partial M$ since $\tau(x) = 0$ for any $x \in \partial M$. As for homotopy, we may use a similar one to H in the proof of lemma 9.1. $\square$

Now we are in a position to state our main claim; that is, homotopy invariance of the modulo 2 intersection number.

Theorem 9.3 *Let M, K be manifolds and Q be a closed submanifold of K. Suppose that M, K and Q satisfy the following conditions.*

(1) M is compact.

(2) $\dim M + \dim Q = \dim K$.

Let $f_0, f_1 : M \to K$ be smooth maps both of which are transversal to Q. If f_0 and f_1 are smoothly homotopic, then $I_2(f_0, Q) = I_2(f_1, Q)$.

Proof. Let $F : M \times I \to K$ be a smooth homotopy between f_0 and f_1. Obviously $M \times I$ is a manifold with boundary whose boundary is $(M \times 0) \cup (M \times 1)$. Since ∂F consists of f_0 on $(M \times 0)$ and f_1 on $(M \times 1)$, ∂F is transversal to Q. Thus, through lemma 9.2, there exists a map $H : M \times I \to K$ smoothly homotopic to F such that both H and ∂H are transversal to Q and that $H = F$ on $\partial(M \times I)$. Note that we may substitute H for F as a smooth homotopy between f_0 and f_1. Then, through theorem 9.1, $H^{-1}(Q)$ is a manifold with boundary and for its boundary we have

$$\partial(H^{-1}(Q)) = H^{-1}(Q) \cup \partial(M \times I)$$
$$= (f_0^{-1}(Q) \times 0) \cup (f_1^{-1}(Q) \times 1).$$

Since $H^{-1}(Q)$ is a compact 1-dimensional manifold, $\partial(H^{-1}(Q))$ con-
sists of an even number of points (see lemma 4.1). Thus $\sharp f_0^{-1}(Q) = \sharp f_1^{-1}(Q)$ $(mod\ 2)$, which implies that $I_2(f_0, Q) = I_2(f_1, Q)$. $\qquad\square$

9.2 Economical Analysis

Here we discuss the number of extended equilibria in regular economies.
The basic idea for the approach is similar to the one given in chapter 4
(esp. 4.2.2). The only difference consists in using the modulo 2 intersection
number in place of the modulo 2 degree. As in chapter 4, it will turn out
that our argument reveals the existence as well as the number of extended
equilibria in regular economies.

9.2.1 *The Basic Idea and Its Attendant Considerations*

The basic idea in our approach is as follows. First, we construct a special
regular economy that possesses a unique extended equilibrium. Then choose
any regular economy. By characterizing the set of extended equilibria for
those economies by means of the modulo 2 intersection number, we are
able to relate those sets through an appropriate homotopy to determine
the number of extended equilibria for an arbitrary regular economy.

Thus, the modulo 2 intersection number and homotopy are the main
tools to investigate the number of extended equilibria in regular economies.
In applying those concepts to our economical issue, however, we have to be
cautious in some respects.

First of all, the framework of our economical issue does not allow the
direct use of the modulo 2 intersection number. It is because the relevant
manifold is not compact in our context, which is the difficulty we have
already experienced in chapter 4. Recall that we got through this difficulty
there by modifying the relevant proposition so as to allow non-compact
manifolds. We are able to follow the same procedure here. Since what will
play a crucial role in our concrete analysis is theorem 9.3, we shall alter the
theorem so as to suit our purpose.

Proposition 9.1 *Let M, K be manifolds and Q be a submanifold of K.
Suppose that $dim\ M + dim\ Q = dim\ K$. Let $f_0, f_1 : M \to K$ be smoothly
homotopic and both be transversal to Q. In addition, let a homotopy $F :
M \times I \to K$ of f_0 and f_1 be both transversal to Q. If $F^{-1}(Q)$ is a compact
1-dimensional manifold, then $I_2(f_0, Q) = I_2(f_1, Q)$.*

Proof. Since both f_0 and f_1 are transversal to Q, ∂F is transversal to Q. Thus, through theorem 9.1, the preimage $F^{-1}(Q)$ is a manifold with boundary satisfying that $\partial(F^{-1}(Q)) = F^{-1}(Q) \cap \partial(M \times I)$. Obviously $F^{-1}(Q) \cap \partial(M \times I) = (f_0^{-1}(Q) \times 0) \cup (f_1^{-1}(Q) \times 1)$. Since $F^{-1}(Q)$ is a compact 1-dimensional manifold, $\partial(F^{-1}(Q))$ consists of an even number of points. Thus $\sharp f_0^{-1}(Q) = \sharp f_1^{-1}(Q) \ (mod\ 2)$, which proves the claim. $\qquad\square$

According to the proposition, we may dispense with the compactness of relevant manifolds at the price of a special homotopy.

Secondly, the use of homotopy in our setting requires us to be concerned with a choice of an appropriate topology for U (space of utility functions), which was unnecessary in chapter 4.

In constructing a homotopy that will play a crucial role in the analysis, we make use of an arc that joins two points in the space of economies $\hat{\mathcal{E}}$. Thus, $\hat{\mathcal{E}}$ is required to be arcwise connected. However, U that makes a part of $\hat{\mathcal{E}}$ would not be arcwise connected with the Whitney C^∞ topology. Thus, we need to adopt the compact open C^∞ topology instead.

More specifically, let (u_0, ω_0) and (u_1, ω_1) be two points in $\hat{\mathcal{E}}$. These points are said to be joined by an arc if there exist two continuous maps $v : [0,1] \to U$ and $w : [0,1] \to \boldsymbol{R}_{++}^{LI}$ such that $v(0) = u_0$, $v(1) = u_1$ and $w(0) = \omega_0$, $w(1) = \omega_1$ respectively. In general, v is not continuous if U is endowed with the Whitney C^∞ topology. Indeed, it is advisable to imagine the case in which the difference between the values of u_0 and u_1 becomes unlimitedly large at infinity. In contrast, the compact open C^∞ topology allows us to have v continuous (for instance, $v(t) = tu_0 + (1-t)u_1$ is continuous in the compact open C^∞ topology).

Therefore, when we speak of a regular economy in the following, each utility function of the economy should be interpreted as an element of a dense set in the compact open C^∞ topology.

Incidentally, the homotopy H that we shall use is constructed by means of a map $h(x; v, w)$ with v, w as its parameters. That is to say,

$$h(x; v, w) = h(x; v(t), w(t)) = H(x,\ t).$$

9.2.2   The Number of Extended Equilibria in Regular Economies

Recall the key argument in 4.2.2. What enabled us to successfully obtain the fruitful consequence despite our abandonment of the compactness of relevant manifolds consisted in assumption 3.1; that is, the boundary condition of the demand function. For this analogy, it is strongly advisable to use the boundary condition of the utility function in the present subject.

We have already referred to the boundary condition of the utility function in 6.2.1, which is, however, based on the utility function without any differentiability (see assumption 6.1).

Here we present a differential version of the boundary condition concerning utility functions. For simplicity of notation, a sequence of the derivative for u with respect to $\{x\}^n$ is expressed by du_{x^n}. Accordingly, $\frac{\partial u}{\partial x_j}(x^n)$ is written by $\frac{\partial u}{\partial x_j^n}$ in the following.

Assumption 9.1 Boundary condition (differential version): For any sequence $\{x^n\}$ ($\subset R_{++}^L$) that converges to some point in $\partial R_{++}^L \setminus 0$, we have

$$lim_{n \to \infty} \frac{du_{x^n}}{\|du_{x^n}\|} \in \partial S,$$

where if $\lim_{n \to \infty} x_j^n > 0$, then

$$lim_{n \to \infty} \frac{\partial u / \partial x_j^n}{\|du_{x^n}\|} = 0.$$

This assumption asserts that the scarcer a good is, the higher the *relative* marginal utility of the good is; thus, alternatively put, the marginal utility of a good that is less scarce becomes less and less, which is just the reason that if $\lim_{n \to \infty} x_j^n > 0$, then

$$lim_{n \to \infty} \frac{\partial u / \partial x_j^n}{\|du_{x^n}\|} = 0.$$

We first show that the boundary condition assures the finiteness of extended equilibria for regular economies.

Proposition 9.2 *Under assumption 9.1, the set of extended equilibria for any regular economy is finite. Thus the set of true equilibria, if any, is also finite.*

Proof. Recall that the set of extended equilibria for any regular economy (u, ω), $E_{ex}(u, \omega)$, is equal to the preimage of $\Delta \times 0$ through the map $F_{(u,\omega)} : R_{++}^{LI} \times S \to S^{I+1} \times R^{I-1} \times R^L$ given by

$$F_{(u,\omega)}(x, p) = (du_{x^1}^1 / \|du_{x^1}^1\|, \dots, du_{x^I}^I / \|du_{x^I}^I\|, p,$$
$$p \cdot x^1 - p \cdot \omega^1, \dots, p \cdot x^{I-1} - p \cdot \omega^{I-1},$$

$$\sum_i^I \boldsymbol{x}^i - \sum_i^I \boldsymbol{\omega}^i).$$

Since $E_{ex}(u,\omega)$ is known to be locally unique (theorem 7.2), we have only to show that the set is compact.

Since $\omega \in \boldsymbol{R}_{++}^{LI}$ is given and S is bounded, $F_{(u,\omega)}^{-1}(\Delta \times 0)$ $(= E_{ex}(u,\omega))$ is bounded. Thus any sequence $\{x^n, \boldsymbol{p}^n\}$ in $E_{ex}(u,\omega)$ has a convergent subsequence, which we also denote $\{x^n, \boldsymbol{p}^n\}$ for simplicity of notation. Let the limit of the convergent sequence $\{x^n, \boldsymbol{p}^n\}$ be $(x^0, \boldsymbol{p}^0)$. In order to prove the compactness of $E_{ex}(u,\omega)$, we should show that $(x^0, \boldsymbol{p}^0) \in \boldsymbol{R}_{++}^{LI} \times S$ since $F_{(u,\omega)}^{-1}(\Delta \times 0)$ is relatively closed. To this end, we have to show that $x^0 \notin \partial \boldsymbol{R}_{++}^{LI}$ and $\boldsymbol{p}^0 \notin \partial S$.

Suppose that $x^0 \in \partial \boldsymbol{R}_{++}^{LI}$. Since ω is strictly positive, $x^0 \neq 0$. Thus there exists an agent, say i, and a set of goods, say J, such that $x_{ij}^0 > 0$ for each $j \in J$ and that $x_{ij}^0 = 0$ for any $j \notin J$. Then, noting that

$$\lim_{n \to \infty} \frac{du_{\boldsymbol{x}_i^n}^i}{\|du_{\boldsymbol{x}_i^n}^i\|} = \lim_{n \to \infty} \boldsymbol{p}^n \tag{9.1}$$

and that u^i satisfies the boundary condition, we have that for each $j \in J$

$$\lim_{n \to \infty} p_j^n = p_j^0 = 0.$$

Thus $\lim_{n \to \infty} \boldsymbol{p}^n \cdot \boldsymbol{x}_i^n = 0$. Then, noting that $\boldsymbol{\omega}^i$ is strictly positive, we have

$$\lim_{n \to \infty} \boldsymbol{p}^n \cdot \boldsymbol{x}_i^n - \boldsymbol{p}^n \cdot (\boldsymbol{\omega}^i) \neq 0,$$

which contradicts the fact that $\boldsymbol{p}^n \cdot \boldsymbol{x}_i^n - \boldsymbol{p}^n \cdot (\boldsymbol{\omega}^i) = 0$ for all n.

Then suppose that $\boldsymbol{p}^0 \in \partial S$. Since equation (9.1) holds for any agent i, we obtain that $\lim_{n \to \infty} \boldsymbol{p}^n \cdot \boldsymbol{x}_i^n = 0$ for each i. Thus we can follow a similar argument to reach the contradiction, which implies that $E_{ex}(u,\omega)$ is compact and completes the proof. $\qquad\square$

The boundary condition, moreover, yields a more significant outcome concerning the set of extended equilibria for regular economies, which is just what we are mainly concerned with in this chapter.

Theorem 9.4   *Under assumption 9.1, the number of extended equilibria for any regular economy is odd.*

Proof. The key idea is to use the homotopy invariance of the modulo 2 intersection number. In particular, proposition 9.1 is crucial. Because the whole proof is fairly long, we separate it into three stages.

Step 1: Here we make an appropriate homotopy. First specify an economy $(\bar{u}, \bar{\omega})$ satisfying that

(1) every agent has the same utility function the form of which is
$u(\boldsymbol{x}) = \ln x_1 x_2 \ldots x_L$;

(2) every agent has the same initial endowment vector that is
$\boldsymbol{\omega} = (1, 1, \ldots, 1)$.

It is easily seen that this economy is actually a regular economy and that it has a unique extended equilibrium; that is, $(1, 1, \ldots, 1)$ is the common equilibrium consumption bundle of each agent and $(1/\sqrt{L}, \ldots, 1/\sqrt{L})$ is the equilibrium price vector (this pair also constitutes the true equilibrium). It is also easily checked by computation that this economy satisfies the boundary condition.

Then choose any regular economy satisfying the boundary condition, which we denote (u, ω). Recall that the set of extended equilibria for the economy $E_{ex}(u, \omega)$ is obtained by means of the map $F_{(u,\omega)} : \boldsymbol{R}_{++}^{LI} \times S \to S^{I+1} \times \boldsymbol{R}^{I-1} \times \boldsymbol{R}^L$ given by

$$F_{(u,\omega)}(x, \boldsymbol{p}) = (du_{\boldsymbol{x}^1}^1 / \|du_{\boldsymbol{x}^1}^1\|, \ldots, du_{\boldsymbol{x}^I}^I / \|du_{\boldsymbol{x}^I}^I\|, \boldsymbol{p},$$
$$\boldsymbol{p} \cdot \boldsymbol{x}^1 - \boldsymbol{p} \cdot \boldsymbol{\omega}^1, \ldots, \boldsymbol{p} \cdot \boldsymbol{x}^{I-1} - \boldsymbol{p} \cdot \boldsymbol{\omega}^{I-1},$$
$$\sum_i^I \boldsymbol{x}^i - \sum_i^I \boldsymbol{\omega}^i).$$

That is to say, $E_{ex}(u, \omega) = F_{(u,\omega)}^{-1}(\varDelta \times 0)$. As for the economy $(\bar{u}, \bar{\omega})$, obviously $E_{ex}(\bar{u}, \bar{\omega}) = F_{(\bar{u},\bar{\omega})}^{-1}(\varDelta \times 0)$ and $\sharp F_{(\bar{u},\bar{\omega})}^{-1}(\varDelta \times 0) = 1$. Thus, in view of proposition 9.1, we are naturally led to the consideration of a homotopy between $F_{(u,\omega)}$ and $F_{(\bar{u},\bar{\omega})}$. To this end, we make use of an arc $\alpha : [0, 1] \to U$ between (u, ω) and $(\bar{u}, \bar{\omega})$ given by

$$\alpha(t) = (tu + (1 - t)\bar{u}, t\omega + (1 - t)\bar{\omega})$$

to obtain the following homotopy $H : \boldsymbol{R}_{++}^{LI} \times S \times I \to S^{I+1} \times \boldsymbol{R}^{I-1} \times \boldsymbol{R}^L$.

$$H(x, \boldsymbol{p}, t) = F_{(tu+(1-t)\bar{u}, t\omega+(1-t)\bar{\omega})}(x, \boldsymbol{p}).$$

Note that H is of C^∞ class and that $\partial H = F_{(u,\omega)} \cup F_{(\bar{u},\bar{\omega})}$, thus ∂H is transversal to $\varDelta \times 0$.

Step 2: Here we show that $H^{-1}(\Delta \times 0)$ is compact in $\boldsymbol{R}_{++}^{LI} \times S \times I$. Since $t\omega + (1-t)\bar{\omega}$ is bounded for all t, $H^{-1}(\Delta \times 0)$ is bounded in $\boldsymbol{R}_{++}^{LI} \times S \times I$. Thus any sequence $\{x^n, p^n, t^n\}$ in $H^{-1}(\Delta \times 0)$ has a convergent subsequence, which we also denote $\{x^n, p^n, t^n\}$ for simplicity of notation. Let the limit of the convergent sequence $\{x^n, p^n, t^n\}$ be (x^0, p^0, t^0). In order to prove the compactness of $H^{-1}(\Delta \times 0)$, we should show that $(x^0, p^0, t^0) \in \boldsymbol{R}_{++}^{LI} \times S \times I$ since $H^{-1}(\Delta \times 0)$ is relatively closed. To this end, we have only to show that $x^0 \notin \partial \boldsymbol{R}_{++}^{LI}$ and $p^0 \notin \partial S$ because obviously $t^0 \in I$.

Noting that $t\omega + (1-t)\bar{\omega}$ is strictly positive for all $t \in I$ and that both u^i and $\bar{u}^i$ satisfy the boundary condition, we can adopt almost the same reasoning as the one stated in the proof of proposition 9.2 to obtain that $H^{-1}(\Delta \times 0)$ is compact.

Step 3: The final stage is just to apply proposition 9.1. There remains, however, one problem to be solved. It is the transversality of H provided above to $\Delta \times 0$. In general, such a property is not guaranteed for H, so that we need to modify it so as to suit our purpose. To this end, we rely on lemma 9.2, which assures that there exists a map $\tilde{H}$ smoothly homotopic to H such that both $\tilde{H}$ and $\partial \tilde{H}$ are transversal to $\Delta \times 0$ and that $\partial \tilde{H} = F_{(u,\omega)} \cup F_{(\bar{u},\bar{\omega})}$. Thus we may replace H by $\tilde{H}$ for our purpose. It is, however, not straightforward because the compactness of $\tilde{H}^{-1}(\Delta \times 0)$ is not assured. Therefore our last job is to establish a specific $\tilde{H}$ that has a compact preimage of $\Delta \times 0$.

In view of the proof of lemma 9.2, we may construct an appropriate map $\tilde{H}$ as follows.

Since S is bounded in $\boldsymbol{R}^L$, there exists the open set S^ϵ in $\boldsymbol{R}_{++}^L$ with distance less than ϵ from S where ϵ is sufficiently small so that each point in S^ϵ possesses a unique closest point in S. Let $\rho : S^\epsilon \to S$ be the smooth map that carries each point of S^ϵ to its closest point in S. Note that $\lim_{\alpha \to 0} \rho(x + \alpha) = x$ for any $x \in S$. Let B_{++} be the strictly positive unit open ball in $\boldsymbol{R}^{L(I+1)+I-1+L}$. Set $v^i = tu^i + (1-t)\bar{u}$ and $\zeta^i = t\omega^i + (1-t)\bar{\omega}^i$ $(i = 1, \ldots, I)$. Note that there exists a strictly positive vector c^i $(\in \boldsymbol{R}_{++}^L)$ such that $\zeta^i > c^i$ for each i since both ω^i and $\bar{\omega}^i$ are given in $\boldsymbol{R}_{++}^L$. Then we consider the map $G : \boldsymbol{R}_{++}^{LI} \times S \times I \times B_{++} \to S^{I+1} \times \boldsymbol{R}^{I-1} \times \boldsymbol{R}^L$ given by

$$G(x, p, t; b) = (\rho(\frac{dv_{x^1}^1}{\|dv_{x^1}^1\|} + \epsilon\tau(x, p, t)b_1), \ldots, \rho(\frac{dv_{x^I}^I}{\|dv_{x^I}^I\|} + \epsilon\tau(x, p, t)b_I),$$

$$\rho(p + \epsilon\tau(x, p, t)b_p), p \cdot x_1 - p \cdot \zeta^1 + \tau(x, p, t)b_1, \ldots,$$

$$p \cdot x_{I-1} - p \cdot \zeta^{I-1} + \tau(x,p,t)b_{I-1},$$

$$\sum_{i=1}^{I} x^i - \sum_{i=1}^{I} \zeta^i + \tau(x,p,t)b_\omega)$$

where $b = (b_1, \ldots, b_I, b_p, b_1, \ldots, b_{I-1}, b_\omega) \in B_{++}$ and $\tau : R_{++}^{LI} \times S \times I \to I$ is the same map as the one given in the proof of lemma 9.2. According to the reasoning provided in the same proof, it is easily checked that for almost all $b \in B_{++}$, $G(x,p,t;b)$ can be qualified as a substitutable homotopy for H. Thus we choose $b \in B_{++}$ sufficiently close to 0 to make a homotopy $\tilde{H}$. Then it can easily be seen that $\tilde{H}^{-1}(\Delta \times 0)$ is relatively closed and bounded. Thus any sequence in $\tilde{H}^{-1}(\Delta \times 0)$ has its own convergent subsequence the limit of which can be seen not to be contained in the boundary according to a similar argument to the above second step. Hence we obtain that $\tilde{H}^{-1}(\Delta \times 0)$ is compact. Since $dim\ S = L - 1$ and $dim\ (\Delta \times 0) = L - 1$, we have that

$$dim\ (R_{++}^{LI} \times S) + dim\ (\Delta \times 0) = dim\ (S^{I+1} \times R^{I-1} \times R^L)$$

and that $\tilde{H}^{-1}(\Delta \times 0)$ is a compact 1-dimensinal manifold. Thus we can apply proposition 9.1 to our situation to obtain the desired outcome. $\square$

This theorem implies the existence of extended equilibria for regular economies.

Corollary 9.1 *Under assumption 9.1, there exists at least one extended equilibrium in every regular economy.*

Proof. In view of the above theorem, this claim is trivial because the odd number does not include zero. $\square$

Part 3

Developments of Regular Economies

Chapter 10

Production Economy with Linear Activities

From now on, we turn toward substantial expansions of the basic exchange model we have so far been dependent upon. First of all, in this chapter we introduce a production system into an economy and consider the existence and the (local) uniqueness of equilibrium from the viewpoint of regular economies. This is a natural extension of forgoing arguments based on an exchange economy. We are especially concerned with the production of linear activities which was initially treated by Kehoe and Mas-Colell. The restriction to such a production system provides us a rich concrete method that is centered on the computable index of each equilibrium.

The method depends on the Lefschetz number and the index of a fixed point for a map on which we will give an adequate exposition in Mathematical Preliminaries. Then, in Economical Analysis, we discuss how those mathematical concepts are applied to a linear production economy to obtain suggestive outcomes from the viewpoint of regular economies.

10.1 Mathematical Preliminaries

Our interest here is in fixed points of a smooth map and their specific properties in relation to the index.

10.1.1 *Local Lefschetz Number and Index of Fixed Points*

First we need to define fixed points of a smooth map.

Definition 10.1 Let M be a manifold and $f : M \to M$ be a smooth map. If it holds that $f(x) = x$, then x is said to be a fixed point of f.

141

It should be noted that, in general, a fixed point does not require a smooth map. In this connection, we should refer to a classical theorem called Brouwer's fixed point theorem.

Theorem 10.1   *Let K be a compact convex set in $\mathbf{R}^n$ and $f : K \to K$ be continuous. Then f has a fixed point.*

For proof of the theorem, see e.g. Border (1989), Chap. 6.

Our particular interest in the following is in an isolated fixed point of a smooth map.

Definition 10.2   Let $x \in M$ be a fixed point of $f : M \to M$. If there exists a neighborhood W around x such that every point in W is not a fixed point of f except x, then x is said to be an isolated fixed point of f.

Let M be a m-dimensional manifold and $\bar{x} \in M$ be an isolated fixed point of a smooth map $f : M \to M$. Then we may assume that there exists a parametrization $\psi : U \to W$ about $\bar{x}$ such that every point in W is not a fixed point of f except $\bar{x}$ where U is, of course, an open subset in $\mathbf{R}^m$. Set $\psi^{-1}(\bar{x}) = \bar{z} \, (\in U)$. We consider the following map $g : U \to \mathbf{R}^m$.

$$g = \psi^{-1} \circ f \circ \psi - I$$

where I is the identity map of $\mathbf{R}^m$ to $\mathbf{R}^m$. Note that $g(z)$ is given by $\psi^{-1} \circ f \circ \psi(z) - I(z)$ for each $z \in U \subset \mathbf{R}^m$. Then g itself can be seen as a smooth vector field on U since the tangent space of U at each point z is nothing but $\mathbf{R}^m$. Thus $\bar{z}$ is an isolated zero of the vector field g (indeed, $\bar{z}$ is a unique zero of g in U). When considering a usual orientation in $\mathbf{R}^m$ (see 5.1.1), we can obtain the index of g at $\bar{z}$, $ind_{\bar{z}}(g)$ (see 5.1.3).

Definition 10.3   Let M be a m-dimensional manifold and $\bar{x} \in M$ be an isolated fixed point of a smooth map $f : M \to M$. When defining g by means of f as above, the index of g at $\bar{z} \, (= \psi^{-1}(\bar{x}))$ is called the local Lefschetz number of f at $\bar{x}$, denoted $L_{\bar{x}}(f)$.

Moreover, through the local Lefschetz number, we attain the notion of the index of an isolated fixed point.

Definition 10.4   Let M be a m-dimensional manifold and $\bar{x} \in M$ be an isolated fixed point of a smooth map $f : M \to M$. Then the index of $\bar{x}$ is defined as $(-1)^m L_{\bar{x}}(f)$, denoted $index(\bar{x})$.

10.1.2 *Index Theorem*

The index theorem is concerned with the sum of indices of isolated fixed points. In order for *the sum* to make sense, however, some conditions are required on the underlying manifold and fixed points themselves.

First we consider the condition that facilitates the computation of the index of a fixed point.

Definition 10.5 Let M be a m-dimensional manifold and $f : M \to M$ be a smooth map. Let $\tilde{I}$ be the identity map of $T_{\bar{x}}M$ to $T_{\bar{x}}M$. If $df_{\bar{x}} - \tilde{I} : T_{\bar{x}}M \to T_{\bar{x}}M$ is a linear isomorphism for a fixed point $\bar{x}$ of f, then $\bar{x}$ is called a Lefschetz fixed point.

Proposition 10.1 *A Lefschetz fixed point is isolated.*

Proof. Let $\bar{x} \in M$ be an arbitrary Lefschetz fixed point of f. Let $G(f)$ be the graph of f and Δ be the diagonal set of $M \times M$. Obviously $(\bar{x}, f(\bar{x}))\ (= (\bar{x}, \bar{x})) \in G(f) \cap \Delta$. Note that both $G(f)$ and Δ are m-dimensional submanifolds in $M \times M$. Thus, if we show that at $(\bar{x}, \bar{x})$, $G(f)$ is transversal to Δ in $M \times M$, our claim is proved.

Let $\Delta_{\bar{x}}$ be the diagonal set of $T_{\bar{x}}M \times T_{\bar{x}}M$. Since $df_{\bar{x}} - \tilde{I}$ is a linear isomorphism, $df_{\bar{x}} : T_{\bar{x}}M \to T_{\bar{x}}M$ has no fixed points but 0, which implies that $G(df_{\bar{x}}) \cap \Delta_{\bar{x}} = \hat{0}$ where $G(df_{\bar{x}})$ indicates the graph of $df_{\bar{x}}$ and $\hat{0}$ is the null vector of $T_{\bar{x}}M \times T_{\bar{x}}M$, i.e $(0,0)$. Since both $G(df_{\bar{x}})$ and $\Delta_{\bar{x}}$ are m-dimensional linear subspaces in $T_{\bar{x}}M \times T_{\bar{x}}M$, $G(df_{\bar{x}}) \oplus \Delta_{\bar{x}} = T_{\bar{x}}M \times T_{\bar{x}}M$ where $\oplus$ designates the direct sum of the linear subspaces. Noting that $G(df_{\bar{x}})$ is equal to the tangent space at $(\bar{x}, \bar{x}) \in M \times M$ to $G(f)$ and that $\Delta_{\bar{x}}$ is nothing but the tangent space at $(\bar{x}, \bar{x}) \in M \times M$ to Δ, we immediately have that at $(\bar{x}, \bar{x})$, $G(f)$ is transversal to Δ in $M \times M$. $\square$

Therefore, a Lefschetz fixed point yields a desirable outcome from the computational viewpoint as follows. In the following $sign|A|$ designates $+1$ (resp. -1) when the determinant $|A|$ $(\neq 0)$ of a matrix A is positive (resp. negative).

Proposition 10.2 *Let M be a m-dimensional manifold and $f : M \to M$ be a smooth map. If $\bar{x} \in M$ is a Lefschetz fixed point of f, then we have*

$$L_{\bar{x}}(f) = sign|df_{\bar{x}} - \tilde{I}|.$$

Proof. Let $g : U \to \mathbf{R}^m$ be the smooth map provided in the previous subsection; that is, $g = \psi^{-1} \circ f \circ \psi - I$. Let $\psi^{-1}(\bar{x}) = \bar{z}\ (\in U)$ as before.

Then obviously

$$dg_{\bar{z}} = d\psi_{\bar{x}}^{-1} \circ df_{\bar{x}} \circ d\psi_{\bar{z}} - \tilde{I}$$
$$= d\psi_{\bar{x}}^{-1} \circ (df_{\bar{x}} - \tilde{I}) \circ d\psi_{\bar{z}}.$$

Thus, if $df_{\bar{x}} - \tilde{I}$ is a linear isomorphism, $dg_{\bar{z}}$ is also a linear isomorphism, which implies that $\bar{z}$ is a regular point for g. Moreover, we have that $sign|dg_{\bar{z}}| = sign|df_{\bar{x}} - \tilde{I}|$. Thus, through proposition 5.2, we obtain

$$L_{\bar{x}}(f) = ind_{\bar{z}}(g)$$
$$= sign|dg_{\bar{z}}|$$
$$= sign|df_{\bar{x}} - \tilde{I}|.$$

$\square$

Definition 10.6 Let M be a m-dimensional manifold and $f : M \to M$ be a smooth map. If all fixed points of f are Lefschetz, f is called a Lefschetz map.

Consequently, if M is compact and $f : M \to M$ is a Lefschetz map, the set of fixed points of f is finite. In the following we are especially concerned with a m-dimensional compact manifold M that can be embedded into $\boldsymbol{R}^m$, where the term 'embedded' means that there exists an into-diffeomorphism called an embedding from M to $\boldsymbol{R}^m$. M is obviously a manifold with boundary. Let $f : M \to M$ be a Lefschetz map. If f has no fixed points on the boundary of M, then we have a remarkable computational outcome concerning the indices of its fixed points.

Since M can be embedded in $\boldsymbol{R}^m$, we may consider M to be a m-dimensional compact manifold in $\boldsymbol{R}^m$. Let $I : M \to M$ be the identity map and consider the map $h : M \to \boldsymbol{R}^m$ given by $h(x) = x - f(x)$. Then h is a smooth vector field on M which has no zeros on the boundary.

Lemma 10.1 *If M is orientable and convex, then the sum of the indices at zeros of h is $+1$.*

Proof. Since f is a Lefschetz map, the set of zeros of h is finite. Since M is convex, h points outward at all boundary points. Thus, through the Poincaré-Hopf theorem (theorem 5.1), the sum of the indices at zeros of h is equal to the Euler number of M, which is $+1$ because M is homeomorphic to D^m (the m-dimensional unit ball). $\square$

Now we are in a position to state the index theorem where a m-dimensional manifold M is considered to be embedded into $\boldsymbol{R}^m$.

Theorem 10.2 *Let M be a m-dimensional orientable, compact and convex manifold in $\mathbf{R}^m$. Let $f : M \to M$ be a Lefschetz map without any fixed point on the boundary of M. Then we have*

$$\sum_{f(x)=x} index(x) = +1.$$

Proof. For any fixed point x of f, we have

$$
\begin{aligned}
index(x) &= (-1)^m L_x(f) \\
&= (-1)^m sign|df_x - \tilde{I}| \\
&= sign|-(df_x - \tilde{I})| \\
&= sign|dh_x| \\
&= ind_x(h).
\end{aligned}
$$

Since there is a one-to-one correspondence between the set of fixed points of f and the set of zeros of h, we obtain through lemma 10.1 that

$$
\begin{aligned}
\sum_{f(x)=x} index(x) &= \sum_{h(x)=0} ind_x(h) \\
&= +1.
\end{aligned}
$$
$\square$

Note that according to Brouwer's fixed point theorem, f in the theorem always has a fixed point.

10.2 Economical Analysis

Although there have been several ways of introducing production into the framework of an economy in the literature of regular economies, it seems possible to separate them into two groups. One is the group which deals with the non-linear production technology and the other treats the linear production technology. For the leading works of the former, see Smale (1974 c), Fuchs (1974) and Villanacci et al. (2002, Chap. 9) whereas for the latter, see Mas-Colell (1975, 1985) and Kehoe (1980, 1982, 1983, 1985, 1991, 1998). Although the former is orthodox in that it just corresponds to the standard Arrow-Debreu model with production, we shall discuss the method of the latter. This is not only because constant returns to scale is important in a practical sense, but also because the method itself is uniquely computational, providing a new scope for regular economies.

10.2.1   *The Basic Idea*

The feature of the approach in this chapter is to grasp an equilibrium for an economy as a fixed point of an appropriate map. To begin with, we show how it is accomplished on the basis of a pure exchange economy model discussed in Part 1.

Let S_+^{L-1} be the non-negative $L-1$-dimensional simplex in $\boldsymbol{R}^L$ and $G_\omega : S_+^{L-1} \to \boldsymbol{R}^L$ be the aggregate excess demand function for an economy ω. Then we consider the map $P^S : \boldsymbol{R}_+^L \to S_+^{L-1}$ which carries each point of $\boldsymbol{R}_+^L$ to its closest point in S_+^{L-1}. Since S_+^{L-1} is closed and convex, P^S is a continuous single-valued map. Note that P^S is the identity map on S_+^{L-1}. By using this map, we obtain the desirable map $g_\omega : S_+^{L-1} \to S_+^{L-1}$ given by

$$g_\omega(\boldsymbol{p}) = P^S(\boldsymbol{p} + G_\omega(\boldsymbol{p})). \tag{10.1}$$

Indeed, if G_ω is continuous on S_+^{L-1}, then g_ω is also continuous; thus, Brouwer's fixed point theorem assures that there exists a fixed point of g_ω; that is, we have a point $\boldsymbol{p}$ satisfying that $g_\omega(\boldsymbol{p}) = \boldsymbol{p}$. It is easily seen that such a $\boldsymbol{p}$ is just an equilibrium price vector for an economy ω.

It is worth noting for this approach that for any given $\boldsymbol{p} \in S_+^{L-1}$, $g_\omega(\boldsymbol{p})$ is the solution for the following quadratic programming problem.

$$\min_{\boldsymbol{x}} \quad \frac{1}{2}\sum_{j=1}^{L}(x_j - p_j - G_{\omega j}(\boldsymbol{p}))^2,$$

$$s.t. \quad \sum_{j=1}^{L} x_j = 1, \; x_j \geq 0 \; (j = 1, \ldots L).$$

Thus if an equilibrium price vector is assured to be strictly positive, then through the Kuhn-Tucker theorem, g_ω can be represented in its neighborhood as follows:

$$g_\omega(\boldsymbol{p}) = \boldsymbol{p} + G_\omega(\boldsymbol{p}) + \alpha e$$

where $\alpha = \frac{1}{L}(1 - \sum_{j=1}^{L}(p_j + G_{\omega j}(\boldsymbol{p})))$ and e is the sum vector of order L, i.e $\overbrace{(1,\ldots,1)}^{L}$. Conveniently, this form of g_ω is differentiable, so that if the equilibrium price vector is a Lefschetz fixed point, its index is computable, which allows the application of the index theorem. This is the procedure for characterizing an equilibrium price vector as a fixed point so as to apply the index theorem.

We should offer some remarks on the procedure just stated.

First of all, a remark on a treatment of regular economies in this approach would be in order. Recall that a regular economy has been characterized as an economy ω for which 0 is a regular value for the map $\tilde{G}_\omega$ (see proposition 3.3). In view of the map g_ω, this view only corresponds to the version where an economy ω is a regular economy if and only if g_ω is a Lefschetz map. Indeed, noting the definition of a Lefschetz map, it is easily seen that if an economy ω makes the derivative of $g_\omega - I$ at each of its zeros linear isomorphic, then $\tilde{G}_\omega$ has 0 as its regular value, and vice versa, as long as equilibrium price vectors are assured to be strictly positive for every economy.

Secondly, although the analytic method in this approach looks unique, it is substantially equivalent to the method stated in chapter 5 that considers the aggregate excess demand function to be a vector field, characterizing an equilibrium price vector as a zero of the vector field so as to use the Poincaré-Hopf theorem. Indeed, it can be shown that for any equilibrium price vector $\boldsymbol{p}$, $index(\boldsymbol{p})$ $(= (-1)^L sign|dg_{\omega,\boldsymbol{p}} - \tilde{I}|)$ derived from the map g_ω is equal to $ind_{\boldsymbol{p}}(H_\omega)$ given by the aggregate excess supply function H_ω (for H_ω and $ind_{\boldsymbol{p}}(H_\omega)$, see 5.2.1 and 5.2.2).

Thus it turns out that the approach introduced here is not substantially different from the forgoing ones; rather, they are closely related. It may be safely said that this approach is a sort of compromise in that it exploits the notion of the index as in chapter 5 while retaining the admissible price vectors in the simplex as in chapters 3 and 4 (note that in chapter 5 the simplex was replaced by the positive unit sphere in order to use the vector field). Then, what is the benefit of this approach? We shall see how effectively it works when we introduce the linear production technology into the framework of an economy.

10.2.2 *The Model of Production Economies*

First we set up the model. We thereafter shall show the existence of equilibria on the basis of the model.

So far we have been considering a pure exchange economy model in which there only exists consumer goods. Here we consider production as well as consumption, thus factors of production (including production goods) should be taken into account. However, for the sake of simplicity, we consider all the L goods to be used as either consumer goods or factors of production. Then for the production technology, we characterize as follows.

Every firm has a finite number of feasible production plans, called activities, each of which is designated as a L-vector with positive entries denoting outputs and negative numbers denoting inputs. A firm can only perform its production by combining nonnegative multiples of its activities. Thus the production of each firm is subject to the constant returns to scale. An activity is interpreted as a column vector in the following.

We consider the matrix consisting of all the feasible activities in an economy as a whole. We call such a matrix the aggregate (or social) activity matrix and denote it by A for which the following assumptions are put.

Assumption 10.1 A is a $L \times k$ matrix satisfying
   (1) A contains $-I$ where I is the unit matrix of order L.
   (2) $A \cdot y = 0$ if $A \cdot y \geq 0$, $y \geq 0$.

In this assumption, (1) means that the free disposal is admitted for every good whereas (2) implies that there are no outputs without any inputs since $A \cdot y$ represents a socially feasible production plan for any $y \geq 0$. Let Y be the set of all socially feasible production plans; that is,

$$Y = \{x \in \boldsymbol{R}^L \mid x = A \cdot y \ for \ some \ y \geq 0\}$$

where the elements of the nonnegative vector $y = (y_1, \ldots, y_k)$ are called activity levels. We presume that k is fixed. Obviously $k > L$. Since A is assumed to contain $-I$, it can be expressed as an element of $[-I] \times \boldsymbol{R}^{L \times (k-L)}$. Let $\mathcal{A}$ be the set of $L \times k$ matrices that fulfill (1) and (2) of the above assumption.

It is worth noting that even if a firm aims at profit maximization, it must enjoy 0 profit at an equilibrium due to the constant returns to scale of production. Thus it turns out that any admissible social activity matrix yields no excess profits at an equilibrium.

Then we turn to the consumer side. We adopt almost the same setting as in chapter 1. That is to say, there exist I consumers and each consumer i ($= 1, \ldots, I$) is characterized by its demand function f^i and initial endowments ω^i. For the sake of simplicity, we relax the foregoing assumptions concerning the demand function to admit it to be defined all over $\boldsymbol{R}^L_+ \setminus 0$; otherwise our setting is the same as before. Thus the aggregate excess demand function on the consumer side $G(\omega, p)$ $(= \sum_{i=1}^I f^i(p, p \cdot \omega^i) - \sum_{i=1}^I \omega^i)$ is subject to the following condition.

Assumption 10.2 $G : \boldsymbol{R}^{LI}_{++} \times \boldsymbol{R}^L_+ \setminus 0 \to \boldsymbol{R}^L$ satisfies
   (1) $G \in C^\infty(\boldsymbol{R}^{LI}_{++} \times \boldsymbol{R}^L_+ \setminus 0, \boldsymbol{R}^L)$.

(2) G is homogeneous of degree 0 with respect to p.

(3) $p \cdot G(\omega, p) = 0$ for any $(\omega, p) \in R_{++}^{LI} \times R_{+}^{L}$.

Consequently, we are allowed to normalize price vectors, restricting them to the $(L-1)$-dimensional unit simplex

$$S^{L-1} = \{p \in R_{+}^{L} \mid \sum_{l=1}^{L} p_l^L = 1\}.$$

Thus G is considered to be continuously differentiable on $R_{++}^{LI} \times S^{L-1}$, which implies that there exists an open set O ($\subset R^L$) containing S^{L-1} and a smooth function F of $R_{++}^{LI} \times O$ to R^L such that the restriction of F to $R_{++}^{LI} \times S^{L-1}$ coincides with G.

Finally we shall specify an economy and describe an equilibrium for it. We consider the demand behavior of each consumer to be given, which naturally yields the view that the parameter of a production economy consists of ω and A. Accordingly, the space of production economies here amounts to $R_{++}^{LI} \times \mathcal{A}$. Then an equilibrium for each production economy is expressed as follows.

Definition 10.7 An equilibrium of a production economy (ω, A) is a price vector p^* that satisfies

(1) $p^* \cdot A \leq 0$,

(2) there exists some y^* ($\in R^k$) such that $G(\omega, p^*) = A \cdot y^*$,

(3) $p^* \in S^{L-1}$.

We should provide some comments concerning the definition. First, (1) implies that each activity makes a profit of, at most, 0 at p^*, thus no excess profit can be made by any combination of activities. The second condition obviously means the clearance of all markets. But, considering the possibility of free goods because of 0 price, it may seem that this should be replaced by the condition that $G(\omega, p^*) \leq A \cdot y^*$. In this respect, it is worth noting that the free disposal can rule out the possibility of excess supply, so that we may set $G(\omega, p^*) = A \cdot y^*$. The third condition is trivial. Finally, note that an equilibrium activity level y^* makes no profit; that is,

$$p^* \cdot A \cdot y^* = 0$$

because of Walras' law.

Now consider characterizing such an equilibrium so as to facilitate our analytical argument in the following. To this end, we define a map $g_{(\omega, A)}$:

$S_+^L \to: S_+^L$ for each production economy (ω, A) as follows:

$$g_{(\omega, A)}(\boldsymbol{p}) = P^{S(A)}(\boldsymbol{p} + G_\omega(\boldsymbol{p})) \tag{10.2}$$

where $S(A) = \{\boldsymbol{p} \in \boldsymbol{R}^L \mid \boldsymbol{p} \cdot A \leq 0, \ \sum_{j=1}^L p_j = 1\}$ and $P^{S(A)}$ is the map which carries a point of $\boldsymbol{R}^L$ to its closest point in $S(A)$. Noting that all $\boldsymbol{p}$ in $S(A)$ are nonnegative because of the free disposal activities in A, we have that $S(A) \subset S_+^L$. Then we obtain

Proposition 10.3   *For any production economy (ω, A), $\boldsymbol{p}$ is an equilibrium price vector if and only if $g_{(\omega, A)}(\boldsymbol{p}) = \boldsymbol{p}$.*

Proof.   It is obvious that $g_{(\omega, A)}(\boldsymbol{p}) = \boldsymbol{p}$ if and only if $\boldsymbol{p}$ is a solution of the following quadratic programming problem problem.

$$\min_{\boldsymbol{x}} \quad \frac{1}{2} \sum_{j=1}^L (x_j - p_j - G_{\omega j}(\boldsymbol{p}))^2$$

$$s.t. \ \boldsymbol{x} \cdot A \leq 0, \ \sum_{j=1}^L x_j = 1.$$

According to the Kuhn-Tucker theorem, the necessary and sufficient conditions for $\boldsymbol{x}^*$ to be a solution for the problem are as follows:

$$\boldsymbol{x}^* - \boldsymbol{p} - G_\omega(\boldsymbol{p}) + A\mu + \lambda e = 0$$

$$\boldsymbol{x}^* \cdot A\mu = 0, \ \boldsymbol{x}^* \cdot A \leq 0, \ \sum_{j=1}^L x_j^* = 1$$

where e is the sum vector of order L and both $\mu \in \boldsymbol{R}_+^k$ and $\lambda \in \boldsymbol{R}_+$ are Lagrange multipliers. Hence, $\boldsymbol{p}$ is a solution for the problem if and only if $G_\omega(\boldsymbol{p}) = A\mu + \lambda e$, $\boldsymbol{p} \cdot A\mu = 0$, $\boldsymbol{p} \cdot A \leq 0$, $\sum_{j=1}^L p_j = 1$. Considering Walras' law, we have

$$0 = \boldsymbol{p} \cdot G_\omega(\boldsymbol{p})$$

$$= \boldsymbol{p} \cdot A\mu + \boldsymbol{p}\lambda e$$

$$= \lambda$$

which implies that $\boldsymbol{p}$ is an equilibrium price vector. Note that the Lagrange multipliers μ indicate the activity levels at the equilibrium. $\qquad\square$

Comparing (10.2) to (10.1), we immediately see that equilibria with production can be characterized just like those without production. Thus we are allowed to follow similar analytical treatments to those addressed in the foregoing subsection.

Since the maps G_ω and $P^{S(A)}$ are both continuous for any (ω, A), we immediately have the existence of equilibria.

Theorem 10.3 *Under assumptions 10.1 and 10.2, there exists an equilibrium for any production economy (ω, A).*

Proof. Since $g_{(\omega,A)}$ is continuous and S^L_+ is compact and convex, through Brouwer's fixed point theorem, the claim follows. $\qquad\qquad\square$

10.2.3 Regular Economies with Linear Production Technology

In order to consider regular economies in the model provided above, the map $g_{(\omega,A)}$ is required to be differentiable at least at equilibria. We need some assumption on a social activity matrix for that purpose.

Assumption 10.3 No column of A can be expressed as a linear combination of less than $L - 1$ other columns.

This assumption is harmless from the generic viewpoint since any matrix of $\mathcal{A}$ can be transformed into a matrix satisfying the above condition by an arbitrarily small perturbation of entries. We denote the set of matrices satisfying assumptions 10.1 and 10.3 by $\mathcal{A}^*$ in the following.

Noting Walras' law, it is easily seen from definition 10.1 that if an activity is actually employed at an equilibrium, then the activity yields no profit. The above assumption generically assures that the converse holds.

Lemma 10.2 *For any $A \in \mathcal{A}^*$, there exists an open and dense set $\Omega \subset R^{LI}_{++}$ such that at every production economy $(\omega, A; \omega \in \Omega)$ the submatrix of activities, say B^*, that earn 0 profit at an equilibrium, say p^*, consists of linearly independent columns, satisfying that $G_\omega(p^*) = B^* \cdot y^*$ for a strictly positive activity level vector y^*.*

Proof. First note that for any economy $(\omega, A; A \in \mathcal{A}^*)$, the submatrix of activities that earn 0 profit at an equilibrium has less than $L - 1$ columns which are linearly independent. Indeed, if the submatrix in question, say B ($\subset A$), consists of more than L columns, B must be of full rank, i.e. $rank(B) = L$ by assumption 10.3. Thus we are allowed to choose L columns out of B which are linearly independent. However, by assumption, $p^* \cdot B = 0$ for an equilibrium price vector $p^* \neq 0$, which is the contradiction.

Now pick an arbitrary economy $(\bar{\omega}, \bar{A}; \bar{A} \in \mathcal{A}^*)$. Let an equilibrium price vector for the economy be p^* and the submatrix of activities that are actually employed at p^* be B, i.e. $G_{\bar{\omega}}(p^*) = B \cdot y^*$, $y^* > 0$. Since $p^* \cdot B = 0$, B consists of less than $L - 1$ columns which are linearly independent. Set $K(B) = \{ p \in \mathbf{R}^L \mid p \cdot B = 0, \sum_{j=1}^{L} p_j = 1 \}$ and $O(B) = \{ p \in \mathbf{R}^L \mid p \cdot B = 0, \sum_{j=1}^{L} p_j = 0 \}$.

If we choose a sufficiently small neighborhood of $\bar{\omega}$, say $N(\bar{\omega})$, then we may assume that for any economy $(\omega, \bar{A}; \omega \in N(\bar{\omega}))$ there exists an equilibrium price vector at which only B is actually employed. In order to characterize such an equilibrium for an economy $(\omega, \bar{A}; \omega \in N(\bar{\omega}))$, we consider the map $f_\omega : K(B) \cap S_+^L \to O(B)$ given by

$$f_\omega(p) = P^{O(B)}(G_\omega(p)).$$

Then $f_\omega(p) = 0$ if and only if p is an equilibrium for $(\omega, \bar{A})$ and $p \cdot B = 0$ since $P^{O(B)}(G_\omega(p)) = P^{K(B)}(p + G_\omega(p)) - p$.

To reach our goal, we consider ω to be a parameter so as to apply the transversality theorem to this map. Accordingly we replace f_ω by the map $F : (K(B) \cap S_+^L) \times N(\bar{\omega}) \to O(B)$ given by $F(p, \omega) = P^{O(B)}(G_\omega(p))$. A straightforward application of the the Kuhn-Tucker theorem shows that $P^{O(B)}$ is represented by $I - C(C^t C)^{-1} C^t$ where the superscript 't' indicates the transpose and $C = [B \; e]$ for the sum vector e interpreted as a column vector. Thus, F is smooth. It can be shown by computation that at any point of $F^{-1}(0)$ the derivative of F with respect to ω is surjective, thus F is transversal to the origin of $\mathbf{R}^L$. Hence, through the transversality theorem, there exists an open and dense set in $N(\bar{\omega})$ such that for each ω of that set f_ω has 0 as its regular value.

Here choose an arbitrary submatrix $\bar{B}$ of $\bar{A}$ which satisfies that $B \subset \bar{B}$ and that $rank(B) < rank(\bar{B})$. Then consider the restriction of F to $K(\bar{B}) \cap S_+^L$ (note that $K(\bar{B}) \subset K(B)$). Let the restriction be $\bar{F}$. Since at each point of $\bar{F}^{-1}(0)$ the derivative of $\bar{F}$ with respect to ω is equal to that of F, $\bar{F}$ is also transversal to the origin of $\mathbf{R}^L$. Thus, through the transversality theorem, there again exists an open and dense set in $N(\bar{\omega})$ such that for each ω of that set the restriction of f_ω to $K(\bar{B}) \cap S_+^L$, say $\bar{f}_\omega$, has 0 as its regular value. However, the dimension of the tangent space of the domain $(K(\bar{B}) \cap S_+^L)$ at each point is strictly less than the dimension of the range $(O(B))$ since $rank(B) < rank(\bar{B})$. Thus for almost all ω of $N(\bar{\omega})$, $\bar{f}_\omega^{-1}(0)$ is empty, which implies that there exists no equilibrium price vector p that satisfies both $p \cdot B = 0$ and $p \cdot \bar{B} = 0$. Considering the notice provided at the outset of the proof, the lemma is proved. □

This lemma generically assures the differentiability of the map $g_{(\omega,A)}$ at equilibria.

Proposition 10.4 *For any $A \in \mathcal{A}^*$, there exists an open and dense set $\Omega \subset \boldsymbol{R}_{++}^{LI}$ such that for every production economy $(\omega, A; \omega \in \Omega)$, $g_{(\omega,A)}$ is expressed as follows in a neighborhood of each equilibrium:*

$$g_{(\omega,A)}(\boldsymbol{p}) = (I - C(C^tC)^{-1}C^t)(\boldsymbol{p} + G_\omega(\boldsymbol{p})) + C(C^tC)^{-1}e_{r+1}$$

where $C = [B \ e]$ in which B consists of all the columns, say r columns, of A that are actually employed at an equilibrium price vector and e is the sum vector interpreted as a column vector while e_{r+1} indicates the column vector $(0, \ldots, 0, 1)$ of order $r + 1$.

Proof. Let $\boldsymbol{p}^*$ be an equilibrium price vector for an economy $(\omega, A; \omega \in \Omega)$. Recall the proof of proposition 10.1. Then, we see that B consists of the columns of A which correspond to strictly positive elements of the solution of μ (Lagrange multiplier vector). Since $\boldsymbol{p}^* \cdot B = 0$, we have that the columns of C are linearly independent.

Step 1: Let $\hat{\boldsymbol{p}}$ be an arbitrary vector in a sufficiently small neighborhood of $\boldsymbol{p}^*$ and consider a similar quadratic programming problem for the $\hat{\boldsymbol{p}}$. We shall show that the signs of the Lagrange multipliers solution for the problem are the same as those of the problem for $\boldsymbol{p}^*$ even without Walras' law.

Let $\boldsymbol{a}_h$ be an activity of A which does not belong to B. Note that the Lagrange multipliers solution $\mu_h(\boldsymbol{p}^*) = 0$. Then $\boldsymbol{p}^*\boldsymbol{a}_h < 0$, which implies that $g_{(\omega,A)}(\boldsymbol{p}^*)\boldsymbol{a}_h < 0$. Since $g_{(\omega,A)}$ is continuous, we have that $g_{(\omega,A)}(\hat{\boldsymbol{p}})\boldsymbol{a}_h < 0$. When solving the quadratic programming problem for the $\hat{\boldsymbol{p}}$, we obtain that $g_{(\omega,A)}(\hat{\boldsymbol{p}})A\mu = 0$, which implies that the solution $\mu_h(\hat{\boldsymbol{p}}) = 0$.

Then consider only activities which belong to B. In this case, the corresponding quadratic programming problem for any $\boldsymbol{p} \in S_+^L$ yields the following condition:

$$g_{(\omega,A)}(\boldsymbol{p}) - \boldsymbol{p} - G_\omega(\boldsymbol{p}) + B\mu(B) + \lambda(\boldsymbol{p})e = 0.$$

Note that $\mu(B) > 0$ if $\boldsymbol{p} = \boldsymbol{p}^*$. Since $g_{(\omega,A)}, G_\omega$ and λ are continuous in $\boldsymbol{p}$, we have that $\mu(B) > 0$ for $\hat{\boldsymbol{p}}$.

As for λ, it is straightforward that $\lambda > 0$ for both $\boldsymbol{p}^*$ and $\hat{\boldsymbol{p}}$.

Step 2: Return to the quadratic programming problem for $\hat{p}$. Then we have, through the Kuhn-Tucker theorem, that

$$x^* - \hat{p} - G_\omega(\hat{p}) + [B\ e](\mu\ \lambda) = 0.$$

Set $z = (\mu\ \lambda)$ for simplicity. Then the above equation turns to

$$\begin{aligned} C^t C z &= C^t(-x^* + \hat{p} + G_\omega(\hat{p})) \\ &= -C^t(x^*) + C^t(\hat{p} + G_\omega(\hat{p})). \end{aligned}$$

In view of the other Kuhn-Tucker conditions, we have that $C^t(x^*) = e_{r+1}$, which leads to

$$z = -(C^t C)^{-1} e_{r+1} + (C^t C)^{-1} C^t(\hat{p} + G_\omega(\hat{p})).$$

Applying these Lagrange multipliers to the initial condition, we obtain

$$x^* = (I - C(C^t C)^{-1} C^t)(\hat{p} + G_\omega(\hat{p})) + C(C^t C)^{-1} e_{r+1}.$$

Since $\hat{p}$ is arbitrarily chosen, the proposition is proved. $\qquad\square$

Now we define the regular production economies. To this end, it is more desirable that we have only manifolds for relevant sets. In particular, the domain of G_ω, that is S_+^L, should be altered. Thus we extend the domain (S_+^L) to X that is a compact convex manifold in the $L-1$ dimensional affine subspace $\{x \in R^L \mid \sum_{j=1}^L x_j = 1\}$, containing S_+^L. Such an extension is always possible because of assumption 10.2.

Definition 10.8 A production economy $(\omega, A) \in R_{++}^{LI} \times \mathcal{A}^*$ is a regular economy if $dg_{(\omega,A)} - \tilde{I} : R^{L-1} \to R^{L-1}$ is a linear isomorphism at every equilibrium.

Note that the definition makes sense owing to proposition 10.4.

Since each equilibrium price vector is a fixed point of the map $g_{(\omega,A)} : X \to O$ where O indicates the set $\{p \in R^L \mid \sum_{j=1}^L p_j = 0\}$, a regular production economy is, roughly speaking, an economy for which the relevant map $g_{(\omega,A)}$ is a Lefschetz map.

We will obtain several desirable properties of regular production economies.

Proposition 10.5 *Every regular production economy has a finite number of equilibria.*

Proof. According to the definition, the map $g_{(\omega,A)} - I$ turns out to be a diffeomorphism in a neighborhood of each equilibrium, which implies that every equilibrium is locally unique. Since the domain of the map is compact, the claim immediately follows. $\qquad\square$

Noting that an equilibrium is equal to a fixed point of the relevant map and that each fixed point is isolated according to the above proposition, we are allowed to have the index of each equilibrium for any regular production economy. In this connection, the index theorem provides us with a significant outcome concerning the sum of the indices.

Theorem 10.4 *For every regular production economy, the sum of the indices of all the equilibria is $+1$.*

Proof. Since the equilibrium set for any regular production economy (ω, A) is finite, $g_{(\omega,A)}$ can be smoothed over some compact and convex manifold containing all the fixed points in its interior without disturbing those fixed points (see Kehoe (1980), lemma 2). Applying the index theorem (theorem 10.1) to the altered smooth map, we immediately have that the sum of the indices of all the equilibria is $+1$. $\qquad\square$

This theorem directly leads to the following claim concerning uniqueness of equilibrium.

Corollary 10.1 *If the index of every equilibrium is positive for a regular production economy, then there exists a unique equilibrium for the economy.*

Lastly, we should investigate to what extent the regular production economies are observable.

Theorem 10.5 *The set of regular production economies is open and dense in the space of economies where the space of economies consists of $\boldsymbol{R}_{++}^{LI} \times \mathcal{A}^*$.*

Proof. For any $A \in \mathcal{A}^*$, we choose any ω, denoted by $\hat{\omega}$, which belongs to an open and dense set in $\boldsymbol{R}_{++}^{LI}$ provided in proposition 10.4. Let $N(\hat{\omega})$ be a sufficiently small neighborhood of $\hat{\omega}$ and consider the map $F : N(\hat{\omega}) \times X \to O$ given by

$$F(\omega, \boldsymbol{p}) = (I - C(C^t C)^{-1} C^t)(\boldsymbol{p} + G(\omega, \boldsymbol{p})) + C(C^t C)^{-1} e_{r+1} - \boldsymbol{p}$$

where $G(\omega, \boldsymbol{p}) = G_\omega(\boldsymbol{p})$ and C is a submatrix of A which corresponds to an equilibrium price vector for the economy $(\hat{\omega}, A)$ (see proposition 10.4).

For any $(\omega, A; \omega \in N(\hat{\omega}))$ an equilibrium price vector $\boldsymbol{p}$ is the vector satisfying that $g_{(\omega,A)}(\boldsymbol{p}) - \boldsymbol{p} = 0$. However, as we have shown, in a neighborhood of each equilibrium price vector the map $g_{(\omega,A)} - I$ can be represented as F by choosing an appropriate C. Thus if we can show that 0 is a regular value of F for a representative C, then through the transversality theorem, we obtain that for almost all $\omega \in N(\hat{\omega})$, $dg_{(\omega,A)} - \tilde{I} : \boldsymbol{R}^{L-1} \to \boldsymbol{R}^{L-1}$ is a linear isomorphism at every equilibrium.

Then we shall show that 0 is a regular value of F for a representative C. Note that C is expressed as $[B \ \boldsymbol{e}]$ for an appropriate submatrix $B \ (\subset A)$ as we have seen. It is easily seen that the derivative of F at any $(\omega, \boldsymbol{p}) \in N(\hat{\omega}) \times X$ is as follows:

$$dF_{(\omega,\boldsymbol{p})} = ((I - C(C^tC)^{-1}C^t)dG_\omega,$$
$$- C(C^tC)^{-1}C^t + (I - C(C^tC)^{-1}C^t)dG_{\boldsymbol{p}}) \cdots (*)$$

where dG_ω (res. $dG_{\boldsymbol{p}}$) is the derivative of G with respect to ω (res. $\boldsymbol{p}$). Note that the submatrix $(I - C(C^tC)^{-1}C^t)dG_\omega$ is to be applied to $T_\omega(N(\hat{\omega}))$ $(= \boldsymbol{R}^{LI})$ while the other submatrix $-C(C^tC)^{-1}C^t + (I - C(C^tC)^{-1}C^t)dG_{\boldsymbol{p}}$ is to be applied to $T_{\boldsymbol{p}}X$. We consider any element of $T_\omega(N(\hat{\omega})) \times T_{\boldsymbol{p}}X$ that has the special form; that is, $(\boldsymbol{y}_1, \boldsymbol{y}_2, 0, \ldots, 0, \boldsymbol{x})$ where $\boldsymbol{y}_1, \boldsymbol{y}_2, 0 \in \boldsymbol{R}^L$ and $\boldsymbol{x} \in T_{\boldsymbol{p}}X$. Then for any $\boldsymbol{y}_1 \in \boldsymbol{R}^L$ and $\boldsymbol{x} \in T_{\boldsymbol{p}}X$ there exists some $\boldsymbol{y}_2 \in \boldsymbol{R}^L$ such that the term $(I - C(C^tC)^{-1}C^t)dG_{\boldsymbol{p}}\boldsymbol{x}$ is cancelled out in $dF_{(\omega,\boldsymbol{p})}(\boldsymbol{y}_1, \boldsymbol{y}_2, 0, \ldots, 0, \boldsymbol{x})$. Note that $(I - C(C^tC)^{-1}C^t)dG_\omega(\boldsymbol{y}_1, \boldsymbol{y}_2, 0, \ldots, 0)$, $\boldsymbol{y}_1 \in \boldsymbol{R}^L$ spans the set $O(B)$ $(= \{ \boldsymbol{p} \in \boldsymbol{R}^L \mid \boldsymbol{p} \cdot B = 0, \sum_{j=1}^{L} p_j = 0\})$ while $-C(C^tC)^{-1}C^t\boldsymbol{x}$, $\boldsymbol{x} \in T_{\boldsymbol{p}}X$ constitutes a r-dimensional subvector space of $sp[C]$ where r is the number of columns of B and $sp[C]$ indicates the subvector space of $\boldsymbol{R}^L$ that the columns of C span. Since $O(B)$ is orthogonal to $sp[C]$, $dF_{(\omega,\boldsymbol{p})}(\boldsymbol{y}_1, \boldsymbol{y}_2, 0, \ldots, 0, \boldsymbol{x})$ covers the subspace of O, of which the dimension is $dim \ O(B) + r = L - 1$. Noting that the dimension of O is also $L - 1$, we have that F is a submersion, thus 0 is a regular value of F.

Since A is arbitrarily chosen from $\mathcal{A}^*$ and $\hat{\omega}$ is also arbitrarily taken out of an open and dense set of $\boldsymbol{R}_{++}^{LI}$, the theorem is proved. $\square$

10.2.4 *Computation of the Index of an Equilibrium in Regular Production Economies*

According to proposition 10.4, for any regular production economy (ω, A) we have a very tractable form of $g_{(\omega,A)}$ in a neighborhood of each equilibrium. It is easily seen that the particular form enables us to calculate the index of every equilibrium. Indeed, by the definition of the index (definition 10.4) and proposition 10.2, we immediately have that at any equilibrium price vector $\boldsymbol{p}^*$ for a regular production economy (ω, A)

$$index(\boldsymbol{p}^*) = (-1)^L sign \mid (I - C(C^tC)^{-1}C^t)(I + dG_\omega, \boldsymbol{p}_*) - I \mid.$$

Conveniently, the index is furthermore simplified by making use of the following lemma.

Lemma 10.3 *Let C be a $n \times k$ matrix $(n \geq k)$ and J be a $n \times n$ matrix. If C is of full rank, then the sign of the determinant of $(I - C(C^tC)^{-1}C^t)(I + J) - I$ is the same as the one of the following determinant.*

$$\begin{vmatrix} J & C \\ C^t & 0 \end{vmatrix}.$$

For proof of the lemma, see Kehoe (1980), lemma 4.

Consequently, the index is expressed as follows:

$$(-1)^L sign \begin{vmatrix} dG_\omega, \boldsymbol{p}_* & B^* & \boldsymbol{e} \\ B^{*t} & 0 & 0 \\ \boldsymbol{e}^t & 0 & 0 \end{vmatrix}$$

where B^* indicates the submatrix of activities that earn 0 profit at $\boldsymbol{p}^*$.

The above expression seems easy to calculate. We should, however, notice that the derivative $dG_\omega, \boldsymbol{p}_*$ is applied *not* to $\boldsymbol{R}^L$ itself *but* to a $L - 1$ dimensional subspace of $\boldsymbol{R}^L$. Thus the numerical expression of the derivative is not as easy to obtain as it appears.

In order to cope with this difficulty, we consider an extension of G_ω, which we may also denote G_ω without any confusion, that is differentiable on a L-dimensional compact and convex manifold Z containing X. It is worth noting that all the properties concerning regular production economies provided before still hold even if we redefine a regular production economy by way of this new map G_ω. Indeed, for the new map proposition 10.5, theorem 10.4 and corollary 10.1 are trivial, thus we shall only show the genericity property, i.e. theorem 10.5. To this end, it suffices to show that 0 is a regular value of the map $F : N(\hat{\omega}) \times Z \to O$ given by

$$F(\omega, \boldsymbol{p}) = (I - C(C^tC)^{-1}C^t)(\boldsymbol{p} + G(\omega, \boldsymbol{p})) + C(C^tC)^{-1}\boldsymbol{e}_{r+1} - \boldsymbol{p}$$

for a representative C where $N(\hat{\omega})$ and $\boldsymbol{e}_{r+1}$ are the same as before (see the proof of theorem 10.5). We can follow a similar method to the one provided in the proof of theorem 10.5. Obviously the form of the derivative of the above map F is identical with $(*)$ in the proof of theorem 10.5 although the domain changes from $\mathbf{R}^{LI} \times T_p X$ to $\mathbf{R}^{LI} \times \mathbf{R}^L$ since $T_p Z = \mathbf{R}^L$. Then for any $\mathbf{y}_1,\ \mathbf{x} \in \mathbf{R}^L$ we may choose some $\mathbf{y}_2 \in \mathbf{R}^L$ in such a way that the term $(I - C(C^t C)^{-1} C^t) dG_{\mathbf{p}} \mathbf{x}$ is cancelled out in $dF_{(\omega,\mathbf{p})}(\mathbf{y}_1, \mathbf{y}_2, 0, \ldots, 0, \mathbf{x})$. Since $(I - C(C^t C)^{-1} C^t) dG_\omega(\mathbf{y}_1, \mathbf{y}_2, 0, \ldots, 0)$, $\mathbf{y}_1 \in \mathbf{R}^L$ spans the set $O(B)$ while $-C(C^t C)^{-1} C^t \mathbf{x}$, $\mathbf{x} \in \mathbf{R}^L$ spans $sp[C]$, $dF_{(\omega,\mathbf{p})}$ is surjective, which implies that 0 is a regular value of the map F.

Based on the new version of regular production economies, we are able to further simplify the form of the index of an equilibrium as follows.

Theorem 10.6 *For a regular production economy based on the extended G_ω, the index of each equilibrium price vector $\mathbf{p}^*$ is expressed as follows:*

$$index(\mathbf{p}^*) = sign \begin{vmatrix} -\bar{J} & -\bar{B}^* \\ \bar{B}^{*t} & 0 \end{vmatrix}$$

where $\bar{J}$ is the matrix constructed by deleting the last column and row of $dG_\omega,\, \mathbf{p}_*$ and $\bar{B}^*$ is the matrix obtained by deleting the last row of B^*.

Proof. First note that even if we are based on the extended G_ω, we have the same form of the index as provided before; that is,

$$index(\mathbf{p}^*) = (-1)^L sign \begin{vmatrix} dG_\omega,\, \mathbf{p}_* & B^* & \mathbf{e} \\ B^{*t} & 0 & 0 \\ \mathbf{e}^t & 0 & 0 \end{vmatrix}.$$

Since G_ω is homogeneous of degree 0 with respect to $\mathbf{p}$, through Euler's theorem, we have that $dG_\omega,\, \mathbf{p}_* \cdot \mathbf{p}^* = 0$. Thus, in the determinant of the right side of the above equation, multiply each j-th column from first to L-th by p_j^* $(j = 1, \ldots, L)$ and add them to the last column, the determinant turns into

$$\begin{vmatrix} dG_\omega,\, \mathbf{p}_* & B^* & \mathbf{e} \\ B^{*t} & 0 & 0 \\ \mathbf{e}^t & 0 & 1 \end{vmatrix}.$$

Then subtract the last column from each column through first to L-th and expand the resultant determinant by the last row, we have

$$\begin{vmatrix} dG_\omega,\, \mathbf{p}_* - I & B^* \\ B^{*t} & 0 \end{vmatrix}.$$

Now it is worth noting that through Walras' law and the property of A, we obtain

$$\boldsymbol{p}^* \cdot dG_\omega,\, \boldsymbol{p}_* = -G_\omega(\boldsymbol{p}^*)$$
$$= -\sum_{b \in B^*} y_b \boldsymbol{b},\, y_b > 0. \qquad \cdots \text{(\dag)}$$

We may assume that $p_L^* > 0$ without loss of generality. Thus multiplying L-th row of the above determinant by p_L^* results in another determinant with the same sign. Then for that determinant, after multiplying each j-th column from first to $L-1$-th by p_j^* ($j = 1, \ldots, L-1$) and adding them to L-th column, again multiply each row from $L+1$-th to $L+r$-th by y_b of the equation (\dag) and add them to L-th row, we obtain

$$\begin{vmatrix} J_{11}-1 & J_{12}-1 & \cdots & J_{1L}-1 & B_{11}^* & \cdots & B_{1r}^* \\ J_{21}-1 & J_{22}-1 & \cdots & J_{2L}-1 & B_{21}^* & \cdots & B_{2r}^* \\ \vdots & \vdots & \ddots & \vdots & \vdots & \ddots & \vdots \\ J_{L-1\,1}-1 & J_{L-1\,2}-1 & \cdots & J_{L-1\,L}-1 & B_{L-1\,1}^* & \cdots & B_{L-1\,r}^* \\ -1 & -1 & \cdots & -1 & 0 & \cdots & 0 \\ \hline B_{11}^* & B_{21}^* & \cdots & B_{L1}^* & & & \\ \vdots & \vdots & \ddots & \vdots & & \mathcal{O} & \\ B_{1r}^* & B_{2r}^* & \cdots & B_{Lr}^* & & & \end{vmatrix}$$

where $J = dG_{\omega, \boldsymbol{p}_*}$, $J = (J_{ij})$, $i, j = 1, \ldots, L$ and $B^* = (B_{ij}^*)$, $i = 1, \ldots, L$, $j = 1, \ldots, r$. Then we consider the third determinant that is constructed by multiplying L-th column in the above determinant by $p_L^* (> 0)$. Note that such an operation keeps the sign of the determinant unchanged. We further manipulate the resultant determinant as follows. First multiply each of the first $L-1$ columns by p_j^* ($j = 1, \ldots, L-1$) and add them to L-th column. Secondly subtract that L-th column from each of the first $L-1$ columns. Lastly expand the resultant determinant by L-th row. Then we obtain the following determinant:

$$(-1)\begin{vmatrix} J_{11} & \cdots & J_{1\,L-1} & B_{11}^* & \cdots & B_{1r}^* \\ \vdots & \ddots & \vdots & \vdots & \ddots & \vdots \\ J_{L-1\,1} & \cdots & J_{L-1\,L-1} & B_{L-1\,1}^* & \cdots & B_{L-1\,r}^* \\ \hline B_{11}^* & \cdots & B_{L-1\,1}^* & & & \\ \vdots & \ddots & \vdots & & \mathcal{O} & \\ B_{1r}^* & \cdots & B_{L-1\,r}^* & & & \end{vmatrix}$$

which is equivalent to

$$(-1)^L \begin{vmatrix} -\bar{J} & -\bar{B}^* \\ \bar{B}^{*t} & 0 \end{vmatrix}.$$

This determinant immediately leads to the claim. $\qquad\square$

Therefore each equilibrium is characterized by the computable index. It is, however, worth noting that such an index $(+1 \; or \; -1)$ itself does not convey any particular economic meaning. If we introduce a price adjustment mechanism into the model as in chapter 5, then it will turn out that the index indicates either the local stability or local instability of each equilibrium.

Chapter 11

Incomplete Markets I

In this chapter we introduce uncertainty into the basic model. When we speak of uncertainty here, we mean future uncertainty; that is, the uncertainty which is concerned with the states in the future. People will try to prepare somehow for the future when they recognize this sort of uncertainty. It is this attitude that yields new goods called financial commodities (or, more generally, assets) which enable us to adjust the income distribution among the present and the future. If the number of asset markets is insufficient when compared to conceivable states in the future, those markets are said to be incomplete. We are going to deal with this type of asset market in this and subsequent chapters.

When the asset markets are incomplete, it is known that we experience many inconveniences about the equilibria of the economy. Among other factors, the existence of equilibria is not necessarily assured (see Hart (1974)). This crucial issue is what we are concerned with in this chapter. It will turn out that we can successfully cope with this issue by resorting to the method of regular economies we have so far developed. The mathematical tools employed are the Grassmann manifolds and the modulo 2 Euler number on which we give an adequate exposition in Mathematical Preliminaries. Then, in Economical Analysis, we illustrate the successful approach based on these mathematical appliances which is due to Hirsch, Magill and Mas-Colell (1990).

11.1   Mathematical Preliminaries

11.1.1   *Grassmann Manifolds*

We need a special manifold called the Grassmann manifold for our economical analysis in this chapter in order to provide the definition of the manifold and refer to its topological structure.

To this end, we are first required to extend the definition of a manifold presented in chapter 1. Consider a topological space M instead of a subset in $\boldsymbol{R}^n$. If M is locally homeomorphic to $\boldsymbol{R}^m$, then it is called a m-dimensional topological manifold. To be precise, there is an open covering $\mathcal{U} = \{U_i\}_{i\in\Lambda}$ of M such that for each $i \in \Lambda$ there is a map $\varphi_i : U_i \to \boldsymbol{R}^m$ which maps U_i homeomorphically onto an open subset of $\boldsymbol{R}^m$. A pair (φ_i, U_i) is called a chart (or coordinate system) with domain U_i and the set of charts $\Phi = \{\varphi_i, U_i\}_{i\in\Lambda}$ is an atlas. If an atlas has a differential structure as defined below, then the topological manifold is said to be a C^∞ (or smooth) manifold.

Definition 11.1   An atlas $\Phi = \{\varphi_i, U_i\}_{i\in\Lambda}$ of a topological manifold M is a C^∞ differential structure if for any two charts (φ_i, U_i), (φ_j, U_j) the coordinate change maps $\varphi_j \circ \varphi_i^{-1} : \varphi_i(U_i \cap U_j) \to \varphi_j(U_i \cap U_j)$ and $\varphi_i \circ \varphi_j^{-1} : \varphi_j(U_i \cap U_j) \to \varphi_i(U_i \cap U_j)$ are both C^∞ diffeomorphisms.

It is easy to grasp the image of a C^∞ manifold. See the figure below.

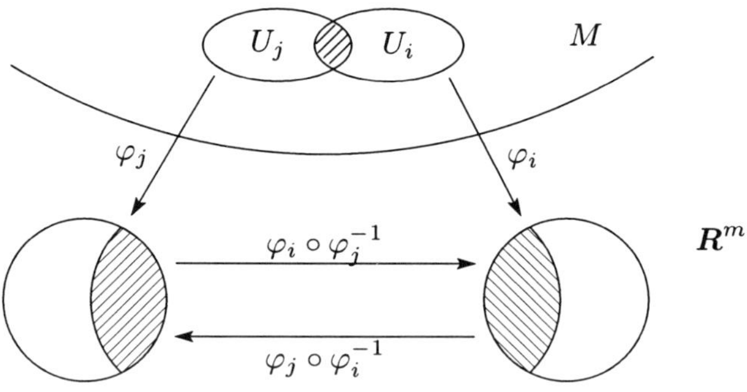

Fig. 11.1

Then we proceed to the Grassmann manifold. Stated simply, it is the set of all k-dimensional linear subspace or k-planes of $\boldsymbol{R}^n$ endowed with a suitable topology and differential structure. We usually denote it by $G_{k,n}$.

The Grassmann manifold $G_{k,n}$ possesses a particular property as follows.

Proposition 11.1 *The Grassmann manifold $G_{k,n}$ is a compact smooth manifold of dimension $(n-k)k$.*

Proof. We shall show how the set of all k-dimensional linear subspace of $\boldsymbol{R}^n$, denoted by G, is evolved into a smooth manifold, which will naturally lead to the claim.

Step 1: For any $V \in G$ we consider a ϵ-neighborhood ($\epsilon > 0$) of V in G as follows. That is, V' is in the neighborhood if and only if for any point $x \in V$ satisfying $\|x\| \leq 1$ there exists some $y \in V'$ such that $\|y\| \leq 1$ and $\|x - y\| \leq \epsilon$. It is easily seen that the family of those neighborhoods generated by ϵ can be qualified as a complete system of neighborhoods at V. Thus G is endowed with a topology.

Step 2: Then we shall relate a neighborhood of V to $\boldsymbol{R}^{(n-k)k}$. Let $V^\perp$ be the orthogonal complement of V and $L(V, V^\perp)$ be the set of all linear transformations of V to $V^\perp$. Since the dimension of V is k and that of $V^\perp$ is $n-k$, $L(V, V^\perp)$ can be identified with $\boldsymbol{R}^{(n-k)k}$ by way of the matrix representation of a linear transformation. Thus we consider an element of $\boldsymbol{R}^{(n-k)k}$ to be a $(n-k) \times k$ matrix. Let U be the set of k-dimensional linear subspaces of $\boldsymbol{R}^n$ that do not intersect $V^\perp$ except the origin. Note that U is a neighborhood of V. We show that every element of U is associated with the graph of a unique element of $L(V, V^\perp)$.

Pick any point $X = (x_{ij})$, $i = 1, \ldots, n - k$, $j = 1, \ldots, k$ out of $\boldsymbol{R}^{(n-k)k}$. Then the graph of the linear transformation represented by X is $\{ (\alpha, X\alpha) \mid \alpha \in \boldsymbol{R}^k \}$. If $(v_1, \ldots, v_k)$ and $(\bar{v}_1, \ldots, \bar{v}_{n} - k)$ are respectively the bases for V and $V^\perp$, then the graph is expressed in $\boldsymbol{R}^n$ as follows.

$$\{\alpha_1(v_1 + \sum_{i=1}^{n-k} x_{i1}\bar{v}_i) + \alpha_2(v_2 + \sum_{i=1}^{n-k} x_{i2}\bar{v}_i) + \ldots + \alpha_k(v_k + \sum_{i=1}^{n-k} x_{ik}\bar{v}_i)$$

$$\mid \alpha = (\alpha_1, \ldots, \alpha_k) \in \boldsymbol{R}^k\}$$

which is nothing but a k-dimensional linear subspace in $\boldsymbol{R}^n$ with the basis of $\{(v_j + \sum_{i=1}^{n-k} x_{ij}\bar{v}_i)\}$, $j = 1, \ldots, k$. This gives a continuous map from $\boldsymbol{R}^{(n-k)k}$ to U.

Conversely, pick any element V' out of U. Since in general any vector of V' can be represented as $\sum_{j=1}^{k} \alpha_j v_j + \sum_{i=1}^{n-k} \beta_i \bar{v}_i$ for some $\alpha \in \boldsymbol{R}^k$ and $\beta \in \boldsymbol{R}^{n-k}$ where $\alpha \neq 0$, it is easily seen that for each j ($j = 1, \ldots, k$) there exists a vector $\bar{\beta}(j) \in \boldsymbol{R}^{n-k}$ such that the vector $v_j + \sum_{i=1}^{n-k} \bar{\beta}_i(j)\bar{v}_i$ belongs to V'. Then we can construct a $(n-k) \times k$ matrix with those $\bar{\beta}(j)$

as its columns. This matrix is uniquely determined. Indeed, if there exists another $(n-k) \times k$ matrix $X' = (x'_{ij})$ such that for every j $(= 1, \ldots, k)$, $v_j + \sum_{i=1}^{n-k} x'_{ij} \bar{v}_i$ belongs to V', each vector $\sum_{i=1}^{n-k} (\bar{\beta}_i(j) - x'_{ij}) \bar{v}_i$, $(j = 1, \ldots, k)$ is contained both in V' and $V^{\perp}$, which implies that $\sum_{i=1}^{n-k} (\bar{\beta}_i(j) - x'_{ij}) \bar{v}_i = 0$, $(j = 1, \ldots, k)$. But $\{(\bar{v}_i)\}_i$ are linearly independent, thus we have that $\bar{\beta}_i(j) = x'_{ij}$, $i = 1, \ldots, n-k$, $j = 1, \ldots, k$. Thus we also have a map from U to $\boldsymbol{R}^{(n-k)k}$ that is easily shown to be continuous.

The two maps we have described are trivially inverse to one another, thus U is homeomorphic to $\boldsymbol{R}^{(n-k)k}$. Since we can take a pair consisting of a neighborhood and a homeomorphism for each V in this way, a family of those pairs over all k-dimensional linear subspace constitutes an atlas. Noting that there is a linear isomorphism between any two same dimensional linear subspaces, it is easily seen that the atlas is a C^{∞} differential structure.

Step 3: It remains to be shown that G is compact. Let $F_{k,n}$ be the set of all k-dimensional linear subspaces with orthonormal bases in $\boldsymbol{R}^n$. Put the set in $\boldsymbol{R}^{nk}$, then it is compact since it is closed and bounded there. Let $V_k(\boldsymbol{R}^n)$ be the set of all linear subspaces up to k-th dimension in $\boldsymbol{R}^n$. We endow the set with the same topology as the one provided in Step 1 and consider the map $f : \boldsymbol{R}^{nk} \to V_k(\boldsymbol{R}^n)$ given by

$$f(x_1, \ldots, x_k) = sp[x_1, \ldots, x_k].$$

This map is continuous. Since $G = f(F_{k,n})$, the claim is proved. $\square$

11.1.2   *Modulo 2 Euler Number*

The modulo 2 Euler number is the notion obtained by applying the modulo 2 intersection number to vector bundles. To begin with, we should review vector bundles (see 3.1.2).

A k-dimensional vector bundle consists of three ingredients; that is, the total space P, the base space M and the projection map $\pi : P \to M$ where $\pi^{-1}(x)$, usually denoted by P_x and called the fibre over x, has the structure of a k-dimensional vector space at every $x \in M$ and the following local triviality condition is satisfied. Each point x of M has an open neighborhood U and a homeomorphism $f : \pi^{-1}(U) \to U \times \boldsymbol{R}^k$ such that for every $x \in U$

$$f|_{\pi^{-1}(x)} : \pi^{-1}(x) \to x \times \boldsymbol{R}^k$$

is a linear isomorphism. Thus we may identify P_x with $\{x\} \times \mathbf{R}^k$.

We need an additional concept concerning vector bundles.

Definition 11.2 A section of a vector bundle (P, π, M) is a map $s : M \to P$ such that $\pi \circ s : M \to M$ is the identity map. In particular, if $s(x)$ is 0-vector of P_x for every $x \in M$, s is called the 0-section of (P, π, M), denoted by s_0.

In short, a section is a map $s : M \to P$ satisfying that $s(x)$ is contained in the fibre over x, i.e. $s(x) \in P_x$ for each $x \in M$. A typical example of a section is a vector field on a tangent bundle.

In the following discussion, we consider P and M to be smooth manifolds. Then the vector bundle (P, π, M) is said to be a smooth vector bundle if π is a submersion and the map f provided above is a diffeomorphism. Note that in this case the dimension of P is equal to $dim\ M + k$.

Let M be a m-dimensional compact manifold. Note that if we speak of a manifold, it is considered to be an ordinary, that is, boundaryless one unless otherwise noted. Suppose that for each $x \in M$ the dimension of the fibre over x is also m. Then, obviously the total space P has the dimension of $2m$. Let S_0 be the image of M by s_0, i.e. $S_0 = s_0(M)$. It is easily seen that S_0 is a m-dimensional closed submanifold of P. Choose a smooth section $s : M \to P$ that is transversal to S_0. Then we can consider the modulo 2 intersection number $I_2(s_0, S_0)$ of s with S_0 since M is compact and S_0 is closed and $dim\ M + dim\ S_0 = dim\ P$ (see definition 9.1). It is worth noting that any two smooth sections are homotopic. Indeed, for any two sections s and s', the map $F : M \times I \to P$ given by $F(x, t) = (1-t)s(x) + ts'(x)$ can be qualified as a smooth homotopy between them. Thus, in view of homotopy invariance of the modulo 2 intersection number (see theorem 9.3), we have the well-defined definition of the modulo 2 Euler number as follows.

Definition 11.3 For a m-dimensional smooth vector bundle (P, π, M) which satisfies that M is compact and that $dim\ M = m$, the modulo 2 intersection number of a smooth section with S_0 is called the modulo 2 Euler number of the bundle, denoted by $E_2(P, \pi, M)$.

For simplicity of notation, we denote a bundle (P, π, M) simply by ξ in the following. Thus the modulo 2 Euler number is expressed as $E_2(\xi)$.

Here we consider the product of two vector bundles $\xi_1 \ (= (P_1, \pi_1, M_1))$ and $\xi_2 \ (= (P_2, \pi_2, M_2))$. That is, we define

$$\xi_1 \times \xi_2 = (P_1 \times P_2,\ \pi_1 \times \pi_2,\ M_1 \times M_2)$$

which is easily checked to be another vector bundle whose dimension is obviously $dim\ \xi_1 + dim\ \xi_2$.

Let ξ_1 be a smooth vector bundle satisfying that M_1 is compact and that $dim\ \xi_1 = dim\ M_1$. Similarly, let ξ_2 be a smooth vector bundle satisfying that M_2 is compact and that $dim\ \xi_2 = dim\ M_2$. Then the modulo 2 Euler number is definable for the product $\xi_1 \times \xi_2$ as well as each ξ_i, $i = 1, 2$. We obtain the following claim concerning those numbers.

Proposition 11.2 *Let ξ_1 be a smooth vector bundle satisfying that its base manifold M_1 is compact and that $dim\ \xi_1 = dim\ M_1$. Let ξ_2 be a smooth vector bundle satisfying that its base manifold M_2 is compact and that $dim\ \xi_2 = dim\ M_2$. Then it holds that*

$$E_2(\xi_1 \times\ \xi_2) = E_2(\xi_1) \times E_2(\xi_2).$$

Proof. Set $\xi_1 = (P_1, \pi_1, M_1)$ and $\xi_2 = (P_2, \pi_2, M_2)$. Let $dim\ \xi_1$ be m_1 and $dim\ \xi_2$ be m_2.

Let S_0^1 be the image of M_1 by the 0-section of ξ_1 and S_0^2 be the image of M_2 by the 0-section of ξ_2. Choose a smooth section s_1 of ξ_1 that is transversal to S_0^1 and a smooth section s_2 of ξ_2 that is transversal to S_0^2. We may represent $s_1(x_1)$ as $(x_1, v_1(x_1))$ for each $x_1 \in M_1$ where $v_1 : M_1 \to \boldsymbol{R}^{m_1}$ is a smooth map. Similarly, $s_2(x_2)$ can be expressed as $(x_2, v_2(x_2))$ for each $x_2 \in M_2$ where $v_2 : M_2 \to \boldsymbol{R}^{m_2}$ is a smooth map. Thus we have

$$
\begin{aligned}
E_2(\xi_1) &= I_2(s_1, S_0^1) \\
&= \sharp\{x_1 \in M_1 \mid v_1(x_1) = 0\}\,mod\ 2, \\
E_2(\xi_2) &= I_2(s_2, S_0^2) \\
&= \sharp\{x_2 \in M_2 \mid v_2(x_2) = 0\}\,mod\ 2.
\end{aligned}
$$

Let $\{x_1 \in M_1 \mid v_1(x_1) = 0\} = \{x_{11}, \ldots, x_{1k}\}$ and $\{x_2 \in M_2 \mid v_2(x_2) = 0\} = \{x_{21}, \ldots, x_{2l}\}$.

Note that the product map $s = s_1 \times s_2 : M_1 \times M_2 \to P_1 \times P_2$ is a section of the product $\xi_1 \times \xi_2$. Moreover, it is easily seen that s is transversal to $S_0^1 \times S_0^2$, thus $E_2(\xi_1 \times \xi_2) = I_2(s, S_0^1 \times S_0^2)$. Then, noting that $s(x_1, x_2)$ can be expressed as $(x_1, x_2, v_1(x_1), v_2(x_2))$, we have

$$
\begin{aligned}
I_2(s, S_0^1 \times S_0^2) \\
&= \sharp\{(x_1, x_2) \in M_1 \times M_2 \mid v_1(x_1) = v_2(x_2) = 0\}\,mod\ 2 \\
&= \sharp\{(x_{1i}, x_{2j}),\ i = 1, \ldots, k,\ j = 1, \ldots, l\}\,mod\ 2 \\
&= [\sharp\{x_1 \in M_1 \mid v_1(x_1) = 0\} \times \sharp\{x_2 \in M_2 \mid v_2(x_2) = 0\}]\,mod\ 2
\end{aligned}
$$

$$= (\sharp\{x_1 \in M_1 \mid v_1(x_1) = 0\} \bmod 2) \times (\sharp\{x_2 \in M_2 \mid v_2(x_2) = 0\} \bmod 2)$$
$$= E_2(\xi_1) \times E_2(\xi_2).$$

$\square$

11.1.3 *Some Modifications of the Modulo 2 Euler Number*

The framework of the economical problem in this chapter does not allow the direct application of the modulo 2 Euler number provided above. This is because the manifold consisting of the vector bundle does not necessarily meet the condition for the modulo 2 Euler number. In our economical analysis this difficulty occurs in the context of the tangent bundle, so that we shall confine ourselves to the tangent bundle, modifying the modulo 2 Euler number.

Let's review the tangent bundle (see example 3.2). Let M be a m-dimensional manifold. The tangent bundle over M is the m-dimensional smooth vector bundle defined by the disjoint union of $T_x M$, i.e. $\bigcup_{x \in M} T_x M$ (the total space), $\pi : \bigcup_{x \in M} T_x M \to M$ given by $\pi(v) = x$ where $v \in T_x M$ (the projection) and M itself (the base space). It is common practice to denote $\bigcup_{x \in M} T_x M$ by TM. We omit showing that TM constitutes a $2m$ dimensional manifold and that (TM, π, M) is actually qualified as a smooth vector bundle. For their proof, see e.g. Hirsch (1976), Chap. 1, § 2. In the following, we consider M (the base manifold) to be a subset of $\boldsymbol{R}^n$ for practical purposes.

In order to obtain the modulo 2 Euler number, the base manifold is required to be compact. However we do not always have such a manifold in applications. In view of the economical analysis in this chapter, our particular interest is in the case where the base manifold is bounded but not compact. We try to make an appropriate version of the modulo 2 Euler number in accordance with this case. To this end, we concentrate on the set of sections that always point inward close to the boundary of the base manifold. To be precise, we only consider a smooth section over the base manifold that gives an inward tangent vector at each point sufficiently close to the boundary of the base manifold (for an inward tangent vector, see 5.1.1). Let the set of those sections be S for the tangent bundle (TM, π, M). Note that we always have a smooth homotopy F_t between any two sections of S such that F_t points inward close to the boundary of M at each $t \in I$ (choose a convex combination of those two sections). Then the constrained modulo 2 Euler number is conceivable because of the following lemma.

Lemma 11.1   *Let s, s' be two sections of S both of which are transversal to S_0. Then we have*

$$I_2(s, S_0) = I_2(s', S_0).$$

Proof.   Let $F : M \times I \to TM$ be a smooth homotopy between s and s' such that F_t points inward close to the boundary of M at each $t \in I$. We may assume that F and ∂F are both transversal to S_0 (see lemma 9.2). Thus, through theorem 9.1, $F^{-1}(S_0)$ is a manifold with boundary, satisfying that

$$\partial F^{-1}(S_0) = (s^{-1}(S_0) \times \{0\}) \cup (s'^{-1}(S_0) \times \{0\})$$

and that $dim\ F^{-1}(S_0) = 1$. Accordingly, we have only to show that $F^{-1}(S_0)$ is compact.

To this end, we shall show that the limit of a convergent sequence of $F^{-1}(S_0)$ does not belong to $\partial M \times I$ (note that $F^{-1}(S_0)$ is bounded and relatively closed in $M \times I$). Let $\{x_n, t_n\}_{n=1}^{\infty}$ be an arbitrary convergent sequence of $F^{-1}(S_0)$ whose limit is (x_0, t_0). Suppose that $(x_0, t_0) \in \partial M \times I$, then for n sufficiently large x_n is sufficiently close to ∂M, thus the tangent vector given by $F(x_n, t_n)$ at x_n points inward, which contradicts the assumption that $(x_n, t_n) \in F^{-1}(S_0)$. Thus the lemma is proved. $\square$

According to this lemma, we obtain

Definition 11.4   Let (TM, π, M) be a tangent bundle satisfying that M is bounded. If M is compact, the modulo 2 Euler number of the bundle is defined as the modulo 2 intersection number of a section with S_0. If M is noncompact, then the modulo 2 Euler number of the bundle is defined as the modulo 2 intersection number of a section of S with S_0 where S is the set of smooth sections that yield tangent vectors pointing inward close to the boundary of M.

For simplicity, we may use the same notation for the modulo 2 Euler number provided above as the previous one.

A similar argument is valid for the product of two tangent bundles. Let (TM_1, π_1, M_1) and (TM_2, π_2, M_2) be the tangent bundles where M_1 and M_2 are bounded. If the modulo 2 Euler number of the tangent bundle is defined as in definition 11.4, then it is easy to check that the modulo 2 Euler number of the product is equal to the product of the modulo 2 Euler numbers of those two tangent bundles; that is

$$E_2(TM_1 \times TM_2, \pi_1 \times \pi_2, M_1 \times M_2) = E_2(TM_1, \pi_1, M_1) \times E_2(TM_2, \pi_2, M_2).$$

Moreover, even when we construct the product vector bundle by picking one general vector bundle (P, π, K) satisfying the conditions in definition 11.3 and one tangent bundle (TM, π', M) with a bounded M, we end up with the same result, i.e.

$$E_2(P \times TM, \pi \times \pi', K \times M) = E_2(P, \pi, K) \times E_2(TM, \pi', M).$$

11.2 Economical Analysis

11.2.1 *Uncertainty and Assets*

There are many kinds of uncertainty in our real economic world although so far we have not taken any of them into account. In other words, the agents in our specific model have been implicitly assumed to have the perfect foresight for everything. Here we consider more realistic people and introduce a specific uncertainty for them; that is, the uncertainty concerning future events. Since no one knows what will happen in the future, this uncertainty is quite universal.

Let's consider how a typical agent will behave in facing this uncertainty. We may safely say that the agent will try to prepare somehow or other for the future. A rational agent would never ignore the future in the present. This propensity to prepare for the future yields new goods called assets. Note that the term 'asset' is a little different than the familiar one in our everyday life. Indeed, an insurance that promises to deliver a certain amount of money contingent on some event in the future is included in the assets and is referred to as a nominal asset. In this connection, we have another kind of asset called a real asset that promises to deliver a bundle of goods contingent on some future event.

Now let's expand the basic model by taking account of these new factors. For the sake of simplicity, we still remain in the pure exchange economy. In order to make matters simple, we consider only two periods, i.e. the present $(t = 0)$ and the future $(t = 1)$. An economic environment which may happen in the future is called a state of nature. For the sake of simplicity, we assume that the conceivable set of states of nature is finite, numbered by $s = 1, \ldots, S$. We call date $t = 0$, state $s = 0$ so that there are $S + 1$ states in all including the present and the future. There are L goods and I consumers that are common in each state. Each consumer i $(i = 1, \ldots, I)$ is characterized by its consumption set C^i, initial endowments ω^i and utility function u^i for which we assume as follows. Since a rational consumer would take account of all future possibilities, C^i can be properly assumed to be a subset of $\mathbf{R}^{L(S+1)}$. Accordingly, u^i turns out to be a map of C^i to $\mathbf{R}$ that is possibly interpreted as a von Neumann-Morgenstern expected utility function given by

$$\sum_{s=1}^{S} \rho_s U^i(x_0^i, x_s^i)$$

in which x_s^i is obviously a consumption vector at state s $(s = 1, \ldots, S)$ and $\rho_s > 0$ denotes the subjective probability of state s and $\sum_{s=1}^{S} \rho_s = 1$. However, our argument below does not depend on this particular type of function. Finally, ω^i is obviously an element of $\mathbf{R}^{L(S+1)}$.

For simplicity of notation, we set $\omega^i = (\omega_0^i, \omega_1^i, \ldots, \omega_S^i)$, $\omega_{\mathbf{1}}^i = (\omega_1^i, \ldots, \omega_S^i)$ and $x^i = (x_0^i, x_1^i, \ldots, x_S^i)$, $x_{\mathbf{1}}^i = (x_1^i, \ldots, x_S^i)$.

Then we turn to the assets that are, as we have mentioned, separated into two groups; that is, real assets and nominal assets. First, we characterize the real assets. A real asset is a contract that promises to deliver a bundle of goods at each state in the future. Let $a_j(s)$ be the bundle of goods $(\in \mathbf{R}^L)$ that a real asset j delivers at state s $(s = 1, \ldots, S)$. Then the whole returns of j are represented by a LS-vector $(a_j(1), \ldots, a_j(S))$.

Example 11.1 contingent claims: A contingent claim (s, l) is the claim for one unit of good l contingent on state s and for nothing otherwise. This is a real asset for which the returns are expressed by such a vector that the corresponding component to (s, l) is 1 but the others are all 0. A contingent claim (s, l) is often called a contingent commodity for good l in state s.

On the other hand, a nominal asset is a contract that promises to deliver an exogenously given stream of money across the states at date 1. Thus, if we denote a given amount of money a nominal asset j delivers at state s by $a_j(s)$, the whole returns of the asset are expressed by a S-vector $(a_j(1), \ldots, a_j(S))$.

Example 11.2 Arrow securities: An Arrow security s is the claim for one unit of money contingent on state s and for nothing otherwise. This is obviously a special nominal asset for which the returns are expressed by such a vector that the corresponding component to s is 1 but the others are all 0.

In the following, we only deal with real assets in our model. For nominal assets, see Balasko and Cass (1989), Cass (1991, 1992). Then, suppose that there exist J real assets. If we see the returns vector $(a_j(1), \ldots, a_j(S))$ of each asset j as a column vector, we have the real asset structure as follows.

Definition 11.5 The real asset structure of J real assets is a $LS \times J$ matrix given by

$$A = \begin{pmatrix} a_1(1) & a_2(1) & \cdots & a_J(1) \\ a_1(2) & a_2(2) & \cdots & a_J(2) \\ \vdots & \vdots & \ddots & \vdots \\ a_1(S) & a_2(S) & \cdots & a_J(S) \end{pmatrix}.$$

Finally we refer to prices. Note that there are spot market prices at each state at date 1 as well as the present market prices. In addition, we need to consider the prices of the real assets. Needless to say, the asset markets are only open at the date 0 (the present) since we only consider two periods. Let p_0 be the price vector of goods at date 0 and p_s be the (spot market) price vector of goods at state s ($s = 1, \ldots, S$) at date 1. The price vector of J assets is denoted by q ($= (q_1, \ldots, q_J)$). We assume that all prices are strictly positive. Similarly to consumption vectors, we set $p = (p_0, p_1, \ldots, p_S)$ and $p_1 = (p_1, \ldots, p_S)$ in the following.

Given a real asset structure A, we obtain the date 1 matrix of revenues brought in by A which is called a dividend matrix.

Definition 11.6 A dividend matrix of a real asset structure A is the matrix given by

$$D(p_1, A) = \begin{pmatrix} p_1 \cdot a_1(1) & \cdots & p_1 \cdot a_J(1) \\ \vdots & \ddots & \vdots \\ p_S \cdot a_1(S) & \cdots & p_S \cdot a_J(S) \end{pmatrix}.$$

Note that this matrix is obviously obtained by premultiplying A by the following $S \times LS$ matrix P consisting of p_s ($s = 1, \ldots, S$).

$$P = \begin{pmatrix} p_1 & 0 & \cdots & 0 \\ 0 & p_2 & \cdots & 0 \\ \vdots & \vdots & \ddots & \vdots \\ 0 & \cdots & \cdots & p_S \end{pmatrix}$$

where each p_s ($s = 1, \ldots, S$) is interpreted as a row vector. Thus, D can be seen as a smooth map with p_1 and A as its independent variables.

It follows from the above argument that the economy with assets is specified by the three kinds of parameters; that is, each consumer's utility function and initial endowments plus an asset structure. Thus, we call a triple $(u, \omega; A)$ an economy with assets where $u = (u^1, \ldots, u^I)$ and $\omega = (\omega^1, \ldots, \omega^I)$.

Let's consider the behavior of each consumer given an economy. Although a consumer faces the uncertainty concerning future events, he/she is able to adjust his/her income among the present and the future through the assets. Thus, he/she will seek to obtain the optimal intertemporal consumption allocation by buying and selling those assets. The demand vector of consumer i for J assets is called a portfolio of i and denoted by $z^i \; (= (z^i_1, \ldots, z^i_J))$. Note that the positive (negative) element of the portfolio implies the demand (supply) of the corresponding asset. For simplicity, we set $z = (z^1, \ldots, z^I)$ in the following.

Considering this course of the behavior of each consumer, the definition of equilibria of an economy with assets is straightforward. Before describing the definition, however, we introduce a specific operation called the box product.

Let a and b be two n sets of k-vector; that is, $a = (a_1, \ldots, a_n)$, $b = (b_1, \ldots, b_n)$ where $a_i, b_i \in R^k$, $i = 1, \ldots, n$. Then the box product $a \,\Box\, b$ of a and b is defined as

$$a \,\Box\, b = (a_1 b_1, \ldots, a_n b_n).$$

We are now in a position to state the definition of an equilibrium for an economy with assets.

Definition 11.7　For an economy with assets $(u, \omega; A)$, an equilibrium is a pair of prices and actions $(p, q; x, z)$ satisfying that

(1) (x^i, z^i) is a solution for the following optimization problem $(i = 1, \ldots, I)$,

$$\begin{aligned}
\max_{x^i} \quad & u^i(x^i) \\
\text{s.t.} \quad & p_0(x^i_0 - \omega^i_0) + q \cdot z^i \leq 0 \\
& p_1 \,\Box\, (x^i_1 - \omega^i_1) \leq D(p_1, A)z^i,
\end{aligned}$$

(2) $\sum_{i=1}^{I} (x^i - \omega^i) = 0$,
(3) $\sum_{i=1}^{I} z^i = 0$.

Note in the above definition that (1) implies the subjective equilibrium for each consumer and that (2), (3) are the market clearance conditions respectively for goods and assets.

11.2.2 *Complete and Incomplete Markets*

We postulate that the utility function of each consumer satisfies the monotonicity in the following.

Now imagine that there are two assets one of which is low in price but yields much revenue and the other of which is expensive but brings in bad returns. In this case a rational consumer would buy the former asset and sell the latter one so that he/she can increase his/her income as much as desired at every state including the present. When this happens, we say that there exists an arbitrage opportunity. Then it turns out that we always have the excess demand of the former market and the excess supply in the latter, which results in no equilibrium.

The above argument reveals that we need some restriction on the asset structure in order to obtain an equilibrium for an economy with assets. Let's formalize the restriction. Since the income for consumer i obtained by trading the assets consists of $-q \cdot z^i$ for the present and $D(p_1, A)z^i$ for the states of the future, if there exists a portfolio z^i satisfying that

$$\begin{pmatrix} -q \\ D(p_1, A) \end{pmatrix} z^i > 0,$$

then not only i but all consumers desire such a portfolio as much as possible, which prevents the clearance in each asset market. Thus, in order for an equilibrium to exist, we need to require that there exists no portfolio z such that

$$\begin{pmatrix} -q \\ D(p_1, A) \end{pmatrix} z > 0.$$

To this condition the following proposition, called Stiemke's theorem is applicable.

Theorem 11.1   *For each given $n \times m$ matrix A, either*
   (I) $A \cdot x \leq 0$ has a solution $x \in R^m$
or
   (II) $y \cdot A = 0$, $y > 0$ has a solution $y \in R^n$
but never both.

For proof of the theorem, see Mangasarian (1969,1994), Chap.2. § 4.

Thus, there must exist a $S + 1$-vector $\alpha \ (= (\alpha_0, \alpha_1, \ldots, \alpha_S)) > 0$ such that

$$\alpha \begin{pmatrix} -q \\ D(p_1, A) \end{pmatrix} = 0$$

It can be easily seen that we are allowed to normalize the vector $\boldsymbol{\alpha}$, thus we set $\alpha_0 = 1$ for the present and also set $\alpha_1 = (\alpha_1, \ldots, \alpha_S)$. Then we have that $\boldsymbol{q} = \alpha_1 D(p_1, A)$ which is written in component form as follows.

$$q_j = \sum_{s=1}^{S} \alpha_s D_s^j(p_1, A), \quad j = 1, \ldots, J$$

where $D_s^j(p_1, A)$ denotes the dividend brought by asset j at state s. Hence α_1 is a coefficient vector that associates the revenue of each asset at each state with its present price; that is, α_1 is interpreted as the vector of the discount rates. Accordingly, the absence of arbitrage opportunities implies the existence of the vector of the discount rates common to all assets. Such a vector is often called a present value vector. In addition, the presence of such a present value vector is often called the no-arbitrage condition.

Under the no-arbitrage condition, for any portfolio satisfying the budget constraints for consumer i, we immediately have

$$\sum_{s=0}^{S} \alpha_s \boldsymbol{p}_s (\boldsymbol{x}_s^i - \boldsymbol{\omega}_s^i) = 0.$$

Set $\boldsymbol{p}_s^* = \alpha_s \boldsymbol{p}_s$ $(s = 0, 1, \ldots, S)$, which can be interpreted as the present value price vector of spot prices at each state.

Then, noting that the set $\{\, \boldsymbol{z} \in \boldsymbol{R}^J \mid p_1 \,\square\, (x_1 - \omega_1) = D(p_1, A) \cdot \boldsymbol{z}\,\}$ is equal to the set $\{\, \boldsymbol{z} \in \boldsymbol{R}^J \mid p_1^* \,\square\, (x_1 - \omega_1) = D(p_1^*, A) \cdot \boldsymbol{z}\,\}$ since $D(p_1^*, A) \cdot \boldsymbol{z} = \alpha_1 \,\square\, D(p_1, A) \cdot \boldsymbol{z}$, the optimization problem for i can be rewritten as follows.

$$\begin{aligned} \max_{x^i} \quad & u^i(x^i) \\ \text{s.t.} \quad & p^*(x^i - \omega^i) = 0 \\ & p_1^* \,\square\, (x_1^i - \omega_1^i) \in sp[D(p_1^*, A)] \end{aligned}$$

where $sp[D(p_1^*, A)]$ denotes the linear subspace of $\boldsymbol{R}^S$ spanned by the column vectors of $D(p_1^*, A)$.

It is worth noting that in the above formulation z^i and $\boldsymbol{q}$ are excluded; that is, the portfolio selecting behavior of i is put aside.

Moreover, we are allowed to dispense with the market clearance condition of the assets. To be precise, if the subjective equilibrium demand of each consumer for goods, i.e. the solution for the above problem, satisfies the market clearance condition, then there always exists an optimal portfolio allocation $(\bar{z}^1, \ldots, \bar{z}^I)$ such that $\sum_{i=1}^{I} \bar{z}^i = 0$. Indeed, noting that for the solution x^i of the above problem there exists a portfolio z^i $(= (z^i_1, \ldots, z^i_J))$ such that $p^*_s \cdot (x^i_s - \omega^i_s) = \sum_{j=1}^{J} D^j_s(p^*_1, A) z^i_j$ for all s, we may set $\bar{z}^i_j = z^i_j - \sum_{i=1}^{I} z^i_j / I$, $j = 1, \ldots, J$ to obtain that

$$p^*_s \cdot (x^i_s - \omega^i_s) = \sum_{j=1}^{J} D^j_s(p^*_1, A) \bar{z}^i_j, \ i = 1, \ldots I$$

$$\sum_{i=1}^{I} \bar{z}^i_j = 0, \ j = 1, \ldots, J.$$

Hence, under the no-arbitrage condition, we have a simplified definition of an equilibrium for the economy with assets as follows.

Definition 11.8   For an economy with assets $(u, \omega; A)$, an equilibrium under the no-arbitrage condition is a pair of prices and actions (p, x) satisfying that

(1) x^i is a solution for the following optimization problem $(i = 1, \ldots, I)$.

$$\max_{x^i} \quad u^i(x^i)$$
$$s.t. \ \ p \cdot (x^i - \omega^i) = 0$$
$$p_1 \ \Box \ (x^i_1 - \omega^i_1) \in sp[D(p_1, A)],$$

(2) $\sum_{i=1}^{I}(x^i - \omega^i) = 0$.

It is worth noting that we have in the background that the equilibrium price q_j of asset j is equal to $\sum_{s=1}^{S} D^j_s(p_1, A)$, $j = 1, \ldots, J$ where p_1 is the equilibrium prices of goods at date 1. This is because the prices for the goods in the above definition are interpreted as the present value prices. Since we have no equilibrium under the presence of arbitrage opportunities, we may confine ourselves to the no-arbitrage equilibrium in the following.

In light of the above definition, it is easily seen that the term $sp[D(p_1, A)]$ plays a crucial role. Indeed, if $sp[D(p_1, A)] = R^S$, then the second budget constraint for consumer i is always met and is dispensable. Hence, in this case, the equilibrium condition turns out to be the same in form as the one for an economy without assets which we have already discussed. This observation leads to the following dichotomy.

Definition 11.9   In definition 11.8, if $sp[D(p_1, A)] = R^S$, then the asset markets are said to be complete. Otherwise, they are incomplete.

Example 11.3   Suppose that there exists a contingent commodity for every good l at every state s, $l = 1, \ldots, L, s = 1, \ldots, S$. Thus, there are LS

real assets (contingent commodities) in all. Then the asset structure A for them constitutes the $LS \times LS$ unit matrix, which yields P as its dividend matrix. Accordingly, $D(p_1, A)$ is of full rank as long as $p > 0$, which means that the asset markets are complete.

It is quite legitimate for us to concentrate on the case of incomplete markets in the following. However, in contrast to complete markets, incomplete markets give rise to significant difficulties with regard to the fundamental properties of equilibria. Consider the following numerical example due to Geanakoplos (1990).

Example 11.4　There are two consumers (a, b), two goods (x, y), two states of nature $(s = 1, 2)$ at date 1 and two assets $(j = 1, 2)$. At state 1 two goods are both tradable, but only x is tradable at state 2 as well as at state 0 (the present). Let (x_1, y_1) denote the quantity vector of the two goods at state 1 and x_2 denote the one at state 2. The prices for those goods are respectively designated by p_{x_1}, p_{y_1} and p_{x_2}. On the other hand, let q_1, q_2 denote the prices respectively for assets 1 and 2. The asset structure of these assets is given by

$$\begin{pmatrix} 1 & 0 \\ 0 & 1 \\ 1 & 1 \end{pmatrix}$$

where the 1st and the 2nd row respectively designate the quantity of goods x and y delivered at state 1, while the 3rd row indicates the quantity of good x delivered at state 2. Hence, the dividend matrix of these assets is as follows.

$$\begin{pmatrix} p_{x_1} & p_{y_1} \\ p_{x_2} & p_{x_2} \end{pmatrix}.$$

Utilities of consumers a and b are respectively given by the following utility functions.

$$u^a = \ln x_1^a + 2 \ln y_1^a + \ln x_2^a$$
$$u^b = \ln x_1^b + \ln y_1^b + 2 \ln x_2^b.$$

Note that neither consumer cares for x_0. Endowments for them are as follows.

$$\omega^a = (\bar{x}_0^a, \bar{x}_1^a, \bar{y}_1^a, \bar{x}_2^a)$$
$$= (0,\ 1,\ 1,\ 2)$$

$$\omega^b = (\bar{x}_0^b, \bar{x}_1^b, \bar{y}_1^b, \bar{x}_2^b)$$
$$= (0,\ 1,\ 2,\ 1).$$

In this framework, the behavior of each consumer is summarized as the following optimization program. That is, for consumer a

$$\max \quad \ln x_1^a + 2\ln y_1^a + \ln x_2^a$$
$$s.t. \quad q_1\theta_1^a + q_2\theta_2^a = 0$$
$$p_{x_1}(x_1^a - 1) + p_{y_1}(y_1^a - 1) = p_{x_1}\theta_1^a + p_{y_1}\theta_2^a$$
$$p_{x_2}(x_2^a - 2) = p_{x_2}\theta_1^a + p_{x_2}\theta_2^a$$

where θ_j^a $(j = 1,\ 2)$ denotes the quantity demanded by a for asset j whereas for b we have that

$$\max \quad \ln x_1^b + \ln y_1^b + 2\ln x_2^b$$
$$s.t. \quad q_1\theta_1^b + q_2\theta_2^b = 0$$
$$p_{x_1}(x_1^b - 1) + p_{y_1}(y_1^b - 2) = p_{x_1}\theta_1^b + p_{y_1}\theta_2^b$$
$$p_{x_2}(x_2^b - 1) = p_{x_2}\theta_1^b + p_{x_2}\theta_2^b$$

where θ_j^b $(j = 1,\ 2)$ is alike θ_j^a.

On the other hand, the market clearance conditions are as follows.

$$\theta_j^a + \theta_j^b = 0, \quad j = 1,\ 2$$
$$x_1^a + x_1^b = 2$$
$$y_1^a + y_1^b = 3$$
$$x_2^a + x_2^b = 3.$$

Now let's solve for the equilibrium prices and quantities demanded. Considering the homogeneity of degree 0 with respect to the prices, we may set $q_1 = p_{x_1} = p_{x_2} = 1$. Note at the same time that Walras' law makes any three of the market clearance conditions dispensable.

First solve the optimization problem for consumer a to obtain the subjective equilibrium for x_1^a and θ_1^a given q_2 and p_{y_1}. By computation, we have that

$$x_1^a = \frac{q_2(1 + q_2)(1 - p_{y_1})}{4(1 - q_2)}$$
$$\theta_1^a = \frac{q_2((1 + q_2)(1 - p_{y_1})/4(q_2 - p_{y_1}) - 2)}{q_2 - 1}.$$

Similarly we obtain for consumer b that

$$x_1^b = \frac{p_{y_1}(1 - 2q_2) + 1}{4(1 - q_2)}$$

$$\theta_1^b = \frac{q_2((p_{y_1}(1 - 2q_2) + 1)/2(q_2 - p_{y_1}) - 1)}{q_2 - 1}.$$

Combining them with the two market clearance conditions $x_1^a + x_1^b = 2$ and $\theta_1^a + \theta_1^b = 0$, we finally reach the equilibrium which says that $p_{y_1} = q_2 = 1$ but $0/0$ for all the quantities. Consequently, we conclude that there can be no equilibrium in this example.

Note that at equilibrium prices all entries of the dividend matrix of the assets are 1, which implies that the asset markets are incomplete in the example.

The lesson of this example is that we may have no equilibrium in incomplete markets. In view of the fact that the example possesses no abnormal features, this is a very serious problem. We shall discuss this issue in the next subsection.

11.2.3   *Generic Existence of Equilibria in Economies with Incomplete Asset Markets*

Here we consider the existence problem of equilibria in economies with incomplete asset markets. Before proceeding to the issue, we pay attention to the number of assets and states. We distinguish two cases: $J \geq S$ and $J < S$. Considering the structure of the dividend matrix, we have the viability of complete markets for the former case, whereas we have no choice but of incomplete markets for the latter. As example 11.4 has shown, the former does not always yield complete markets but allows us to investigate the existence of equilibria *in relation to complete markets*; that is, the investigation can be centered on what conditions can make the asset markets complete. However, such an approach is impossible for the latter. We deal with the latter in the following. For the former, see Magill and Shafer (1990, 1991).

The following argument is basically an application of the theory of regular economies so far developed. In fact, many authors have delt with this particular issue from the viewpoint of regular economies. The approach described below is due to Hirsch, Magill and Mas-Colell (1990). For other approaches, see, e.g. Duffie and Shafer (1985), Husseini, Lasry and Magill

(1990) and Geanakoplos and Shafer (1990).

To begin with, we slightly modify the definition of an equilibrium for an economy with assets so as to facilitate the following analysis. Recall that we postulated a specific normalization of any given $S+1$-vector $\alpha > 0$ satisfying

$$\alpha \begin{pmatrix} -q \\ D(p_1, A) \end{pmatrix} = 0$$

to obtain definition 11.8 for a no-arbitrage equilibrium. Here, as a $S+1$-vector fulfilling the above equalities we may especially take the optimal values of Lagrange multipliers $(\lambda_0^1, \lambda_1^1, \ldots, \lambda_S^1)$ obtained by solving the optimization problem for consumer 1 presented in definition 11.7. Then, through the same normalization for that vector, we obtain another representation of an equilibrium which alters part (1) of definition 11.8 as follows.

$(1')$ x^1 is a solution for the following optimization problem.

$$\max_{x^1} \quad u^1(x^1)$$
$$s.t. \quad p \cdot (x^1 - \omega^1) = 0.$$

$$(11.1)$$

For other consumers, x^i is a solution for the following optimization problem $(i = 2, \ldots, I)$.

$$\max_{x^i} \quad u^i(x^i)$$
$$s.t. \quad p \cdot (x^i - \omega^i) = 0$$
$$p_1 \ \square \ (x_1^i - \omega_1^i) \in sp[D(p_1, A)].$$

On the basis of the altered definition, we investigate the existence problem of equilibria in economies with incomplete markets from the viewpoint of regular economies. To this end, we need some analytical preliminaries.

First of all, we are required to determine the space of economies. In view of the framework of the model, it is appropriate for us to consider a pair of the initial endowment allocations among consumers and the asset structure to be the parameters describing an economy. Utility functions of consumers could be included in such parameters but, to make the matter simple, we only pick these elements in the following. Moreover, for the sake of simplicity, we assume that only strictly positive endowments are admissible. Thus the space of economies turns out to be $\boldsymbol{R}_{++}^{L(S+1)I} \times \boldsymbol{R}^{LSJ}$, which we denote $\tilde{\mathcal{E}}$.

Secondly we need some conditions including differentiability on a given utility function of each consumer. For the sake of simplicity, we assume the smoothness, the boundary condition, the monotonicity and the strong quasi-concavity for a utility function so that we have a differentiable demand function $f^i : \boldsymbol{R}_{++}^{L(S+1)} \times \boldsymbol{R}_{++} \to \boldsymbol{R}_{++}^{L(S+1)}$ for each consumer i $(i = 1, \ldots, I)$ (see 6.2.1). Note in this setting that each f^i satisfies assumption 3.1 (the boundary condition) as well as assumption 1.3 (see 1.2.1 and 3.2.2).

Now let's proceed to the analysis. First we define an auxiliary notion of equilibria called a pseudo-equilibrium.

Definition 11.10   For an economy $(\omega, A) \in \tilde{\mathcal{E}}$, a pseudo-equilibrium is a triple $(p,\ x,\ L)$ satisfying that

(1) x^1 is a solution for the following optimization problem.

$$\max_{x^1}\quad u^1(x^1)$$
$$s.t.\ \ p \cdot (x^1 - \omega^1) = 0.$$

$$(11.2)$$

For other consumers, x^i is a solution for the following optimization problem $(i = 2, \ldots, I)$:

$$\max_{x^i}\quad u^i(x^i)$$
$$s.t.\ \ p \cdot (x^i - \omega^i) = 0$$
$$p_\mathbf{1} \ \square \ (x^i_\mathbf{1} - \omega^i_\mathbf{1}) \in L.$$

(2) $\sum_{i=1}^{I}(x^i - \omega^i) = 0.$
(3) $sp[D(p_\mathbf{1}, A)] \subset L.$

where L is an element of $G_{J,S}$ (the Grassmann manifold), that is, L is a J-dimensional linear subspace of $\boldsymbol{R}^S$.

Note that if there exists a pseudo-equilibrium such that $sp[D(p_\mathbf{1}, A)] = L$, it is nothing but an equilibrium itself. For a pseudo-equilibrium, we have a remarkable claim as follows.

Proposition 11.3   *There exists a pseudo-equilibrium for every economy* $(\omega, A) \in \tilde{\mathcal{E}}.$

Proof. Step 1: Set $f^i(p, p \cdot \omega^i; L) = f^i(p, L)$ for any given economy $(\omega, A) \in \tilde{\mathcal{E}}$, $i = 2, \ldots, I$. Similarly set $f^1(p, p \cdot \omega^1) = f^1(p)$. By identifying L with an element of $\boldsymbol{R}^{(S-J)J}$ $(= G_{J,S})$, we may consider $f^i : \boldsymbol{R}_{++}^{L(S+1)} \times G_{J,S} \to \boldsymbol{R}_{++}^{L(S+1)}$ to be smooth $(i = 1, \ldots, I)$. Let $F : \boldsymbol{R}_{++}^{L(S+1)} \times G_{J,S} \to \boldsymbol{R}^{L(S+1)}$ be an aggregate excess demand function, i.e.

$$F(p, L) = f^1(p) - \omega^1 + \sum_{i=2}^{I} (f^i(p, L) - \omega^i).$$

Then a pseudo-equilibrium for the economy is obviously expressed as a pair (p, L) such that $F(p, L) = 0$ and $sp[D(p_1, A)] \subset L$. It can be easily seen that F is homogeneous of degree 0 with respect to p and that $p \cdot F(p, L) = 0$ for any $p \in \boldsymbol{R}_{++}^{L(S+1)}$ and any $L \in G_{J,S}$. Moreover, noting the boundary condition of f^1, we obtain that for any sequence $p^k \subset \boldsymbol{R}_{++}^{L(S+1)}$ that is convergent to a point in $\partial \boldsymbol{R}_{++}^{L(S+1)}$, $\lim_{k \to +\infty} \|F(p^k, L)\| = +\infty$.

Step 2: Since F is homogeneous of degree 0 with respect to p, we may restrict p to the strictly positive $L(S+1) - 1$-dimensional unit sphere in $\boldsymbol{R}^{L(S+1)}$ which we denote S_{++}. Then obviously S_{++} is a noncompact and bounded manifold on which F constitutes a vector field pointing inward everywhere close to the boundary.

Here we consider two vector bundles ξ_1 and ξ_2 defined as follows. That is, $\xi_1 = (\Gamma, \pi_1, G_{J,S})$ where $\Gamma = \{ (L, y) \in G_{J,S} \times \boldsymbol{R}^{SJ} \mid y = (\boldsymbol{y}_1, \ldots, \boldsymbol{y}_J), \boldsymbol{y} \in L^{\perp} \subset \boldsymbol{R}^S, j = 1, \ldots, J\}$. Note that $L^{\perp}$ indicates the orthogonal complement of L in $\boldsymbol{R}^S$ as we have stated before. On the other hand, $\xi_2 = (TS_{++}, \pi_2, S_{++})$, i.e. the tangent vector bundle on S_{++}. Then construct their product vector bundle $\xi_1 \times \xi_2 = (\Gamma \times TS_{++}, \pi_1 \times \pi_2, G_{J,S} \times S_{++})$ and restrict admissible sections to those which yield tangent vectors pointing inward close to the boundary of S_{++}. In this setting, we have that

$$E_2(\xi_1 \times \xi_2) = E_2(\xi_1) \times E_2(\xi_2)$$

(see the last statement in 11.1.3.).

Step 3: We shall show that $E_2(\xi_1) = E_2(\xi_2) = 1$. First we deal with $E_2(\xi_2)$. Let s_0^2 be the zero section and S_0^2 be the image of S_{++} by s_0^2. For any given $\boldsymbol{p}^* \in S_{++}$, consider the smooth section $s : S_{++} \to TS_{++}$ given by

$$s(\boldsymbol{p}) = (\boldsymbol{p}, \frac{\boldsymbol{p}^*}{\boldsymbol{p} \cdot \boldsymbol{p}^*} - \boldsymbol{p}).$$

Note that $s^{-1}(S_0^2) = \{(\boldsymbol{p}^*)\}$ is a singleton. It is easy to check that the map $f : S_{++} \to \boldsymbol{R}^m$ given by

$$f(\boldsymbol{p}) = \frac{\boldsymbol{p}^*}{\boldsymbol{p} \cdot \boldsymbol{p}^*} - \boldsymbol{p}$$

is a submersion at $\boldsymbol{p}^*$, which implies that s is transversal to S_0^2. Thus we have that $E_2(\xi_2) = 1$.

Then we work on $E_2(\xi_1)$. Just like $E_2(\xi_2)$, let s_0^1 denote the zero section and S_0^1 be its image. Fix an arbitrary $L^* \in G_{J,S}$. Let $(\boldsymbol{v}_1, \ldots, \boldsymbol{v}_J)$ be the orthonormal base of L^*. We consider the following section $s : G_{J,S} \to \Gamma$.

$$s(L) = (L, \; \Pi(L^\perp)\boldsymbol{v}_1, \ldots, \Pi(L^\perp)\boldsymbol{v}_J)$$

where $\Pi(L^\perp)$ is the projection of $\boldsymbol{R}^S$ to $L^\perp$. Obviously $s^{-1}(S_0^1) = L^*$. Thus, as in the case of $E_2(\xi_2)$, we have only to show that s is transversal to S_0^1 at L^*. Let $U(L^*)$ be the set of J dimensional linear subspaces of $\boldsymbol{R}^S$ that do not intersect $L^{*\perp}$ except at the origin. Note that $U(L^*)$ is a neighborhood of L^* and can be identified with $L(L^*, L^{*\perp})$, the set of all linear transformations of L^* to $L^{*\perp}$ (see the proof of proposition 11.1). For any $L \in G_{J,S}$, let $T_L \in L(L^*, L^{*\perp})$ be the linear transformation corresponding to L and consider expressing $\Pi(L^\perp)\boldsymbol{v}_j$ of $s(L)$ by using T_L, $j = 1, \ldots, J$. First note that there exists $\lambda_j \in \boldsymbol{R}$ and $\boldsymbol{w}_j \in \boldsymbol{R}^S$ such that $\Pi(L^\perp)\boldsymbol{v}_j = \boldsymbol{v}_j - \boldsymbol{w}_j$, $\boldsymbol{w}_j = \lambda_j(\boldsymbol{v}_j + T_L\boldsymbol{v}_j)$ (see the figure in the next page).

Since $\|\boldsymbol{v}_j\|/\|\boldsymbol{v}_j + T_L\boldsymbol{v}_j\| = \|\boldsymbol{w}_j\|/\|\boldsymbol{v}_j\|$ and $\|\boldsymbol{v}_j\| = 1$, $\|\boldsymbol{w}_j\| = 1/\|\boldsymbol{v}_j + T_L\boldsymbol{v}_j\|$, which implies that $\lambda_j = 1/\|\boldsymbol{v}_j + T_L\boldsymbol{v}_j\|^2$. Thus we obtain that

$$\Pi(L^\perp)\boldsymbol{v}_j = \boldsymbol{v}_j - \frac{\boldsymbol{v}_j + T_L\boldsymbol{v}_j}{\|\boldsymbol{v}_j + T_L\boldsymbol{v}_j\|^2}, \quad j = 1, \ldots, J.$$

In order to investigate the property of the derivative for s, it is sufficient for us to check the directional derivative of each $\Pi(L^\perp)\boldsymbol{v}_j$ in the direction of L. For simplicity, set $\sigma_j(L) = \Pi(L^\perp)\boldsymbol{v}_j$. Then, we have that

$$\frac{d\sigma_j(tL)}{dt}\Big|_{t=0} = -T_L\boldsymbol{v}_j, \; j = 1, \ldots, J$$

which is orthogonal to $\boldsymbol{v}_j$. Since L is arbitrarily chosen, we obtain that s is transversal to S_0^1.

Step 4: Since $E_2(\xi_1 \times \xi_2)$ has been shown to be equal to 1, the image of S_{++} by any section that yields vectors pointing inward close to the

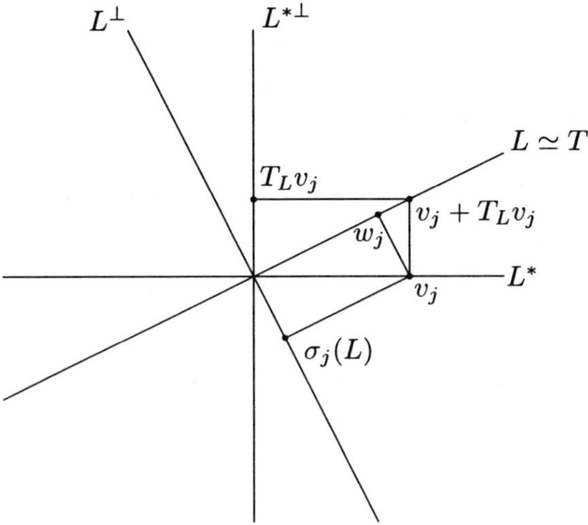

Fig. 11.2

boundary always intersects $S_0^1 \times S_0^2$. We especially consider the smooth section s^* given by

$$s^*(L,p) = (L,\ p,\ \Pi(L^\perp)D^1(p_1, A), \ldots, \Pi(L^\perp)D^J(p_1, A),\ F(p, L))$$

where $D^j(p_1, A)$ denotes the j-th column of $D(p_1, A)$, $j = 1, \ldots, J$. This section obviously yields vectors pointing inward close to the boundary because of the property of F. Thus there exists p and L such that $F(p, L) = 0$ and that $\Pi(L^\perp)D^1(p_1, A) = \ldots = \Pi(L^\perp)D^J(p_1, A) = 0$, which implies that each $D^j(p_1, A)$ is included in L; that is $sp[D(p_1, A)] \subset L$. This completes the proof. $\qquad\square$

As we have noticed before, if $D(p_1, A) = L$ at a pseudo-equilibrium, then the pseudo-equilibrium is a real equilibrium. It is, however, easily seen that this condition is equivalent to the following,

$$rank\ D(p_1, A) = J$$

which means that $D(p_1, A)$ is of full rank in our setting. In this connection, it is worth noting that the set $\{(p, A) \in S_{++} \times \boldsymbol{R}^{LSJ} \mid rank\ D(p_1, A) = J\}$ constitutes an open and dense subset in $S_{++} \times \boldsymbol{R}^{LSJ}$ because of the following two observations: (1) the set of full rank matrices forms an open and dense subset in the set of all $S \times J$ matrices, and (2) the smooth map $D : S_{++} \times \boldsymbol{R}^{LSJ} \to \boldsymbol{R}^{SJ}$ is a submersion. This fact suggests that a pseudo-equilibrium is not so far from a real equilibrium. In other words, a slight perturbation of an economy may bring a pseudo-equilibrium to a real equilibrium. Therefore we are reasonably tempted to investigate the issue from the viewpoint of the genericity, which implies that we should adopt the method of regular economies here. By doing so, we actually obtain the following result.

Theorem 11.2 *For almost all economies with incomplete asset markets, there exists an equilibrium.*

Proof. Let Θ denote the set $\{(p, A) \in S_{++} \times \boldsymbol{R}^{LSJ} \mid rank\ D(p_{\mathbf{1}}, A) = J\}$, which is an open and dense set in $S_{++} \times \boldsymbol{R}^{LSJ}$ as we have shown above. We consider a map that associates each economy $(\omega, A) \in \tilde{\mathcal{E}}$ with its pseudo-equilibria.

Step 1: First we check if this map is well-defined. To this end, pick the smooth section $s^* : G_{J,S} \times S_{++} \to \Gamma \times TS_{++}$ for the product vector bundle $\xi_1 \times \xi_2$ given in the proof of the above proposition, i.e.

$$s^*(L, p) = (L,\ p,\ \Pi(L^{\perp})D^1(p_{\mathbf{1}}, A), \ldots, \Pi(L^{\perp})D^J(p_{\mathbf{1}}, A),\ F(p, L)).$$

We construct from this section a particular smooth map $\gamma : G_{J,S} \times S_{++} \times \boldsymbol{R}_{++}^{L(S+1)I} \times \boldsymbol{R}^{LSJ} \to \boldsymbol{R}^{SJ} \times \boldsymbol{R}^{L(S+1)}$ defined by

$$\gamma(L, p, \omega, A) = (\Pi(L^{\perp})D^1(p_{\mathbf{1}}, A), \ldots, \Pi(L^{\perp})D^J(p_{\mathbf{1}}, A),\ F(p, L)).$$

Noting the derivative of the map with respect to (ω, A), it is easily seen that γ is a submersion. Thus $\gamma^{-1}(0)$ is a submanifold with the dimension of $L(S + 1)I + LSJ$. This manifold consists of the pairs $\{(an\ economy,\ corresponding\ pseudo-equilibria)\}$, and is therefore properly called the pseudo-equilibrium manifold (see 3.2.1), which we denote by Λ for simplicity.

We follow the same procedure as the one provided in 3.2.1. That is, take the projection $\pi : G_{J,S} \times S_{++} \times \boldsymbol{R}_{++}^{L(S+1)I} \times \boldsymbol{R}^{LSJ} \to \boldsymbol{R}_{++}^{L(S+1)I} \times \boldsymbol{R}^{LSJ}$ restricted to Λ and consider the set of regular values of the restricted projection. Needless to say, such a regular value is just a regular economy of the incomplete market version. Thus the set constitutes an open and dense set in $\boldsymbol{R}_{++}^{L(S+1)I} \times \boldsymbol{R}^{LSJ}$ (the space of economies) and yields a smooth map which associates a regular economy with a pseudo-equilibrium (see theorem 3.3 and theorem 3.4). Note that the set of pseudo-equilibria is finite for every economy since the number of the set is shown in the proof of proposition 11.1 to be odd. Thus, if we choose any regular economy, we locally have a particular odd number, say H, of smooth map $p_h(\omega, A)$ and $L_h(\omega, A)$ which carry (ω, A) to each pseudo-equilibrium (p_h, L_h), $h = 1, \ldots, H$.

Step 2: Here we especially pay attention to the smooth map $p_h(\omega, A)$ provided above. This is because real equilibria only depend on whether (p, A) belongs to Θ. Concretely, we ask if $(p_h(\omega, A), A)$ belongs to Θ for each regular economy. First we shall show that each $p_h(\omega, A)$ is a submersion. For simplicity of notation, we omit suffix h in the following. Since we locally have that

$$\gamma(L(\omega, A), p(\omega, A), \omega, A) \equiv 0,$$

$$d\gamma_{(L,P)} \circ (dL_{(\omega,A)}; dp_{(\omega,A)}) = -d\gamma_{(\omega,A)}$$

where $(dL_{(\omega,A)}; dp_{(\omega,A)})$ is the matrix obtained by putting $dL_{(\omega,A)}$ and $dp_{(\omega,A)}$ (both matrix-representation) vertically. Since γ is a submersion, the rows of $-d\gamma_{(\omega,A)}$ are linearly independent. Noting that each of the rows of $-d\gamma_{(\omega,A)}$ is expressed as a linear combination of the rows of $(dL_{(\omega,A)}; dp_{(\omega,A)})$, we obtain that the rows of $(dL_{(\omega,A)}; dp_{(\omega,A)})$ are also linearly independent, thus particularly the rows of $dp_{(\omega,A)}$ are linearly independent; that is to say, $p(\omega, A)$ is a submersion.

Now choose any regular economy and consider in its neighborhood the smooth map $\zeta(\omega, A) = (p_h(\omega, A), A)$, $h = 1, \ldots, H$ where H is the (odd) number of equilibria which is locally constant. Since each $p_h(\omega, A)$ is a submersion, so is ζ. Thus, $\zeta^{-1}(\Theta)$ constitutes an open and dense subset. Since the set of regular economies constitutes an open and dense subset in the space of economies, we obtain that for almost all economies a pseudo-equilibrium is equal to a real equilibrium, which completes the proof. $\quad\square$

It turns out from the proof of the theorem that the method of regular economies enables us to successfully resolve the existence problem of equilibria in the economies with incomplete markets and get over the crisis of the non-existence of equilibria.

Chapter 12

Incomplete Markets II

In this chapter, we consider the welfare property of equilibria in the economies with incomplete markets. In a complete market economy, the equilibrium allocations are known to have a desirable welfare property called Pareto efficiency. However, in contrast, incomplete market equilibria are not necessarily Pareto efficient, as Hart (1975) first pointed out. In view of the argument in the previous chapter, it is interesting to investigate this issue from a generic viewpoint.

Unfortunately, it turns out that we are not able to succeed in overcoming the difficulty this time. However, we shall see another significant aspect of the theory of regular economies in examining the issue. Specifically, the main tool of the theory, that is the transversality theorem, will play a role of the impossibility theorem to show the failure of the equilibrium to be Pareto efficient, which is especially distinguished in section 2 of this chapter.

We do not need any additional mathematics for the analysis in this chapter.

12.1 Welfare Problem of Incomplete Markets: Pareto Efficiency and Inefficiency of Equilibria

It is well known that in the basic Arrow-Debreu model (without assets) of competitive economies the resource allocation realized through the market mechanism, that is an equilibrium allocation, possesses a desirable property from the welfare viewpoint. That property is the so-called Pareto efficiency (or Pareto optimality). Loosely speaking, a Pareto efficient (optimal) allocation is one such that there is no other feasible allocation that makes everyone better-off, which is precisely defined as follows. For the sake of simplicity, we postulate the pure exchange economy with I consumers.

187

Definition 12.1 An allocation $\bar{x} = (\bar{x}^1, \ldots, \bar{x}^I)$ is Pareto efficient (optimal) if (1) $\bar{x}$ is feasible (2) there does not exist $x = (x^1, \ldots, x^I)$ such that x is feasible and that $u^i(x^i) \geq u^i(\bar{x}^i)$, $i = 1, \ldots, I$ with strict inequality for at least one i where u^i indicates the utility function of consumer i.

The observation that equilibrium in competitive markets is Pareto optimal, which is known as the first theorem of welfare economics, is especially considered significant in that it corresponds to the consequence of Adam Smith's invisible hand. Moreover, in the framework of the basic Arrow-Debreu model without assets, we can establish the inverse of the theorem under the assumption of the concavity of utility functions, which is known as the second theorem of welfare economics.

However, once we enter the economy with incomplete markets, the Pareto optimality of equilibrium becomes dubious. The difficulty is easily understandable when we think of the specific feature of the basic model in terms of its welfare. It follows from the two theorems mentioned above that we may presume equilibrium allocations in the basic Arrow-Debreu model without assets to be virtually equivalent to Pareto optimal allocations. Thus if the exchange model with asset markets can be transformed into the basic Arrow-Debreu model without assets, then we could hold that equilibrium in the initial model is Pareto optimal. Such a transformation is, however, admissible only if the asset markets are complete (see definition 11.8 and 11.9). Therefore, so long as we have incomplete asset markets, there is little chance for equilibrium, if any, to be Pareto optimal. Indeed, Magill and Quinzii (1996) have shown generic inefficiency of equilibrium in the economies with incomplete asset markets by way of the method of regular economies, which provides a useful starting point for our argument, so that we shall illustrate their discussion in the following.

The model is almost the same as the one provided in the previous chapter except for one point; that is, it is assumed in this model that there is a single consumption good in each state. It follows that the consumption set of each consumer is R_{++}^{S+1} instead of $R_{++}^{L(S+1)}$ and that an asset structure A is not a $LS \times J$ but only a $S \times J$ matrix. Now we fix each u^i $(i = 1, \ldots, I)$ and an asset structure A where u^i is assumed to fulfill the smoothness, the boundary condition, the monotonicity and the strong quasi-concavity as before and $rank\ A = J\ (< S)$. Thus the space of economies, denoted by $\tilde{\mathcal{E}}$, solely consists of distributions of initial endowments among the consumers, i.e. $\tilde{\mathcal{E}} = R_{++}^{(S+1)I}$. In this setting the following proposition holds.

Proposition 12.1 *In a single consumption good economy, if each utility function satisfies the smoothness, the boundary condition, the monotonicity and the strong quasi-concavity and the rank of the asset structure is equal to $J \ (< S)$, then for almost all economies, the equilibrium allocation is Pareto inefficient.*

Proof. We give a sketch of the whole proof.

(1) The equilibrium condition is represented by the equations system with regard to the asset prices and the initial endowments distribution. To this end, the asset demand function z^i of each i is considered. Let $q \ (\in \mathbf{R}^J)$ denote the price vector of the assets and set $W(q)$ as follows:

$$W(q) = \begin{pmatrix} -q \\ A \end{pmatrix}.$$

Then, owing to the properties of the utility function, we have the well-defined asset demand function $z^i : Q \times \tilde{\mathcal{E}} \to \mathbf{R}^J$, $i = 1, \ldots, I$, given by

$$z^i(q, \omega^i) = arg \ max \ u^i(\omega^i + W(q) \cdot z^i)$$

where Q is the set of no-arbitrage asset prices defined as

$$Q = \{ \, q \in \mathbf{R}^J \mid q = \pi_1 \cdot A, \ \pi_1 \in \mathbf{R}^S_{++} \}.$$

Note that z^i is smooth. The equilibrium condition of the economy is now given by

$$\sum_{i=1}^{I} z^i(q, \omega^i) = 0,$$

since if this equation holds, the good markets are automatically cleared.

(2) Consider the present value vector of each consumer. Since the vector designates the gradient vector of the utility function at the subjective equilibrium, equality among those vectors leads to Pareto optimality. Noting that the present value vector $(\pi_1^i, \ldots, \pi_S^i)$ of consumer i is expressed at the subjective equilibrium $\bar{x}^i$ as follows

$$\pi_s^i(\bar{x}^i) = \frac{\partial u^i(\bar{x}^i)/\partial x_s^i}{\partial u^i(\bar{x}^i)/\partial x_0^i}, \quad s = 1, \ldots, S,$$

we can define the map $\pi_1^i : Q \times \tilde{\mathcal{E}} \to \mathbf{R}^S$, $i = 1, \ldots, I$, given by

$$\pi_1^i(q, \omega^i) = (\pi_s^i(\omega^i + W(q) \cdot z^i(q, \omega^i))), \quad s = 1, \ldots, S.$$

Then in order for the equilibrium to be Pareto optimal, the following equations must hold:

$$\pi_1^i(q, \omega^i) - \pi_1^j(q, \omega^j) = 0, \quad i, \, j = 1, \ldots, I.$$

(3) The goal is to show that for any pair i, j with $i \neq j$, the system of equations

$$\sum_{i=1}^{I} z^i(q, \omega^i) = 0$$

$$\pi_1^i(q, \omega^i) - \pi_1^j(q, \omega^j) = 0$$

has no solution for almost all $\omega \in \tilde{\mathcal{E}}$. For simplicity of notation, set $f(q, \omega) = \sum_{i=1}^{I} z^i(q, \omega^i)$. Since the asset markets are incomplete, there exists some $\pi_1 \in \mathbf{R}^S$ such that π_1 belongs to the orthogonal complement of $sp[A]$ and that $\pi_1 \neq 0$, thus $\pi_{\bar{s}} \neq 0$ for some $\bar{s} \in \{1, \ldots, S\}$. Then, instead of the above system of equations, we consider the simplified one given by

$$f(q, \omega) = 0$$

$$\pi_{\bar{s}}^i(q, \omega^i) - \pi_{\bar{s}}^j(q, \omega^j) = 0.$$

Defining the function $h : Q \times \tilde{\mathcal{E}} \to \mathbf{R}^{J+1}$ by

$$h(q, \omega) = (f(q, \omega), \; \pi_{\bar{s}}^i(q, \omega^i) - \pi_{\bar{s}}^j(q, \omega^j)),$$

the problem reduces to showing that the equation $h(q, \omega) = 0$ has no solution for almost all $\omega \in \tilde{\mathcal{E}}$.

Here is a theorem concerning the non-existence of solutions (see Magill and Quinzii (1996), chapter 2, 11.3 Theorem):

Let $Q \subset \mathbf{R}^J$, $\Omega \subset \mathbf{R}^K$ be open sets and let $h : Q \times \Omega \to \mathbf{R}^{J+1}$ be a smooth map. If, for all $(\bar{q}, \bar{\omega}) \in Q \times \Omega$ such that $h(\bar{q}, \bar{\omega}) = 0$ we have that

$$rank[dh_{(q,\omega)}(\bar{q}, \bar{\omega})] = J + 1,$$

then for almost all $\omega \in \Omega$ the set $\{q \in Q \mid h(q, \omega) = 0\}$ is empty.

According to the above theorem, we have only to show that $rank[dh_{(q,\omega)}(\bar{q}, \bar{\omega})] = J + 1$ for all $(\bar{q}, \bar{\omega}) \in Q \times \tilde{\mathcal{E}}$ such that $h(\bar{q}, \bar{\omega}) = 0$.

(4) The problem just presented above is resolved by showing the existence of $(\Delta q, \Delta \omega) \in \mathbf{R}^J \times \mathbf{R}^{(S+1)I}$ such that

$$dh_{(q,\omega)}(\bar{q}, \bar{\omega})(\Delta q, \Delta \omega) = e^j$$

for each j ($j = 1, \ldots, J + 1$) where $e^1, \ldots, e^{J+1}$ denote the standard basis for $\mathbf{R}^{J+1}$. For $j = 1, \ldots, J$, it can be shown that $\Delta \omega^1 = (\bar{q}_j, -A_1^j, \ldots, -A_S^j), \Delta \omega^i = 0$, $i = 2, \ldots, I$ and $\Delta q = 0$ satisfy the requirement. For $j = J+1$, we need some preparation. Let $\bar{x}^i$ be the equilibrium consumption vector of consumer i corresponding to $(\bar{q}, \bar{\omega})$. Note that $\pi_1^i(q, \omega^i) = (\pi_s^i(\omega^i + W(q) \cdot z^i(q, \omega^i))) = \pi_1^i(x^i)$. Then, first establish that there exists some $\Delta x^i \in \mathbf{R}^{S+1}$ such that $\pi_{\bar{s}}^i(\bar{x}^i + \Delta x^i) = \pi_{\bar{s}}^i(\bar{x}^i) + 1$. This is proved by using a lemma concerning the local controllability of the present-value vector (see Magill and Quinzii (1996), chapter 2, 11.7 Lemma). Then it can be shown that $\Delta q = 0, \Delta \omega^i = \Delta x^i$ and $\Delta \omega^j = 0$, $j \neq i$ fulfill the requirement for $j = J + 1$ where Δx^i is the one just provided above.

(5) Let $\Omega_{i,j}$ be an open and dense subset of $\tilde{\mathcal{E}}$ in which the system of equations

$$\sum_{i=1}^{I} z^i(q, \omega^i) = 0$$

$$\pi_1^i(q, \omega^i) - \pi_1^j(q, \omega^j) = 0$$

has no solution. Then it is evident that $\bigcap_{i \neq j} \Omega_{i,j}$ is also open and dense in $\tilde{\mathcal{E}}$, which proves the proposition. $\qquad\square$

According to the proposition, even a single consumption good economy would scarcely have a Pareto optimal equilibrium with incomplete markets, which properly implies that in multi-goods economies it is hopeless to achieve Pareto optimal equilibria as long as the asset markets are incomplete.

12.2 Inefficiency of Equilibria of Incomplete Markets without Concavity

The consequence of the previous section is very serious. But we should notice that the result obtained there is crucially dependent on the assumption of the concavity of utility functions. If we lack the assumption, then the (virtual) equivalence of market equilibrium allocations and Pareto optimal allocations fails, which prevents us from the straight insight of inefficiency of equilibria in incomplete market economies. It is worth noting that the argument in the proof of the proposition 12.1 is no more valid for the case without concavity since we would not be able to have well-defined demand functions without concavity of utility functions.

Let's consider the matter in a drastically simplified situation. See Fig. 12.1 below where a well-known Edgeworth box diagram is depicted.

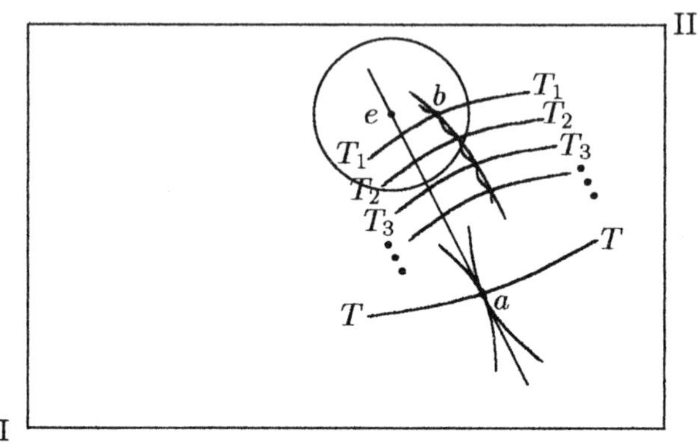

Fig. 12.1

The south-west corner of the box indicates the origin for agent I while the north-east corner indicates the origin for agent II. Let the curve TT denote the (part of) contract curve when the given utility function of each agent is strictly quasi-concave. Now suppose that an initial endowment distribution is located at e in the box. If we have complete markets, then the equilibrium is realized at a which is obviously Pareto optimal. However, if we have incomplete markets, the trade opportunity is limited for each agent in that the free exchange between all the goods is not permitted (see definition 11.9), which implies in our simple situation that the agents are only allowed to trade inside the restricted area including e. We may consider the area to be a circle with e as the center like the one depicted in the box. Then, it is evident from the diagram that a Pareto optimal allocation is unattainable through the market equilibrium. It can be easily seen that the same argument is valid for many other initial endowment distributions than e.

Next, consider what would happen without concavity of utility functions. In that case, we are allowed to have multi-contract curves, say, T_1T_1, $T_2T_2, \ldots$ in the diagram. Thus, as the figure is showing, a Pareto optimal equilibrium allocation is obtainable, say, like b. We can apply the similar argument to other initial endowment distributions than e. This observation implies that if we dispense with the assumption of concavity, equilibrium allocations are more liable to be Pareto optimal even with incomplete markets.

Consequently, we are naturally led to the question to what extent utility functions without concavity can yield Pareto optimal equilibria.

To this issue our genericity analysis so far discussed is again applicable. More specifically, we adopt the admissible set of utility functions to expand the space of economies on which we practice the genericity analysis concerning Pareto optimality of equilibria, though remaining in a single consumption good model.

Thus the model to be considered is as follows. The consumption set and the admissible set of initial endowments of each consumer are, as before, both R_{++}^{S+1}. As for utility functions, we make the following assumption.

Assumption 12.1 the utility function u^i of consumer i $(i = 1, \ldots I)$ satisfies

(1) $u^i \in C^\infty(R_{++}^{S+1}, R)$.
(2) $du_{\boldsymbol{x}}^i \in R_{++}^{S+1}$ for each $\boldsymbol{x} \in R_{++}^{S+1}$.

That is to say, we only require the monotonicity for a utility function. For simplicity , set $u = (u^1, \ldots, u^I)$ and $\omega = (\omega^1, \ldots, \omega^I)$ in the following.

An asset structure A is described as a $S \times J$ matrix $(J < S)$ where each column is denoted by $\boldsymbol{a}^j$ $(j = 1, \ldots, J)$. Let $\boldsymbol{q}$ $(= (q_1, \ldots, q_J))$ be the price vector of the assets. Since we adopt the generic viewpoint with respect to u and ω , A is fixed so that we may assume that rank $A = J$ without loss of generality.

Thus the space of economies consists of permissible u and ω. Let U be the set of functions satisfying assumption 12.1 and let $\mathcal{U}$ be I-product of U, that is, U^I. Then the space is represented as $\mathcal{U} \times R_{++}^{(S+1)I}$ which is denoted by $\check{\mathcal{E}}$ in the following.

To $R_{++}^{(S+1)I}$ a standard Euclidean topology is given whereas $C^\infty(R_{++}^{S+1}, R)$ is endowed with the Whitney C^∞ topology so that $C^\infty(R_{++}^{S+1}, R)^I$ is considered to be a product topological space. Then, through proposition 6.8, we obtain that $\mathcal{U}$ is an open subset of $C^\infty(R_{++}^{S+1}, R)^I$ in the Whitney C^∞ (product) topology.

Given the asset structure A, each agent has a chance to purchase amounts of J assets and adjust his income stream so that he can optimize his intertemporal consumptions. Let $\boldsymbol{z}^i = (z_1^i, \ldots, z_J^i) \in R^J$ be a portfolio of agent i. Then the problem consumer i has to solve is as follows:

$$\max_{\boldsymbol{x}^i, \boldsymbol{z}^i} \quad u^i(\boldsymbol{x}^i)$$

$$s.t. \ \ x_0^i = \omega_0^i - q \cdot z^i, \ \ \ z^i \in \boldsymbol{R}^J \qquad \qquad \cdots (*)$$
$$x_1^i = \omega_1^i + A \cdot z^i$$

where x_1^i and ω_1^i denote $(x_1^i, \ldots, x_S^i)$ and $(\omega_1^i, \ldots, \omega_S^i)$ respectively as before. Note that there is only one good in the economy so that the price of the good is normalized to be unity (the good at date 0 is interpreted as a numeraire). Now we define the equilibrium for an economy $(u, \omega) \in \check{\mathcal{E}}$.

Definition 12.2 An asset market equilibrium for (u, ω) is a tuple $((x^i, z^i)_i, q)$ such that (1) (x^i, z^i) is a solution of the problem (), $i = 1, \ldots, I$. (2) $\sum_{i=1}^{I} x^i = \sum_{i=1}^{I} \omega^i$ (3) $\sum_{i=1}^{I} z^i = 0$.

Next we consider the efficiency of allocations. Given u and ω, a Pareto optimal allocation is defined as follows.

Definition 12.3 An allocation $x = (\bar{x}^1, \ldots, \bar{x}^I) \in \boldsymbol{R}_{++}^{(S+1)I}$ is a Pareto optimum if (1) $\sum_{i=1}^{I} \bar{x}^i = \sum_{i=1}^{I} \omega^i$ (2) there does not exist $x = (x^1, \ldots, x^I) \in \boldsymbol{R}_{++}^{(S+1)I}$ such that $\sum_{i=1}^{I} x^i = \sum_{i=1}^{I} \omega^i$ and $u^i(x^i) \geq u^i(\bar{x}^i), i = 1, \ldots, I$ with a strict inequality for at least one i.

Lastly we consider a particular feasibility for the economy (u, ω).

Definition 12.4 An allocation $x = (x^1, \ldots, x^I) \in \boldsymbol{R}^{(S+1)I}$ is pseudo-A-feasible if (1) $\sum_{i=1}^{I} x^i = \sum_{i=1}^{I} \omega^i$ (2) $x_1^i \in \langle A \rangle + \omega_1^i, i = 1, \ldots, I$ where $\langle A \rangle$ indicates a vector subspace spanned by the columns of A.

Let $F_A(\omega)$ denote the set of pseudo-A-feasible allocations with respect to ω. Indeed only the intersection of $F_A(\omega)$ and $\boldsymbol{R}_{++}^{(S+1)I}$ makes sense, but we will use the whole set of $F_A(\omega)$ for analytical convenience in the following. If a tuple $((x^i, z^i)_i, q)$ is an asset market equilibrium for (u, ω), then obviously $(x^i)_i$ is an element of $F_A(\omega)$. $F_A(\omega)$ will play a very critical role in the analysis.

The following analysis is a little complicated so that we give the scenario for our discussion below. First we consider the set of allocations which satisfy the first order necessary condition for a Pareto optimum. To characterize the set we can use the Thom Transversality Theorem in 1-jet space and obtain the result that the set constitutes a definite dimensional manifold generically in u. Then we work on $F_A(\omega)$. It can be easily seen that $F_A(\omega)$ is also a manifold for every ω. To examine transversality between $F_A(\omega)$ and the set previously mentioned we can use the transversality theorem (theorem 8.1) in turn and conclude that for almost all ω the intersection of those sets is empty, which implies the consequence to be shown.

The last use of the transversality theorem is suggestive in that it works as an impossibility theorem.

Now let us consider the first order necessary conditions of Pareto optimal allocations.

Proposition 12.2   *Given $(u, \omega) \in \check{\mathcal{E}}$, a Pareto optimal allocation $\bar{x} = (\bar{x}^1, \ldots, \bar{x}^I) \in \boldsymbol{R}_{++}^{(S+1)I}$ satisfies the following equation:*

$$du_{\bar{x}^1}^1 / \sum_{s=0}^{S+1} du_{\bar{x}^1,s}^1 = \ldots = du_{\bar{x}^I}^I / \sum_{s=0}^{S+1} du_{\bar{x}^I,s}^I.$$

Proof.   Since a Pareto optimal allocation can be characterized as a solution of the next maximization problem,

$$\max_{\boldsymbol{x}^1} \ u^1(\boldsymbol{x}^1)$$

$$s.t. \ u^i(\boldsymbol{x}^i) \geq \bar{u}^i, \quad i = 2, \ldots, I$$

$$\sum_{i=1}^{I} \boldsymbol{x}^i = \sum_{i=1}^{I} \omega^i$$

the claim is easily deduced using the Lagrange multiplier method. $\square$

Let the set of allocations which satisfy the equation in the proposition be $P(u)$. Note that an element of $P(u)$ is not required to fulfill feasibility (i.e. condition (1) of definition 12.3).

We are going to apply the Thom Transversality Theorem to characterize $P(u)$ generically in u. To this end, we are concerned solely with 1-jet space $J^1(\boldsymbol{R}_{++}^{S+1}, \boldsymbol{R})$ which is naturally identified with $\boldsymbol{R}_{++}^{S+1} \times \boldsymbol{R} \times \boldsymbol{R}^{S+1}$. Let $J_+^1(\boldsymbol{R}_{++}^{S+1}, \boldsymbol{R})$ denote $\boldsymbol{R}_{++}^{S+1} \times \boldsymbol{R} \times \boldsymbol{R}_{++}^{S+1}$ which is obviously an open submanifold of $J^1(\boldsymbol{R}_{++}^{S+1}, \boldsymbol{R})$. Then we define the map $\phi : J_+^1(\boldsymbol{R}_{++}^{S+1}, \boldsymbol{R}) \to \boldsymbol{R}_{++}^{S+1} \times \boldsymbol{R} \times \Delta_+^S$ given by

$$\phi(a, b, c_1, \ldots, c_{S+1}) = (a, b, c_1 / \sum_{i=1}^{S+1} c_i, \ldots, c_{S+1} / \sum_{i=1}^{S+1} c_i)$$

where Δ_+^S indicates strictly positive S-simplex. I-product function of ϕ (denoted by $\Phi : J_+^1(\boldsymbol{R}_{++}^{S+1}, \boldsymbol{R})^I \to (\boldsymbol{R}_{++}^{S+1} \times \boldsymbol{R} \times \Delta_+^S)^I)$ is defined in such a way that $\Phi(y^1, \ldots, y^I) = (\phi(y^1), \ldots, \phi(y^I))$. In view of proposition 8.2, lemma 8.4 and lemma 8.5, we immediately obtain the following claim:

Proposition 12.3   *Let W be a submanifold of $(\boldsymbol{R}_{++}^{S+1} \times \boldsymbol{R} \times \Delta_+^S)^I$. Then*

$$\mathcal{T} = \left\{ u \in \mathcal{U} \,|\, \Phi \circ j_I^1 u \text{ is transversal to } W \right\}$$

is dense in $\mathcal{U}$.

Proof. Note that when u is an element of $\mathcal{U}$, then the range of $j_I^1 u$ is not $J^1\big(\boldsymbol{R}_{++}^{S+1}, \boldsymbol{R}\big)^I$ but $J_+^1\big(\boldsymbol{R}_{++}^{S+1}, \boldsymbol{R}\big)^I$. Take $\boldsymbol{R}_{++}^{(S+1)I}$, $J_+^1\big(\boldsymbol{R}_{++}^{S+1}, \boldsymbol{R}\big)^I$ and $\big(\boldsymbol{R}_{++}^{S+1} \times \boldsymbol{R} \times \Delta_+^S\big)^I$ for X,Y and Z in Lemma 8.5. Then if we show that Φ is a submersion, the proof is completed by Lemma 8.5 and proposition 8.2. But by the structure of Φ, to show its submersiveness we have only to show that the map $\zeta : \boldsymbol{R}_{++}^{(S+1)I} \to \Delta_+^{SI}$ defined by

$$\zeta(\boldsymbol{c}^1, \boldsymbol{c}^2, \ldots, \boldsymbol{c}^I) = \left(\frac{\boldsymbol{c}^1}{\sum_{i=1}^{S+1} c_i^1}, \frac{\boldsymbol{c}^2}{\sum_{i=1}^{S+1} c_i^2}, \ldots, \frac{\boldsymbol{c}^I}{\sum_{i=1}^{S+1} c_i^I} \right)$$

is a submersion. By applying Lemma 8.4 we see that this map is indeed a submersion. $\qquad\square$

We have a consequence regarding $P(u)$.

Proposition 12.4   *There exists a dense subset $\mathcal{U}^*$ of $\mathcal{U}$ such that for any u in $\mathcal{U}^*$, $P(u)$ constitutes a $S+I$ dimensional submanifold in $\boldsymbol{R}_{++}^{(S+1)I}$.*

Proof.   Let W be the set $\{ (\boldsymbol{a}^i, b^i, \boldsymbol{c}^i)_i \in (\boldsymbol{R}_{++}^{S+1} \times \boldsymbol{R} \times \Delta_+^S)^I \,|\, \boldsymbol{c}^1 = \boldsymbol{c}^2 = \ldots = \boldsymbol{c}^I \}$. It is obvious that W is a $(S+1)I + I + S$ dimensional submanifold of $(\boldsymbol{R}_{++}^{S+1} \times \boldsymbol{R} \times \Delta_+^S)^I$. Since $\mathcal{U}$ is an open subset of $C^\infty\big(\boldsymbol{R}_{++}^{S+1}, \boldsymbol{R}\big)^I$, there exists a dense subset $\mathcal{U}^*$ of $\mathcal{U}$ such that for any u in $\mathcal{U}^*$, $\Phi \circ j_I^1 u$ is transversal to W. Thus for those u, $\Phi \circ j_I^1 u^{-1}(W)$ constitutes a $S + I$ dimensional submanifold of $\boldsymbol{R}_{++}^{(S+1)I}$. Since $\Phi \circ j_I^1 u^{-1}(W) = P(u)$, the proof is completed. $\qquad\square$

Now we turn to $F_A(\omega)$. A particular property of $F_A(\omega)$ is obtainable with an additional assumption on the numbers of agents, assets and states.

Assumption 12.2 $(J+1)I > S+1$.

Proposition 12.5   *Under assumption 12.2, $F_A(\omega)$ constitutes a $(J+1)I - (S+1)$ dimensional submanifold of $\boldsymbol{R}^{(S+1)I}$ for each $\omega \in \boldsymbol{R}_{++}^{(S+1)I}$.*

Proof.   Let X^i be the set $\{(x_0, x_1, \ldots, x_S) \in \boldsymbol{R}^{S+1} \,|\, (x_1, \ldots, x_S) \in \langle A \rangle + \omega_{\boldsymbol{1}}^i \}$. It can be easily seen that X^i is a $J + 1$ dimensional submanifold of $\boldsymbol{R}^{S+1}$ since rank $A = J$. Define a map $g : \prod_i X_i \to \boldsymbol{R}^{S+1}$ by $g(\boldsymbol{x}^1, \ldots, \boldsymbol{x}^I) = \sum_i^I \boldsymbol{x}^i - \sum_i^I \boldsymbol{\omega}^i$. Since $\dim \prod_i X_i = (J+1)I > \dim \boldsymbol{R}^{S+1} = S+1$ by assumption 12.2, $dg_{(\boldsymbol{x}^1, \ldots, \boldsymbol{x}^I)}$ is surjective at each $(\boldsymbol{x}^1, \ldots, \boldsymbol{x}^I) \in \prod_i X_i$ so that g is a submersion. Since 0 is a regular value of g, $g^{-1}(0) = F_A(\omega)$ is a $(J+1)I - (S+1)$ dimensional submanifold of $\boldsymbol{R}^{(S+1)I}$. $\qquad\square$

Finally we investigate the transversality between $P(u)$ and $F_A(\omega)$. To this end, we may use the transversality theorem which was introduced as theorem 8.1.

We fix $P(u)$ for any given u of $\mathcal{U}^*$ and consider the inclusion map $\iota : P(u) \to \mathbf{R}^{(S+1)I}$. Then the image of ι, i.e. $P(u)$, can be interpreted as a $(S+I)$ dimensional submanifold of $\mathbf{R}^{(S+1)I}$. We are going to check if $F_A(\omega)$ is transversal to $P(u)$ generically in ω. To this end, we first pick an arbitrary ω out of $\mathbf{R}^{(S+1)I}_{++}$ and fix it. Then define the map $\psi : F_A(\omega) \times N_1^+(\omega) \to \mathbf{R}^{(S+1)I}$ by $\psi(x,y) = x + y$ where $N_1^+(\omega) = \{y \in \mathbf{R}^{(S+1)I}_{++} \mid \|y - \omega\| < 1\}$.

Proposition 12.6 *For almost all $y \in N_1^+(\omega)$, $\psi(\cdot, y) : F_A(\omega) \to \mathbf{R}^{(S+1)I}$ is transversal to $P(u)$.*

Proof. It is obvious from the structure of ψ that ψ is a submersion. Thus ψ is transversal to any submanifold of $\mathbf{R}^{(S+1)I}$, especially $P(u)$. Here we apply the transversality theorem mentioned above to ψ and obtain the desired result. $\square$

Proposition 12.7 *For each $y \in N_1^+(\omega)$, $\psi(F_A(\omega), y) = F_A(\omega + y)$.*

Proof. Since $F_A(\omega)$ is the set of $x = (x^1, \ldots, x^I) \in \mathbf{R}^{(S+1)I}$ that satisfies (1) $\sum_{i=1}^{I} x^i = \sum_{i=1}^{I} \omega^i$, (2) $x_1^i \in \langle A \rangle + \omega_1^i, i = 1, \ldots, I$, it is easily seen that the image of $F_A(\omega)$ by ψ is $F_A(\omega + y)$. $\square$

Now we are in a position to state our main claim.

Theorem 12.1 *Under assumptions 12.1 and 12.2, for almost all (u, ω) in $\tilde{\mathcal{E}}$, each equilibrium allocation of the economy (u, ω) is Pareto inefficient.*

Proof. Let u be an element of $\mathcal{U}^*$. For any given $\omega \in \mathbf{R}^{(S+1)I}_{++}$, define $N_1^+(\omega)$. Let y be an element of $N_1^+(\omega)$ such that $\psi(\cdot, y)$ is transversal to $P(u)$. Note that from proposition 12.6 such an y is an element of a dense set of $N_1^+(\omega)$. Now suppose that $F_A(\omega + y) \cap P(u) \neq \emptyset$. Since $\psi(\cdot, y)$ is transversal to $P(u)$, it follows from proposition 12.7 that at any $x \in F_A(\omega + y) \cap P(u)$, $T_z F_A(\omega) + T_x P(u) = \mathbf{R}^{(S+1)I}$ where T indicates a tangent space and $z = \psi(\cdot, y)^{-1}(x)$. But considering proposition 12.4, proposition 12.5 and assumption 12.2, we have

$$\begin{aligned}
dim F_A(\omega) + dim P(u) &= (J+1)I - (S+1) + S + I \\
&\leq SI + I - 1 \\
&< (S+1)I \\
&= dim \mathbf{R}^{(S+1)I},
\end{aligned}$$

which is a contradiction. Thus $F_A(\omega + y) \cap P(u) = \emptyset$; that is to say, there exist no Pareto optimal allocations fulfilling pseudo-A-feasibility. Since each equilibrium allocation of (u, ω) is obviously pseudo-A-feasible, it is Pareto inefficient. Noting that ω is arbitrarily taken from $\boldsymbol{R}_{++}^{(S+1)I}$ and that u and y are respectively arbitrary elements of the dense sets, our claim immediately follows. $\qquad\square$

Therefore, even though utility functions are free of concavity, equilibrium allocations in incomplete markets are mostly Pareto inefficient. In addition, we obtain two suggestive findings from the proof of the theorem. One is that the generic inefficiency of equilibrium allocations is caused by the fact that for almost all u and ω, $P(u)$ is disjoint with $F_A(\omega)$ which contains the set of equilibrium allocations. Otherwise stated, it is not the utility maximization behavior of each agent but its pseudo-A-feasibility that yields Pareto inefficiency; thus, as long as each consumer trades on incomplete asset markets under assumptions 12.1 and 12.2, Pareto optimal allocations are hardly attainable whether he/she is engaged in the individual optimization or not.

The other finding is concerned with the likelihood of the inefficiency of equilibrium allocations. When $J = S$, then the incomplete markets model turns into a complete markets model so that every equilibrium allocation is Pareto optimal by the first fundamental theorem of welfare economics. Therefore, even if the asset markets are incomplete, the likelihood of the inefficiency of equilibrium allocations is intuitively expected to be dependent on how much J differs from S. It is thereby conjectured that equilibrium allocations with incomplete markets are more likely to be Pareto optimal when J is close to S than when J is far below S. But it is revealed from our argument that such an intuition is wrong. The reason is as follows. It is always true that $F_A(\omega)$ is transversal to $P(u)$ generically in u and ω. The number J has an effect on $\dim F_A(\omega)$; that is, the more the number grows, the larger $\dim F_A(\omega)$ becomes. However, as long as $J < S$, $\dim F_A(\omega)+\dim P(u) < (S+1)I$, which necessarily yields that $F_A(\omega) \cap P(u) = \emptyset$, i.e., equilibrium allocations are always inefficient.

12.3 Constrained Optimality

We established that the criterion of Pareto optimality is too much to ask of incomplete market equilibria. Then, is there any less demanding criterion concerning the welfare of those equilibria? In studying this issue, it is useful to introduce the idea of a fictional planner. The planner is viewed as having access to feasible allocations of goods independently of the price mechanism. If he can choose a dominant allocation over the equilibrium allocation, then the equilibrium allocation is judged to be inefficient. It is true in our incomplete market model that such a planner could find a dominant allocation over the equilibrium allocation, but we should note that he can do it only when he is given the freedom to *ignore the existence of the assets.* If he is not permitted to have such a freedom and takes it for granted that only assets allow the transfer of the goods between the present and the future, then the feasibility of allocations is restricted, which might alter the consequence provided above. This course of thinking leads to the following constrained optimality.

Definition 12.5 Let A be a given asset structure. An allocation of goods and assets $(\bar{x}^i,\ \bar{z}^i)_i$ is constrained Pareto optimal relative to A if

(1) it satisfies that $\sum_i^I x_0^i = \sum_i^I \omega_0^i$, $x_s^i - \omega_s^i \leq a(s)z^i$, $i = 1,\ldots,I$, $s = 1,\ldots,S$, $\sum_i^I z^i = 0$ where $a(s) = (a^1(s),\ldots,a^J(s))$,

(2) there does not exist $(x^i,z^i)_i$ satisfying (1) such that $u^i(x^i) \geq u^i(\bar{x}^i)$, $i = 1,\ldots,I$ with strict inequality for at least one i.

As far as a single good model is concerned, incomplete market equilibria are shown to rehabilitate themselves in terms of this constrained optimality.

Proposition 12.8 *Let a tuple $((\bar{x}^i,\bar{z}^i)_i,\ \bar{q})$ be an equilibrium in the single good model provided in the previous section. Then, the allocation $(\bar{x}^i,\bar{z}^i)_i$ is constrained Pareto optimal relative to A.*

Proof. Noting that the price of the good at date 1 is normalized to be unity, it is obvious that the equilibrium allocation meets condition (1) in the above definition.

Now, suppose that the allocation $(\bar{x}^i,\bar{z}^i)_i$ is not constrained Pareto optimal relative to A. Then there exists $(x^i,z^i)_i$ satisfying (1) such that $u^i(x^i) \geq u^i(\bar{x}^i)$, $i = 1,\ldots,I$ with strict inequality for at least one i, say i'. Obviously $(\bar{x}^i,\bar{z}^i)_i$ is a solution to the following problem

$$\max_{x^i,z^i} \quad u^i(x^i)$$

$$s.t. \quad x_0^i = \omega_0^i - q \cdot z^i, \ z^i \in R^J$$

$$x_1^i = \omega_1^i + A \cdot z^i.$$

Thus, for each $i \neq i'$ we have

$$x_0^i \geq \omega_0^i - \bar{q} \cdot z^i$$

and for i'

$$x_0^{i'} > \omega_0^{i'} - \bar{q} \cdot z^{i'}.$$

Summing these inequalities and noting that $\sum_i^I z^i = 0$, we obtain that $\sum_i^I x_0^i > \sum_i^I \omega_0^i$, which contradicts that $(x^i, z^i)_i$ satisfies (1) in the above definition. $\qquad\square$

There is another concept of constrained optimality that is obtained by strengthening the one stated in definition 12.5. This was initially presented by Diamond (1967), then through the work of Stiglitz (1982), elaborated and extended to the general model of the incomplete markets by Geanakoplos and Polemarchakis (1986).

Imagine that the fictional planner takes into account the existence of *goods markets* as well as the existence of the assets. Then, the planner could only control the portfolio allocation among the consumers, leaving the allocation of goods to the price mechanism. This course of thinking leads to another constrained feasibility; that is, a constrained feasible allocation is the allocation (x, z) in which $\sum_i^I z^i = 0$ and x is the allocation of goods realized through the price mechanism given the portfolio z. However, in view of incomplete market equilibria, a difficulty occurs concerning this feasibility. Given some portfolio allocation by the planner, any consumer would not care about income transfer from the present to the future. At date 0 (the present) he/she has only to fulfill the budget constraint by the initial endowment alone, which implies that an incomplete market equilibrium is not necessarily constrained feasible. Thus, in order for the concept of constrained feasibility to be consistent with incomplete market equilibria, we put another factor under the control of the planner; that is, a *fee* (payable at date 0) of a portfolio. Before defining a consistent feasibility, a preliminary but simple notion of equilibria is in order, which is free of assets.

Definition 12.6   A state-constrained equilibrium for a two-period economy (u, ω) is a pair $(\bar{x}, \bar{p})$ such that

(1) $\bar{x}^i$ is a solution for the following problem, $i = 1, \ldots, I$

$$\max_{x^i} \quad u^i(x^i)$$

$$s.t. \quad \bar{p}_0 \cdot (x_0^i - \omega_0^i) = 0$$

$$\bar{p}_1 \,\square\, (x_1^i - \omega_1^i) = 0.$$

(2) $\sum_{i=1}^I (\bar{x}^i - \omega^i) = 0.$

By way of this notion, we obtain the following definition of constrained feasibility.

Definition 12.7   An allocation $\bar{x}$ $(= (\bar{x}^1, \ldots, \bar{x}^I))$ is constrained feasible for an economy (u, ω, A) if there exists $\bar{p} \in \boldsymbol{R}_{++}^{L(S+1)}$ and $(\bar{\gamma}, \bar{z}) \in \boldsymbol{R}^I \times \boldsymbol{R}^{JI}$ such that

(1) $\sum_{i=1}^{I} \bar{\gamma}^i = 0$ where $\bar{\gamma} = (\bar{\gamma}^1, \ldots, \bar{\gamma}^I)$,

(2) $\sum_{i=1}^{I} \bar{z}^i = 0$ where $\bar{z} = (\bar{z}^1, \ldots, \bar{z}^I)$,

(3) a pair $(\bar{x}, \bar{p})$ is a state-constrained equilibrium for the economy $(u, \tilde{\omega})$ where $\tilde{\omega}^i = (\omega_0^i - \bar{\gamma}^i e_{01}, \ \omega_1^i + A \cdot z^i)$, $i = 1, \ldots, I$ and $e_{01} = (1, \ 0, \ldots, 0) \in \boldsymbol{R}^L$.

In the above definition, we may regard γ as a fee system corresponding to the portfolio allocation z both of which are, as we have stated, under the control of the fictional planner. Note that the fee is assumed to be paid in units of good 1, which is just for convenience. It is easily seen that if $((\bar{x}, \bar{z}), (\bar{p}, \bar{q}))$ is an incomplete market equilibrium, then $\bar{x}$ is constrained feasible with $\bar{\gamma}^i = \bar{q} \cdot \bar{z}^i$, $i = 1, \ldots, I$.

On the basis of the above constrained feasibility, we are naturally led to the following constrained Pareto optimality.

Definition 12.8   An allocation $\bar{x}$ $(= (\bar{x}^1, \ldots, \bar{x}^I))$ is constrained Pareto optimal (or constrained efficient) for an economy (u, ω, A) if it is constrained feasible and there does not exist any other constrained feasible allocation x $(= (x^1, \ldots, x^I))$ such that $u^i(x^i) > u^i(\bar{x}^i)$, $i = 1, \ldots, I$.

Note that the set of constrained feasible allocations is included in the set of allocations satisfying (1) of definition 12.5. Thus, in the single good model, an incomplete market equilibrium is obviously constrained Pareto optimal by proposition 12.8. Otherwise stated, a constrained Pareto optimal allocation *relative to* A implies the constrained Pareto optimal one in a sense of definition 12.8.

Hence, as far as the single good model is concerned, the concept of constrained Pareto optimality, definition 12.5 or definition 12.8, seems a satisfactory substitute for the pure Pareto optimality. However when there are two or more goods, the situation becomes quite different. Following Magill and Shafer (1991), we shall show that incomplete market equilibria are generically constrained inefficient in a sense of definition 12.8 in the multiple goods model, which automatically implies the generic constrained inefficiency in a sense of definition 12.5. We are going to give a sketch of the proof with some assumptions simplifying the story.

Assumption 12.3 Separability of utility functions. Each utility function $u^i : R_+^{L(S+1)} \to R$ is additively separable as follows:

$$u^i(x^i) = u_0^i(x_0^i) + u_1^i(x_1^i), \quad i = 1, \ldots, I.$$

Let U be the set of utility functions satisfying the smoothness, the boundary condition, the monotonicity, the strong quasi-concavity and assumption 12.3. Let $\mathcal{U}$ be the I-product of U.

Assumption 12.4 Numeraire assets. Each asset j delivers contingent amounts of good 1. Thus the asset structure A is virtually a $S \times J$ matrix.

Note that absolute price levels do not matter in the real asset economy. Thus, by normalizing the spot prices so that $p_{s1} = 1$, $s = 0, 1, \ldots, S$, we may always have A as the dividend matrix under assumption 12.4.

Theorem 12.2 *Let A be a numeraire asset structure and rank $A = J$. If $0 < J < S$, $L > 1$, $I > (L-1)S$, then every equilibrium allocation for an economy (u, ω, A) is constrained inefficient generically in (u, ω) where $\mathcal{U}$ is given the compact open topology.*

Proof. We give a sketch of the proof. For the details, see Magill and Shafer (1991), theorem 27. The proof proceeds as follows.

(1) Let $\Gamma = \{\gamma \in R^I \mid \sum_i^I \gamma^i = 0\}$ and $Z = \{z = (z^1, \ldots, z^I) \in R^{JI} \mid \sum_i^I z^i = 0\}$. For any given $(\omega, A) \in R_{++}^{L(S+1)I} \times R^{LSJ}$, let $g_{\omega,A} : \Gamma \times Z \to R^{LI} \times R^{LSI}$ be the function given by

$$g_{\omega,A}(\gamma, z) = (\omega_0^i - \bar{\gamma}^i e_{01}, \ \omega_1^i + A \cdot z^i)_i^I.$$

Given an economy (u, ω, A), any constrained feasible allocation is represented as a state-constrained equilibrium for the economy $(u, g_{\omega,A}(\gamma, z))$ for some $(\gamma, z) \in \Gamma \times Z$, which allows us to have the differential characterization (the first-order condition) for the constrained feasible allocation. It says as follows:

$$du_{\bar{x}^i}^i = \bar{\lambda}^i \ \square \ \bar{p}, \quad i = 1, \ldots, I$$

where $\bar{x}$ is the constrained feasible allocation and $\bar{p}$ is the state-constrained equilibrium price system for the corresponding economy while $\bar{\lambda}^i$ indicates the Lagrange-multiplier vector $(\bar{\lambda}_0^i, \bar{\lambda}_1^i, \ldots, \bar{\lambda}_S^i)$.

(2) Then the necessary condition for a constrained feasible allocation $\bar{x}$ induced by some $(\bar{\gamma}, \bar{z})$ to be constrained Pareto optimal is stated as

follows: let $(\Delta\gamma, \Delta z)$ be a marginal change satisfying $\sum_i^I \Delta\gamma^i = 0$ and $\sum_i^I \Delta z^i = 0$. Then any state-constrained equilibrium for an economy $(u, g_{\omega,A}(\bar{\gamma} + \Delta\gamma, \bar{z} + \Delta z))$ for any $(\Delta\gamma, \Delta z)$ can not improve every consumer's utility if the constrained feasible allocation $\bar{x}$ is constrained Pareto optimal. By way of the differential characterization for the constrained feasible allocation, we are allowed to have an appropriate representation of this necessary condition. By virtue of assumptions 12.3, 12.4, it is known that the following expression for the condition is obtainable generically in ω.

$$\sum_i^I \frac{1}{\bar{\lambda}_0^i} \Delta u_1^i = \sum_i^I \bar{\pi}_1^i A \cdot \Delta z^i - \sum_i^I \bar{\pi}_1^i (\Delta p_1 \,\square\, (\bar{x}_1^i - \tilde{\omega}_1^i)) = 0,$$

for all $\Delta z \in \mathbf{R}^{JI}$ satisfying $\sum_i^I \Delta z^i = 0$ where $\bar{\pi}_1^i = (\bar{\lambda}_1^i/\bar{\lambda}_0^i, \ldots, \bar{\lambda}_S^i/\bar{\lambda}_0^i)$ and $\tilde{\omega}_1^i$ designates the second component of i-th element of $g_{\omega,A}(\bar{\gamma}, \bar{z})$, $i = 1, \ldots, I$.

(3) Finally, we show that an allocation of any incomplete market equilibrium does not meet the above necessary condition generically in (u, ω). In view of the condition of an incomplete market equilibrium, the necessary condition provided above can be simplified as follows:

$$\sum_i^I \bar{\pi}_1^i (\Delta p_1 \,\square\, (\bar{x}_1^i - \tilde{\omega}_1^i)) = 0,$$

for all Δp_1 induced by Δz provided above. Note that owing to assumption 12.3, the excess demand function $F(p; \omega)$ consists of $F_0(p_0; \omega_0)$ and $F_1(p_1; \omega_1)$ and that the spot prices can be normalized so that $p_{s1} = 1$, $s = 0, 1, \ldots, S$. Then the above necessary condition can be shown to reduce to the orthogonality condition

$$\left(-(\partial\hat{F}_1/\partial\hat{p}_1)^{-1} \sum_{h=1}^{I-1} Q_h A \Delta z^h\right) \cdot \bar{\xi} = 0,$$

for all $(\Delta z^1, \ldots, \Delta z^{I-1}) \in \mathbf{R}^{J(I-1)}$ where $\hat{p}_1$ denotes the truncation of p_1 obtained by omitting the price of good 1 at date 1 and $\hat{F}_1$ is also the truncation of $F_1(p_1; \omega_1)$ obtained by omitting good 1 whereas Q is the $(L-1)S \times S$ matrix of differences in the income effects between consumer I and others without good 1 and $\bar{\xi} = \sum_i^I \bar{\pi}_1^i \,\square\, (\hat{x}_1^i - \hat{\omega}_1^i)$ in which $(\hat{x}_1^i, \hat{\omega}_1^i)$ denotes the similar truncation of $(\bar{x}_1^i, \bar{\omega}_1^i)$.

Here it can be shown that the $(L-1)S \times J(I-1)$ matrix $[Q_1 A, \ldots, Q_{I-1} A]$ has generically *rank* $(L-1)S$ and that $\bar{\xi}$ is generically non-zero, thus we obtain that an incomplete market equilibrium allocation generically does not meet the necessary condition for the constrained Pareto optimality. $\qquad\square$

This theorem suggests that if there exists the planner having good control of portfolios among the consumers, the planner could Pareto improve upon the incomplete market equilibria. In this connection, Villanacci, et. al, (2002) discuss a general methodology to analyze the successful intervention of a planner in an incomplete market economy. They show that Pareto improvement can be accomplished by using few taxes and subsidies.

From the above arguments, we must conclude that incomplete market equilibria are generally irrelevant to Pareto optimality, whether in a pure or constrained sense. Then, is there any other optimality notion than Pareto efficiency that supports incomplete market equilibria? To this inquiry, Grossman produced the notion called social Nash optimality. Loosely speaking, an allocation $\bar{x}$ is a social Nash optimum if it is impossible to improve every consumer's utility by reallocating only $(\bar{x}_s^i)_i$ at state s with $(\bar{x}_k^i)_i$, $k \neq s$ unchanged, $s = 0, 1, \ldots, S$. Grossman has shown that an incomplete market equilibrium allocation is virtually equivalent to a social Nash optimal allocation. For the details, see Grossman (1977).

Bibliography

Abraham, R. and J. Robbin, (1967), *Transversal Mappings and Flows*, New York: W.A. Benjamin.

Adachi, M. (1976), *Differential Topology*, Tokyo: Kyoritu Publ (in Japanese).

Aliprantis, C.D., D.J. Brown and O. Burkinshaw (1990), *Existence and Optimality of Competitive Equilibria*, Berlin: Springer-Verlag.

Arrow, K.J. and F.J. Hahn (1971), *General Competitive Analysis*, San Francisco:Holden Day.

Auslander, L. and R.E. Mackenzie (1977), *Introduction to Differentiable Manifolds*, New York: Dover.

Balasko, Y. (1975a), "The Graph of the Walras Correspondence", *Econometrica*, 43, pp. 907-912.

Balasko, Y. (1975b), "Some Results on Uniqueness and on Stability of Equilibrium in General Equilibrium Theory", *Journal of Mathematical Economics*, 2, pp. 95-118.

Balasko, Y. (1978a), "Economic Equilibrium and Catastorophe Theory", *Econometrica*, 46, pp. 557-569.

Balasko, Y. (1978b), "The Transfer Problem and the Theory of Regular Economies", *International Economic Review*, 19, pp. 687-694.

Balasko, Y. (1979), "A Geometric Approach to Equilibrium Analysis", *Journal of Mathematical Economics*, 6, pp. 217-228.

Balasko, Y. (1980), "Number and Definiteness of Economic Equilibria", *Journal of Mathematical Economics*, 7, pp. 215-225.

Balasko, Y. (1989), *Foundations of the Theory of General Equilibrium*, New York: Academic Press.

Balasko, Y. (1992), "The Set of Regular Equilibrium", *Journal of Economic Theory*, 58, pp. 1-8.

Balasko, Y. and D. Cass (1989), "The Structure of Financial Equilibrium with Exogeneous Yields: The Case of Incomplete Markets", *Econometrica*, 57, pp. 135-162.

Barten, A. N. and V. Böhm (1982), "Consumer Theory", in K.J. Arrow and M.D. Intriligator eds., *Handbook of Mathematical Economics, vol U*, New York: North-Holland.

Berge, C. (1963), *Topological Spaces*, London: Oliver and Boyd.

Border, K.C. (1989), *Fixed Point Theorems with Applications to Economics and Game Theory*, Cambridge: Cambridge University Press.

Bourbaki, N. (1965), *Elements de Mathematique: Topologie Generale*, Chap. 1, 2, Paris: Hermann.

Bredon, G.E. (1993), *Topology and Geometry*, New York: Springer-Verlag.

Brocker, TH. and K. Janich (1982), *Introduction to Differential Topology*, London: Cambridge University Press.

Cass, D. (1991), "Perfect Equilibrium with Incomplete Financial Markets: An Elementary Exposition", in L.W. Mckenzie and S. Zamagni eds., *Value and Capital: Fifty Years Later*, London: Macmillan.

Cass, D. (1992), "Incomplete Financial Markets and Indeterminacy of Competitive Equilibrium ", in J-J. Laffont, ed., *Advances in Economic Theory-Sixth World Congress, vol U*, Cambridge: Cambridge University Press.

Chichilnisky, G. and G. Heal (1996), "On the Existence and the Structure of the Pseudo-Equilibrium Manifold", *Journal of Mathematical Economics*, 26, pp. 171-186.

Chillingworth, D.R.J. (1978), *Differential Topology with a View to Applications*, London: Pitman.

Debreu, G. (1970), "Economies with a finite Set of Equilibria", *Econometrica*, 38, pp. 387-392.

Debreu, G. (1974), "Four Aspects of the Mathematical Theory of Economic Equilibrium", in *Proceedings of the International Congress of Mathematicians, vol T*, Vancouver:Canadian Mathematical Society.

Debreu, G. (1975), "The Rate of Convergence of the Core of an Economy", *Journal of Mathematical Economics*, 2, pp. 1-7.

Debreu, G. (1976), "Regular Differentiable Economies", *American Economic Review*, 66, pp. 280-287.

Delbaen, F. (1970), "Economies with a Finite Set of Equilibria", CORE Discussion Papers,7008, Louvain, Belugium.

Delbaen, F. (1971), "Limit Theorems for Economies with a Finite Number of Equilibria", *Econometrica*, 39, p.59.

Diamond, P.A. (1967), "The Role of a Stock Market in a General Equilibrium Model with Technological Uncertainty", *American Economic Review*, 57, pp. 759-776.

Dierker, E. (1972), "Two Remarks on the Number of Equilibria of an Economy", *Econometrica*, 40, pp. 951-953.

Dierker, E. (1974), *Topological Methods in Walrasian Economics*, Berlin: Springer-Verlag.

Dierker, E. (1977), "Regular Economies: A Survey", in M.D.Intriligator ed., *Frontiers of Qualitative Economics VA*, New York: North-Holland.

Dierker, E. (1982), "Regular Economies", in K.J. Arrow and M.D. Intriligator eds., *Handbook of Mathematical Economics, vol U*, New York: North-Holland.

Dierker, E. and H, Dierker (1972), "The Local Uniqueness of Equilibria". *Econometrica*, 40, pp. 867-881.

Dierker, H. (1975), "Smooth Preferences and the Regularity of Equilibria", *Journal of Mathematical Economics*, 2, pp. 43-62.

Dubrovin, B.A. ,A.T. Fomenko and S.P. Novikov (1985), *Modern Geometry–Methods and Applications: Part U*, New York: Springer-Verlag.

Dugundji, J. (1966), *Topology*, Boston: Allyn Bacon.

Duffie, D. (1992), "The Nature of Incomplete Security Markets", in J-J. Laffont ed., *Advances in Economic Theory: Sixth World Congress vol U*, Cambridge: Cambridge University Press.

Duffie, D. and W. Shafer (1985), "Equilibrium in Incomplete Markets: T", *Journal of Mathematical Economics*, 14, pp. 285-300.

Duffie, D. and W. Shafer (1986), "Equilibrium in Incomplete Markets:U", *Journal of Mathematical Economics*, 15, pp. 199-216.

Fuchs, G. (1974), "Private Ownership Economies with a Finite Number of Equilibria", *Journal of Mathematical Economics*, 1, pp. 141-158.

Fuchs, G. (1977), "Continuity of Equilibria for Production Economies: New Results", *Econometrica*, 45, pp. 1777-1796.

Gaal, S. A. (1964), *Point Set Topology*, New york: Academic Press.

Geanakoplos, J. (1990), "An Introduction to General Equilibrium with Incomplete Asset Markets", *Journal of Mathematical Economics*, 19, pp. 1-38.

Geanakoplos, J,M. Magill, M. Quinzi and J. Dreze (1990), "Generic Inefficiency of Stock Market Equilibrium When Markets are Incomplete", *Journal of Mathematical Economics*, 19, pp. 113-151.

Geanakoplos, J. and A. Mas-Colell (1989), "Real Indeterminacy with Financial Assets", *Journal of Economic Theory*, 47, pp. 22-38.

Geanakoplos, J and H. polemarchakis (1986), "Existence, Regularity and Constrained Suboptimality of Competitive Allocations When the Asset Market is Incomplete", in W. Hellar, R. Starr and D. Starrett, *Uncertainty, Information and Communication*, New York: Cambridge University Press.

Geldrop, J. H. V. (1978), "Extension of a Theorem of Smale on Equilibria for Pure Exchange Economies", *Journal of Mathematical Economics*, 5, pp. 245-253.

Gibson, C. G. (1979), *Singular Points of Smooth Mappings*, London: Pitman.

Golubitsky, M. and V. Guillemin (1973), *Stable Mappings and Their Singularities*, New York: Springer-Verlag.

Grodal, B. (1975), "The Rate of Convergence of the Core for a Purely Competetive Sequence of Economies", *Journal of Mathematical Economics*, 2. pp. 171-186.

Grossman, A. (1977), "A Characterization of the Optimality o Equilibrium with Incomplete Markets", *Journal of Economic Theory*, 15, pp. 1-15.

Guillemin, V. and A. Pollack (1974), *Differential Topology*, Englewood Cliffs,NJ: Prentice-Hall.

Hahn, F. (1991), "General Equilibrium in an Imperfect World: Incomplee Markets", in K. J. Arrow ed., *Issues in Contemporary Economics, vol 1*, London: Macmillan.

Hart, O. (1974), "On the Existence of Equilibrium in Securities Models", *Journal of Economic Theory*, 9, pp. 293-311.

Hart, O. (1975), "On the Optimality of Equilibrium When the Market Structure is Incomplete", *Journal of Economic Theory*, 11, pp. 418-443.

Hattori, A. (1976), *Manifolds*, Tokyo: Iwanami.

Hens, T. (1998), "Incomplete Markets", in A. Kirman ed., *Elements of General Equilibrium Analysis*, Oxford: Blackwell.

Hildenbrand, K. (1972), "Continuity of the Equilibrium-Set Correspondence", *Journal of Economic Theory*, 5, pp. 152-162.

Hildenbrand, W. (1974), *Core and Equilibria of a Large Economy*, Princeton: Princeton U.P.

Hirsch, M. D., M. Magill and A.Mas-Colell (1990), "A Geometric Approach to a Class of Equilibrium Existence Theorems", *Journal of Mathematical Economics*, 19, pp. 95-106.

Hirsch, M. W. (1976), *Differential Topology*, New York: Springer-Verlag.

Husseini, S. Y., J-M. Lasry and M. Magill (1990), "Existence of Equilibrium with Incomplete Markets", *Journal of Mathematical Economics*, 19, pp. 39-67.

Ichiishi, T. (1997), *Microeconomic Theory*, Oxford: Blackwell.

Izumiya, S. and G. Ishikawa (1998), *Applied Theory of Singular Points*, Tokyo: Kyoritu Publ (in Japanese).

Kahn, D. W. (1980), *Introduction to Global Analysis*, New York: Academic Press.

Kalman, P. J., and K-P. Lin (1978), "Applications of Tom's Transversality Theory and Brouwer Degree Theory to Economics", in J. Green ed., *Some Aspects of Foundations of General Equilibrium Theory*, Berlin: Springer-Verlag.

Kawada, K. (1956), *Topology*, Tokyo: Kyoritu Publ (in Japanese).

Kehoe, T. (1980), "An Index Theorem for General Equilibrium Models with Production", *Econometrica*, 48, pp. 1211-1232.

Kehoe, T. (1982), "Regular Production Economies", *Journal of Mathematical Economics*, 10, pp. 147-176.

Kehoe, T. (1983), "Regularity and Index Theory for Economies with Smooth Production Technologies", *Econometrica*, 51, pp. 895-919.

Kehoe, T. (1984), "Computing All of the Equilibria of Economies with the Factors of Production", *Journal of Mathematical Economics*, 13, pp. 207-223.

Kehoe, T. (1985), "Multiplicity of Equilibria and Comparative Statics", *Quarterly Journal of Economics*, 51, pp. 895-919.

Kehoe, T. (1991), "Computation and Multiplicity of Equilibria", in W. Hildenbrand and H. F. Sonnenschein eds., *Handbook of Mathematical Economics, vol W*, Amsterdam: North-Holland.

Kehoe, T. (1998), "Uniqueness and Stability", in A. Kirman ed., *Elements of General Equilibrium Analysis*, Oxford: Blackwell.

Kolstad, C. D., and L. Mathiesen (1987), "Necessary and Sufficient Condition for Uniqueness of a Cournot Equilibrium", *Review of Economic Studies*, LIV, pp. 681-690.

Lang, S. (1969), *Analysis T*, 2nd ed., Reading, MA.: Addison-Wesley.

Lang, S. (1972), *Differential Manifolds*, Reading, MA.: Addison-Wesley.

Laroque, G. and H. Polemarchakis (1978), "On the Sturucture of the Set of Fixed Price Equilibria", *Journal of Mathematical Economics*, 5, pp. 53-69.

Lu, Y-C. (1976), *Singular Theory and An Introduction to Catastrophe Theory*, New York: Springer-Verlag.

Magill, M. and M. Quinzii (1996), *Theory of Incomplete Markets, vol 1*, Cambridge, MA.: MIT Press.

Magill, M. and W. Shafer (1990), "Characterization of Generically Complete Real Asset Structures", *Journal of Mathematical Economics*, 19, pp. 167-194.

Magill, M. and W. Shafer (1990), "Incomplete Markets", in W. Hildenbrand and H. Sonnenschein eds., *Handbook of Mathematical Economics, vol W*, Amsterdam: North-Holland.

Majthay, A. (1985), *Foundations of Catastrophe Theory*, Boston: Pitman.

Malinvaud, E. (1977), *Leçons de Théorie Microéconomique*, 4th ed., Paris: Dunod.

Mangasarian, O. (1969,1994), *Nonlinear Programming*, New York: McGraw-Hill.

Mas-Colell, A. (1975), "On the Continuity of Equilibrium Prices in Constant-Returns Production Economies", *Journal of Mathematical Economics*, 2, pp. 21-33.

Mas-Colell, A. (1977a), "On the Equilibrium Price Set of an Exchange Economy", *Journal of Mathematical Economics*, 4, pp. 117-126.

Mas-Colell, A. (1977b), "Regular,Nonconvex Economies", *Econometrica*, 45, pp. 1387-1407.

Mas-Colell, A. (1985), *The Theory of General Economic Equilibrium: A Differentiable Approach*, Cambridge: Cambridge University Press.

Mas-Colell, A. (1991), "Indeterminacy in Incomplete Market Economies", *Economic Theory*, 1, pp. 45-61.

Mas-Colell, A. (1996), "The Determinacy of Equilibria 25 Years Later", in B. Allen ed., *Economics in Changing World, Vol 2: Microeconomics*, London: Macmillan.

Mas-Colell, A., M. D. Whinston and J. R. Green (1995), *Microeconomic Theory*, New York: Oxford University Press.

Matsumoto, Y. (1989), *Foundations of Manifolds*, Tokyo: Tokyo University Press (in Japanese).

Matsushima, Y. (1965), *Introduction to Manifolds*, Tokyo: Shokabo (in Japanese).

Milnor, J. W. (1969), *Topology from the Differentiable Viewpoint*, Charlottesville, VA: The University Press of Virginia.

Mityagin, V. S. (1972), "Notes on Mathematical Economics", *Russian Mathematical Surveys*, 27, pp. 1-19.

Munkres, J. R. (1966), *Elementary Differential Topology*, revised ed., Princeton, NJ: Princeton University Press.

Nagata, R. (2001a), *A Frontier of Mathematical Economics: the Theory of Regular Economies*, Tokyo: Waseda University Press (in Japanese).

Nagata, R. (2001b), "An Introduction to Regular Economies", in Nagata, R. ed., *Mathematical Methods and Logics in Economics*, Tokyo: Waseda University Press (in Japanese).

Nagata, R. (2000), "An Intersection-based Approach to Genericity Analysis for the Equilibrium Set: With an Application to Lindahl Equilibrium", *the Japanese Economic Review*, 51, pp. 431-447.

Nagata, R. (1998), "The Degree of Indeterminacy of Equilibria with Incomplete Markets", *Journal of Mathematical Economics*, 29, pp. 109-123.

Nakaoka, M. (1971), *Introduction to Topology*, Tokyo: Asakura (in Japanese).

Nakamura, K. (1966), *Topology*, Tokyo: Kyoritu Publ (in Japanese).

Nicola, P-C. (2000), *Mainstream Mathematical Economics in the 20th Century*, Berlin: Springer-Verlag.

Nishimura, K. (1978), "A Further Remark on the Number of Equilibria of an Economy", *International Economic Review*, 19, pp. 679-685.

Noguchi, H. and T. Fukuda (1976), *Elementary Catastrophe*, Tokyo: Kyoritu Publ (in Japanese).

Rudin, W. (1976), *Principles of Mathematical Analysis*, 3rd ed., Tokyo: McGraw-Hill Kogakusha.

Scarf, H. E. (1960), "Some Examples of Global Instability of the Competitive Equilibrium", *International Economic Review*, 1, pp. 157-172.

Schecter, S. (1979), "On the Structure of the Equilibrium Manifold", *Journal of Mathematical Economics*, 6, pp. 1-5.

Schofield, N. (1984), "Existence of Equilibrium on a Manifold", *Journal of Operations Research*, 9, pp. 545-557.

Shiga, K. (1976), *Manifolds I, II, III*, Tokyo: Iwanami (in Japanese).

Singer, I. M. and J. A. Thorpe (1967), *Lecture Notes on Elementary Topology and Geometry*, Glenview,IL: Scott, Foresman.

Smale, S. (1974a), "Global Analysis and Economics UA: Extension of a Theorem of Debreu", *Journal of Mathematical Economics*, 1, pp. 1-14.

Smale, S. (1974b), "Global Analysis and Economics V: Pareto Optima and Price Equilibria", *Journal of Mathematical Economics*, 1, pp. 107-117.

Smale, S. (1974c), "Global Analysis and Economics W: Finiteness and Stability of Equilibria with General Consumption Sets and Production", *Journal of Mathematical Economics*, 1, pp. 119-127.

Smale, S. (1974d), "Global Analysis and Economics X: Pareto Theory with Constraints", *Journal of Mathematical Economics*, 1, pp. 213-221.

Smale, S. (1976a), "Global Analysis and Economics Y: Geometric Analysis of Pareto Optima and Price Equilibria under Classical Hypotheses", *Journal of Mathematical Economics*, 3, pp. 1-14.

Smale, S. (1976b), "Dynamics in General Equilibrium Theory", *American Economic Review*, 66, pp. 288-294.

Spivak, M. (1968), *Calculus on Manifolds: A Modern Approach to Classical Theorems of Advanced Calculus*, New York: Benjamin.

Spivak, M. (1979), *A Comprehensive Introduction to Differential Geometry, vol 1*, 2nd ed., Houston: Publish or Perish.

Stiglitz, J.E. (1982), "The Inefficiency of Stock Market Equilibrium", *Review of Economic Studies*, 49, pp. 241-261.

Suzuki, H. (1979), *Introduction to Differential Manifolds*, Tokyo: Science-sha (in Japanese).

Tamura, I. (1977/1978), *Differential Topology I, II, III*, Tokyo: Iwanami (in Japanese).

Varian, H. (1975), "A Third Remark on the Number of Equilibria of an Economy", *Econometrica*, 43, pp. 985-986.

Villanacci, A., L. Carosi, P. Benevieri and A. Battinelli (2002), *Differential Topology and General Equilibrium with Complete and Incomplete Markets*, Boston: Kluwer Academic Publ.

Vives, X. (1999), *Oligopoly Pricing*, Cambridge, MA.: MIT Press.

Werner, J. (1985), "Equilibrium in Economies with Incomplete Financial Markets", *Journal of Economic Theory*, 36, pp. 110-119.

Werner, J. (1990), "Structure of Financial Markets and Real Indeterminacy of Equilibria", *Journal of Mathematical Economics*, 19, pp. 217-232.

Wiesmeth, H. (1979), "Regular Competitive Equilibria in Disequilibrium Economics", *Journal of Mathematical Economics*, 6, pp. 23-29.

Zhou, Y. (1997a), "The Structure of the Pseudo-equilibrium Manifold in Economies with Incomplete markets", *Journal of Mathematical Economics*, 27, pp. 91-111.

Zhou, Y. (1997b), "Genericity Analysis on the Pseudo-equilibrium Manifold", *Journal of Economic Theory*, 73, pp. 79-92.

Index